Bullets at the Border

Unforgettable Lessons Learned from the
Most Unexpected Place on Earth

Robert D. Messick

insight
PUBLISHING GROUP

Tulsa, Oklahoma

BULLETS AT THE BORDER
© 2008 by Robert D. Messick

Published by Insight Publishing Group
8801 S. Yale, Suite 410
Tulsa, OK 74137
918-493-1718

1st Printing

ISBN 978-1-932503-71-5
Library of Congress catalog card number: 2007934148

Printed in the United States of America

TESTIMONIALS AND ENDORSEMENTS

"Robert has expressed in this book an eternal truth, and one most of us have been taught from our youth. We should never pre-judge our circumstances or others. If we do so, we only hurt ourselves."

Matt Salmon – Former U.S. Congressman (Arizona)

"I know Robert personally and can verify that he lives a life of overcoming. Robert's story is a great illustration that although bad situations happen to all of us, it's what we make of these experiences that really count."

Brian Klemmer – author of "If How-To's Were Enough, We Would All Be Skinny Rich and Happy", president of Klemmer & Associates, national speaker and trainer

"Reading Robert Messick's story reminds us that it is not the pressure that matters, but what comes out of us when we are stressed and squeezed. "Bullets at the Border" gives an insightful view into how Robert not only survived the perils of prison, but revived his passion for life."

Jon McHatton – Chaplain for the Arizona Legislature and President of CARE INC.

"A great example of creating something positive out of a negative situation...an inspirational story about courage and determination, despite struggle and fear."

Jim Stovall – Author of "The Ultimate Gift" President of Narrative Television Network, winner of Entrepreneur of the Year and recipient of the Humanitarian of the Year awards

"The willingness to offer his heart & insight through his words provides a space for humor and inspiration for all of us."

Kimberly Zink – Lead Facilitator for Advanced Leadership Seminars

"Regardless of the situation, each one of us has the power to exercise choice every day and we're responsible for how we handle the outcomes. Through a series of real life stories, Robert Messick leads us to an understanding of this important fact of life that is not only well worth remembering - but it is essential."

Lance Giroux – Founder, Allied Ronin Leadership Training & Consulting

"I'm so glad I didn't know about this until after the fact!"

Haline Messick – Robert's Mom

ACKNOWLEDGEMENTS

After working quite a while on this book, several people have influenced and encouraged me to continue onward through the process. I am truly grateful to them and to everyone who's supported me.

My dad, Sam has been a constant example of being a man of compassion. Without him, the story would not have been the same. I'm still indebted to him for all he has done for me. I'm proud to be called his son.

My mom has been a wonderful source of feedback for the story. A red pen in her hand has been mightier than any sword. She has been a fountain of encouragement, and a valuable second pair of eyes.

My wife, Tara is the best support a husband could ever have. To read and listen to my story without judgment has been heartwarming. For her to accept a past experience in my life and help me create a positive meaning forward has been a blessing to our family.

I think of Christina and her family often. She is a noble lady and I think her family is as royal and gallant as you could get. Their love and support, council and coaching were a wonderful chapter in my life. I hope that by sharing my story, it will show their influence on me was truly valuable.

To all my friends, colleagues, and family members who've said, "Robert, we would have never expected that to happen to you!" I am truly grateful. You have been the reason why I chose to write this story.

TABLE OF CONTENTS

AUTHOR'S NOTE

The following story contains conversations spoken in English and *Spanish*. Words in English are written in normal text, words in *Spanish are in italics*.

A number of people have come up to me and asked if this story is really true. The answer is, yes. And that's why it makes it so humorous and insightful.

CHAPTER 1

MONDAY

Trouble at the Border

The following story I am about to share is a result of my own stupidity. Now that time has healed many wounds I can disclose that I've taken full responsibility for my actions. However, I consider myself a better man for having gone through the following chain of events, even if they were what could be labeled as "trials and tribulations".

It was the beginning of December and all of society was getting ready for the Christmas holiday. Having just graduated from College six months previously, I was hired by a large investment company in Phoenix Arizona.

I was on top of the world. Work was going well and by the beginning of December, I had also completed company training allowing me to be a full-fledged registered broker.

Part of my positive enthusiasm was that I also had a girlfriend. She was a brilliant beautiful business woman who took your breath away when she walked in the room with red hair and a light complexion. Christina and I had been going out for about two months and I felt pretty good about the situation. We were hired by the same company and had gone through the training together, which was how we met. We leaned on each other through the whole ordeal and it was nice to have some companionship to encourage me along.

That fateful Monday, both Christy and I had finished the company training, and we discussed the possibility of doing something that night to celebrate. However, I had different plans. Because of the past three weeks of training, my regular schedule was thrown off somewhat, giving me Tuesday and Wednesday off and I would return to my normal work team on Thursday.

My dad was in Mexico at a timeshare and my plan was to join him for the couple of days I would be off work. Mom had made reservations for her and dad, but was interrupted with a business trip in England since November and wouldn't be back for a couple of more months. Dad had to use the vacation or loose the use of the timeshare.

These timeshares are prepaid weeks that could be used at a network of hotels. If they weren't used by the end the year they would be lost. So while Mom was away and the timeshare already reserved, Dad thought Rocky Point, Mexico would be a nice place to spend the week.

Dad didn't want to spend the whole time alone, so I was happy to join him for my time off. There was also an incentive of great Mexican food involved. Dad had planned on shopping for shrimp at the local Mexican markets and I would take advantage once I got there. So my plan was to leave after work on Monday afternoon, drive down there and meet up with Dad.

I took off from work as fast as I could and headed south from Phoenix. I had packed that morning and already had my bags in the car. That Monday morning was a little rushed before work, so I didn't have a chance to clean the car as I had wanted to. I thought about bringing my passport, but in my hurry, forgot that too. I figured my driver's license was good enough. Our family had gone down to Mexico a number of times when I was younger and had no problem crossing the border. Besides, I figured my lighter skin and red hair would be a dead give-away that I was, no doubt a US citizen.

I headed south. It turned nighttime and I felt confident I was making good time. After a couple hours driving, I started thinking about crossing the Mexican border. I knew I had to be getting close, although I really didn't know just how far it would be now. Along the road, I passed a set of flashing red lights on top of a green Ford Bronco. The border patrol was in the area and obviously they were checking the car it had pulled over. I reduced my speed and planned on getting to the international border without being stopped.

The Mexican border actually came upon me a little quicker than I had expected. On the American side, there's a gas station followed by a set of buildings on both sides of the road. A thought flashed though my mind to pull over at the gas station first before crossing into Mexico. I dismissed the idea prematurely, thinking that nothing was wrong. It was getting late, about 8:30 PM and I just wanted to get on my way into Rocky Point.

I headed on, slowing again to cross into Mexico. The Mexican Border Patrol guard gestured me to stop as I rolled down my window. I greeted him with a smile and he asked me in broken English and in an "official tone" where I was going.

"Rocky Point," was my reply.

He looked in the windows of my car and asked me to pull over to a parking space just ahead of me. I didn't think anything of it so I obliged him and pulled over. I understood he was doing his job and I wanted to cooperate. My family had been stopped before while going into Mexico, but after the Mexican border patrol took a good look at us, they always let us pass. It never occurred to me that as a young, single, American, male I looked a little more suspicious than a family on vacation. It still didn't ring any bells that I might be any type of risk.

The guard instructed me to get out of the car, open the doors and the trunk. I got out, and popped the trunk.

The guard quickly looked in the back seat, and then went to the trunk. Opening zippers, he looked into the bag that held my clothes. He found nothing out of the ordinary until he went through a different small bag that I had forgotten was in my car. To both of our surprise, the border guard pulled out a box marked "AMMUNITION"!

Es Una Problema

My mind started to race, why did I have a box of bullet shells in my car, and why did I bring them over the border into Mexico? Answers came as quickly as the questions, I recalled that I had gone target shooting with some friends over the Thanksgiving weekend a week and a half before. I had the bag in my car at the time, along with my handgun and accompanying 9mm bullets. We had a good time at a local gravel pit shooting various cans and cardboard targets. When I got home, I took the gun out of the bag and back into its place at home. However, I neglected to finish up by taking the bullets out of the car. With the fact that I had not cleaned the car before I came over the border, this chain of events resulted in a box of bullets coming with me into Mexico.

> Why did I have a box of bullet shells in my car, and why did I bring them over the border into Mexico?

The border guard opened the ammunition box, looked at me, looked back into the box and then back at me. Both of us didn't know what to make of this. This was a surprise to me as well and I wanted to display innocence as long as I could. "Oh, I'm very sorry," I said.

The Border Patrol guard called to another guard standing nearby to come over. They started talking in Spanish and by then, it had aroused enough attention that other border guards came over. This became the focus of attention for the whole group of guards. After looking in the blue bag and everything else in my car, the Border patrol found a total of thirty-two bullets and a magazine clip for my handgun.

I was then asked a number of questions while the border guards started an in depth search of my car. The first and most important question was: "Where is the gun?" They seemed to be getting a little frustrated by not finding the handgun as they seemed determined that it was here too. I told them it was at home in Arizona, there was no gun in the car because I didn't bring it with me. If that's the case, they then asked why I brought bullets into Mexico? I really didn't have a good answer because deep down, I really didn't know myself.

"Oh, Es Una Problema, Senior" one guard responded when I asked what was going on. After a few more questions, they then invited me into a small office nearby to try to resolve this. While walking, one of the guards said that I would go inside with them to make a report, while others would bring out dogs to sniff my car.

I was truly amazed. My first thought was that I'm no drug courier. I felt that this was the first exciting thing that had happened to them in a while and they were going all out, dogs and all.

Nearby was a small storefront office with a glass door. With one guard behind me, another guard in front of me opened the door to the office. Once inside, they offered me a chair. Wait a minute, I thought to myself. What is going on? My mind started to race as I sat down and began watching other guards go in and out of the door. The office was tiny, no more than 10 feet by 10 feet. I sat in a corner in the chair I was offered behind an old folding table. Across the room where I was seated was a desk, with some mismatched chairs around the edges of the room. Other than this, the room was really quite bare. However, it was stuffy, and by this time five guards had followed me into the barely adequate office, resulting in standing room only.

I took inventory of my thoughts and tried to find what was so important that I must be detained. This had to be some mix up or something. I thought I'd say I'm sorry, give the bullets up and then I could go. I knew dad was waiting as the clock on the wall displayed 8:30. With any luck, I would be out of here in no time and into Rocky Point perhaps by 10 PM.

It wasn't the case. I didn't know what was in store for me, but it didn't take long for me to know this didn't look good. A woman sat in front of a computer at the desk. She was typing away, but I couldn't read what was being written. I looked at the guard who originally pulled me over when I came to the border. *"What's going on?"* I asked.

"We need to write a report," he responded.

"A report? Why?" I questioned. I was trying to be polite, but I was getting a bit confused trying to understand the Spanish around me.

"We need to make sure that everything is correct." He was then prompted by the woman at the computer to ask, *"Do you have Identification?"*

I pulled my wallet from my back pocket and reached for my driver's license. I remembered my decision not to bring my passport and now wished I had. But, when I packed this morning, I didn't think I would be held by the Mexican Border Patrol. I gave my license to the guard and watched him pass it to the woman at the desk. She took her time to look it over and started copying information into her system.

The mood changed when another man walked into this already crowded office. He was an older gentleman, with dress slacks on and a collared shirt. He came directly over to me. *"How are you doing?"* He asked me.

I nodded my head and said, *"Fine thank you,"* he seemed really nice and gave me a kind smile. It put me at ease just to have this man be friendly to me. I was in a strange place having a strange report written up in front of a bunch of strange border patrol guards.

"Can I go soon?" I asked. I figured he had to be someone in authority.

Without answering, he shrugged his shoulders and asked me to stick my hands out. I looked at him and asked him what he was doing. *"I am a doctor"* He replied. The guards had asked him to come because they had stopped an American and they guessed I needed a check up.

"A doctor? What for?" I asked. The question was directed to both the doctor and the guards looking over his shoulders.

He responded back to me that everyone stopped had to get looked over by a doctor just to make sure that they were OK. I guess this was done as a safety issue. It seemed like the guards have a doctor inspect you so that you can't say they neglected you or beat you while you were in custody. This seemed confusing, but hey, if it meant me going on my way, I'd comply with what the doctor ordered.

The friendly doctor shined a light in my eyes, checked my pulse, checked my head and ears and said "OK". Well, at least I was happy that he gave me a clean bill of health! He nodded an official OK to the others and signed his signature on a clipboard that the guards produced. As quickly as he came, he now left with one of the guards. That was that. I hoped he wouldn't send me a bill for the check up but figured I was in no position to refuse his services.

I decided to relax a bit. If the girl had to write a report I would just calm down a bit and see what happens, besides, it's not everyday I would get to see the policies and procedures of the Mexican Border Patrol. While I waited, a number of guards passed in and out of this storefront office. Through the front window, I could see my car was still parked on the side of road, the trunk and doors still open. I wondered when they would bring the dogs in.

Just like clockwork, my thoughts were interrupted by a commotion outside. Even with the glass door closed, I could hear the yips of dogs barking. But there was more than one, in fact there was so many dogs barking it sounded like an English fox hunt! Good heavens, I thought to myself, how many dogs does it take to sniff my little car? I guess they'd be sure of finding something if they brought in more dogs!

To my surprise a pack of five little, feisty Chihuahua dogs slowly passed within my view. They were busy sniffing each other and causing a bunch of ruckus outside. A few of the guards in the room looked out the glass door too. They chuckled as the dogs passed by.

I silently questioned if these were my Sniffing Drug Dogs. These were small little dogs, the size of footballs and definitely seemed out of the ordinary. Yet, they looked like they didn't have a care in the world. The yapping pack of dogs passed by the office door and across the street. It didn't take long to see that these were a pack of local mutts that nobody cared about. Still the amusing idea that the border patrol could possibly use Taco Bell dogs to sniff cars for drugs passed the time away.

I snapped back to reality when I looked at the clock and realized that this was taking a bit longer than I had anticipated. The clock hanging on the wall reported that it was now 9:00 PM. This was getting crazy. I thought they were writing a report and I could be on my way.

I was then met by another group of new guards that were not around when I first crossed the border. These three new guards came in the room and began speaking to the lady at the computer and others still in the room. It got really cozy in here as it was now crowded and it seemed like everyone was inside again. Probably to see the gringo who had gotten caught with bullets in his car and to get warm from the December night.

One of the new guards looked at me and said "Hello," in English.

I looked back with innocent raised eyebrows and replied a hello back. He seemed like he had taken an honest interest in me, not just the job he was doing. He was clean shaven, and had a defined jaw line.

After talking with the others, he looked back and in English but with a heavy Mexican accent, asked: "Are you the one with bullets in the car?" This guard was the first one I met that had a good English vocabulary.

I didn't know what to say. Was this an incriminating question? If I said yes, did that mean I was guilty by acknowledgment? If I denied what was already apparent, how stupid would that be? I raised my eyebrows meekly and nodded my head yes. "This was an accident. Is it possible for me to give the bullets away and then I can go?"

The guard looked at me, I could tell he was trying to interpret my English into his Spanish mind. But he got the main points of my question and asked the woman at the computer a couple of questions. After a couple of exchanged phrases, he turned back to me with a shrug of the shoulders and said, "She has to finish her report."

I figured that one out already. "And then what's next?" I was hoping he would say that I could go. But he shrugged his shoulders again. He seemed like he really didn't want to get involved with this. I think he just came in to get warmed up a bit from the cool December night. Now that I knew he spoke English, I think he had second thoughts about coming inside and joining the situation.

"Well, then you have to see," he hesitated for the right words, "how you say, a judge. He can then let you go." So I now had to see a judge. My heart sank into my stomach. There seemed to be another step in this process other than just writing a report. I had to see a judge. OK, I thought to myself. We'll just get this report done and then I can see the judge tonight, and hopefully I can get down to Dad sometime yet tonight. My focus was still on getting back on the road. This was not in my schedule and I was still trying to stay on course.

You Have to Sing

The lady border patrol guard printed some papers and brought them over to the table where I was sitting. With a flash of ease, she pushed the papers to me to review. All the words were in Spanish. What else would they be written in? However, whether in French or Spanish or Chinese, I still couldn't read what was before me.

I looked at the new English speaking guard and asked for some direction. At this point, all the guards in the room were looking at me. What did they want me to do? I could only guess. I decided to ask my translating guard. "What is this?" I asked, pointing to the papers in front of me.

His next remark threw me for a loop. He thought for a moment for the right words and said in an off hand cool way with another shrug of the shoulders, "You need to sing," He still had a really heavy Mexican accent, but I thought I heard him correctly.

"You want me to sing?" I asked. What in the world, I thought to myself. They want me to sing? I have heard of cruel and unusual punishment, but this took the cake! "Sing what?" I thought to myself. I had the vocal ability to sing, but why in the world would they want me to sing and what?

"Yes, you need to sing," he replied back. It seemed like this was no big deal and a requirement.

I thought to myself this has got to be a mistake. What do I sing and how bizarre can we get? If I didn't, am I in bigger trouble than if I sung really badly?

"Sing what?" I asked with a big lump in my throat. This felt like dipping my toe in the water to feel how cold it was.

"Sing your name," He didn't get what I was asking. "You need to sing your name on the paper." He raised his hand and wrote in the air.

Oh, now I got it. I figured that was it, but his English vocabulary apparently switched some letters around. I guess they wanted me to SIGN my name rather than SING. How interesting it was to think that for just a couple of letters to get mixed around in his head and the message comes out all wrong. For a moment I was glad I hadn't sung yet.

"Oh," I replied back, "you want me to sign the papers?" I pointed down to the sheets of Spanish text before me.

There was a big expression of relief on his face. He had got his message across. "Yes," he cheerfully replied, "You need to Sign your name," he said without missing a beat and enunciating his new word.

I smiled at the situation. The others guards couldn't quite get what the holdup was about until I spoke to all of them in the best Spanish I could muster. *"I thought you asked me to SING (cantar), but you want me to SIGN (escribir)."* At that, the group of guards before me burst into laughter. It seemed like such a ridiculous request, but under the stress of the situation, I didn't really know what they wanted me to do until I had to ask this guy if I was to SING or SIGN my name. The others started chattering about what had just happened. I could almost imagine what they were saying "Maybe we should make him sing!"

> Now I was in a different dilemma. I was signing my name to something I couldn't read.

Luckily the request before me was to sign my name. A big relief came over me created by everyone's laughing. I can do that, I thought. I looked over the papers. I still couldn't read the words. Now I was in a different dilemma.

I was signing my name to something I couldn't read. What in the world was I signing my name to?

"Ok," I said back to the guard. "What does this say?" I asked. I wanted to know what I was putting my name on before I signed.

"Oh, Es nothing" he said in his accent. He then went on to explain in better English that the text was the report declaring that they had stopped me and found the bullets. It continued that there were no other problems found with the car and that I had provided my license and other papers for the car. The report concluded that I would be turned over to the judge and gave other general information.

The guard's interpretation satisfied me a little, however, I still had some trepidation about signing my name to a Spanish document. I remembered stories of people getting in trouble internationally and signing papers that they couldn't understand. This allowed their captors or the government to hold them based upon the fact that they had signed an incriminating document.

But wait a second, I thought to myself. I merely brought over and handful of spare bullets and no gun anyway. How official do we have to get? Couldn't they just take the bullets away from me with my apologies? My paradigm was that I really didn't mean any harm, I didn't mean to bring them, it just happened. In my mind, I knew that I had done something wrong, but it was a simple mistake. So now I had the choice of signing or not signing. What harm would it do if I signed? What harm would it do if I didn't? The questions raced through my mind.

I asked one more question on the subject. "Ok, if I sign, can I go?" I was hoping it would be that easy, why not!

The guard looked back at the others and spoke a couple of words I couldn't understand. He then looked back at me and shrugged his shoulders again. "Si, after you sign, we see the judge." I studied his eyes for a bluff. It didn't come. Well, I guess if I sign these papers, then we can get over this and on to the next step. Hopefully I would be able to get to Dad by midnight. Who knows? Besides how hard is it to sign papers? It wasn't like I was transporting a nuclear weapon or a backpack of cocaine.

OK, if signing these papers gets me on the road quicker, then I will sign. After the fact, I realize how naïve I was. Deep down inside I was quite embarrassed about bringing these bullets across the border in the first place. The fact that I didn't mean to do such a crime didn't lessen my embarrassment, and if they requested me to sign the papers, then I would. I knew I might be a little too trusting, but I decided to sign my name. I reached for the pen on the table and looked over the papers for a bit. Why I took some time to look over strange unfamiliar words, I didn't know. Maybe I was trying to show that I knew what I was signing, maybe I was just bluffing. Well, I was bluffing, and probably bluffing myself too. It was a 6 page report. Man, this lady had gone into endless detail. After pausing for a moment, I signed at the bottom.

Going to the Bathroom

My bladder told me it finally had enough. I needed a break and needed to go to the bathroom. All this questioning, signing papers and trouble I had gotten into went right into the large soda I consumed on the trip down. It was now in my bladder and I needed to relieve myself.

I communicated to my temporary captors *"I need to go to the bathroom"*. That was one of my first Spanish sentences I learned when I was young. I looked at the English speaking guard to see if he understood my Spanish. The guards looked at each other and talked quickly. I couldn't quite tell what they were saying. I figured the worst. Would they let me even go? How long could I really hold 32 ounces of soda? I guess I would find out soon enough.

After some deliberation, the guards reached a decision and finally agreed it would be ok for me to use the bathroom. The English speaking guard motioned for me to follow him. I got up from my chair and we started towards the door. He took me outside to the border driveway and started to cross the street. I was at his side and wondering where he was taking me. Behind me, not 50 yards away was the US border. I had no thought of running, why should I? I needed to go to the bathroom, not run. Besides, I figured that as soon as I started running like a fugitive, my Mexican guard wouldn't have any hesitation with taking his gun and using me for target practice. I decided just to follow wherever he was leading.

As we walked, my mind turned to this Border Guard escorting me to the bathroom. He was a fair skinned man with curly brown hair. He kept his hands in the pockets of his uniform jacket and seemed pretty easy-go-lucky. I decided to strike up a conversation. "Where are you from?" I asked.

"Mexico City," he replied. I was surprised with his answer as this was quite a long way from central/southern Mexico. I asked some follow up questions and he started telling me how he had just come up to the border recently as there was a campaign to increase quality at the Mexican border patrol. President Fox had just been elected President of Mexico and had established some new programs which had resulted in this guard's move up to the border town. I figured his use of English helped with the job interview.

He wasn't really happy about being here. He referred to his new location as "this hellhole". I was surprised that he knew the English word, but I guess misery translates into any language. For a brief moment I felt sorry for him. Wait a minute. I'm the one in trouble here. What's the deal?

"Why couldn't I just give the bullets to you guys and go? I didn't mean to have them, I didn't remember I had them either. Can I go?" I was trying to figure out how I could get out of this and was grasping for straws. He didn't look at me and just shook his head.

"We have to make this official", he said with another shrug of his shoulders.

We crossed the street and headed for a wall of a nearby building. A wall. By now I needed to go pretty bad and it started going to my head. I wondered why this guy was taking me to the bathroom on a wall. Where was the toilet? Did he want me to go right here? My internal questions were soon answered when we walked around the corner and saw an entrance to a tiled room. The bathroom was one of those public areas that hadn't seen a janitor since it was made. But after a moment I was relieved and was glad that I didn't have to go on a public wall.

Closing the Border

We returned to the office just as the others announced it was finally time to leave. One of the guards took out a pair of handcuffs from the desk drawer and came toward me. I looked at him. It didn't take long to figure it was his intention to put them on me, but I wanted to have some sort of explanation first.

"*Why?*" I asked.

"*Because we are taking you outside,*" was the reply. It seemed like a tongue in cheek answer, but I was not that amused with his response.

"*Is this necessary?*" I questioned. We were both a bit frustrated about the situation, but I wanted him to know I didn't want to be put in handcuffs. Besides, I had already been outside a couple minutes ago for my bathroom experience, now I failed to see why I needed to be handcuffed now.

"*Si, we have to close the border and go into town.*"

I turned to the English speaking guard. "Ok, what's next?" I asked. I wanted to know what the procedures were and I wanted to talk to the guy in English so I could have an upper hand.

The guard shrugged. It still seemed to him like it was no big deal as he kept his hands in his pockets. "We need to take you to the jail in Sonoyta where you will see the judge." I guessed that Sonoyta was the nearby local border town.

"Then can I go?" I pushed the question. I still didn't know specifically what I had to do and what needed to be done for me to be set free.

"Si, whatever the judge says," he shrugged his shoulders again. I was beginning to realize that this guard used his shoulders as much as his English. I looked back at the original guard and put my arms forward and complied with the request.

I really wasn't happy about this but I now had to follow them. This was the first time handcuffs were officially put on me other than playing around with friends and really didn't like the knot in my stomach that accompanied.

I followed the English speaking border guard as he walked me out of the office into the open. Once again, just 20 yards away I could see the imaginary line that divided the United States from Mexico created by the chain link fence that created the border. I had no inclination to run back, I had no reason to. I still felt strongly I didn't do anything terrible other than make the mistake of not cleaning out my car. So I decided to stay and work this thing out. Besides how would I get my car back if I ran away as the car was now parked a ways off in a parking space and I didn't know where my keys were.

Once outside, two other guards approached the road way of the entrance to Mexico and proceeded to close the border of the chain link fencing with a chain and a padlock. I was really surprised that the Mexican guards closed the gate and thereby "officially" closing the border. There was a big sign on both sides of the fence stating that the border was open 8AM to 11PM. So, if the guards were closing the gates, then it must be 11 PM. I realized I had been detained for a little less than three hours.

The lights were dimmed and the border looked much different from when I entered. I heard an engine start up and a pickup truck pulled around from behind one of the buildings. A fourth guard was driving this dark colored truck.

"Get in," said my Mexican escort. I looked at him and suddenly it dawned on me that he was serious. This was how I was going to be transported? I'm going to see the judge in this? There wasn't anything official about this car or my surroundings in the late night. Well, if this was the only means of transportation, I might as well make the best of it. I opened the door and looked into the cab before I got in. The driver was expecting me to simply get in but this seemed a bit strange. The cab was untidy and seemed like some farmer's truck, rather than an official border patrol vehicle.

With my hands still in cuffed together, I reached up and climbed in, only to be pushed over to the center of the cab by my English speaking guard as he started to get in too. What in the world, I thought. It was really crowded with the three of us, but what could I do about it? I was stuck between "Mr. I don't want to be here" and a driver who looked like a Mexican Hillbilly driving his beat up clunker. All that was missing was a hound dog in the back. By this time, they knew I was complying with what they wanted, but they still didn't want to take changes on be being dumb enough to run away.

Both guards in the cab with me looked over their shoulder to the back of the pickup. By that time, the two others finished securing the gate and also headed to the truck. They jumped in the back of the bed and banged on the top of the cab to let us know they were ready to roll.

The driver started away with a jolt. Over my shoulder, I said goodbye to my car that was still parked nearby and farewell to the border gate where all the prob-

lems had begun. I turned my attention to my current situation and where I might be going as the future looked really
bleak. We were driving down a road and I had no clue where
I was being taken to, other than to see some judge. My traveling companions weren't very enthusiastic either. Although
they were border patrol officials they looked more like
Mexican Rednecks, especially in a pickup with two passen-
gers riding down the road in the back.

A strange thought came to my mind. Growing up, the
word 'official' meant something, especially in the United
States. Most of us grow up in regular situations where we
see some official person to show us where to go. The street
crossing lady, the motor division person who calls "next",
there is always someone everywhere to direct us what we
need to do and how. I concluded that Americans are over-
worked with procedure. There has to be procedures for
everything, and that's what defines 'official' to most.

However, these guys were official too; the most important thing was that they were doing the best they could do
with the resources they had. They were doing their best job
trying to survive and help keep some kind of order. Besides,
I was the one who entered into their country bringing in
bullets. Whether by accident or not, whether regretful or
not, I was the one who had broken their law and now was in
trouble.

Even though it felt like this was by the seat of their
pants, these guys were trying to proceed with this situation
as officially as they could. Still, deep inside I had to smile. It
felt like a drive with Uncle Fester, Dr. Jeckle and the Mad
Hatter. At no time in my right mind did I ever think that I
would be stuffed tightly in between Mexican men, driving
in a pickup truck. Twilight Zone doesn't even come close!

As we kept going down the road, it felt as if we were
in the middle of nowhere. I remembered a couple of times
back home as I would take my girlfriend to someplace new,
she would ask, "Where are you taking me?" I would tease

her by replying back "somewhere where they won't find your body!" We would laugh about the joke, but now I was on the other side of it. I really wanted to ask them where they were taking me, but worried they would respond back the way I had.

The headlights led us down the road finally into the border town of Sonoyta, Mexico. We turned a couple of corners and by this time my sense of direction was lost. I regretted that I couldn't tell where I was. We finally pulled up to a relatively small building. The driver turned the engine off and both doors to the truck opened. I guessed we were getting out here.

Following the guard out of the truck, I looked up at the building but couldn't see any signs or markings. I was expecting a large sign saying "municipal" anything, but no such luck.

The Local Jail

I was escorted by the Border Patrol up a set of stairs leading into the building. There was a single porch light on the side of the building, but the rest of the building was dark including inside the windows. I didn't like the feeling of it. Nevertheless, I was still being led into this un-welcoming place.

A few stairs led up to a sliding glass door. As soon as we approached someone from inside slid the door open. I could barely see a shape of our doorman in the darkness as I could only make out a figure in a bulky coat. We had entered into waiting room overlooking the small parking lot.

At the back of this entrance room was another sliding glass door. Both sets of doors seemed a bit out of place, they were just single pane sliding glass doors. There was nothing really secure about them. If I wanted to be angry, I could easily shatter them with a strong kick. I wasn't planning on breaking any glass doors, but I really couldn't understand where I was.

The second set of doors slid open by another figure I couldn't recognize very well. Once again, the border patrol guards pushed me though as they followed behind. This time, the entrance opened into a rather larger but also dark room. This second room was bare with a single metal desk in the center. The floor was linoleum, and at one corner, there was a stack of about 15-20 couch cushions, with a TV set nearby. My eyes started to adjust to the darkness. The light on the side of the building was shining through a side window, but it was the only light. There were several of us total in the room, but no lights on. This was really weird.

As soon as my eyes adjusted, I noticed four other men in the room. They all appeared quite un-kept. Several had snow caps pulled really low, all had bulky jackets and wore cowboy boots. One of them really startled me. He had a machine gun under his arm. With my little knowledge, I recognized it as a shortened version of an M-16 Machine gun. The rifle really didn't bother me, it was the fact that HE had it. "Oh, great," I thought to myself, I'm going to be executed by a Mexican Hoodlum. Why was he walking around with this kind of a gun in the first place?

> The more I looked around the room, the more these guys looked like gang members rather than anything official.

The more I looked around the room, the more these guys looked like gang members rather than anything official. They really looked out of the ordinary. One of them wore an Oakland Raiders jacket, the others were dressed in similar clothes. I kept silent, not knowing what would happen next.

One of them came forward and started speaking Spanish to the border patrol guards. I guessed he was some sort of leader. One of the border patrol guards replied back and handed him a clip board. I don't see you he could read as he looked it over and then turned to me. "Where is the gun?" He asked me in English.

"I don't have it, I didn't bring it," I replied. It was a fair enough question, even though the Border Patrol guards had already accepted this fact. He looked back to the guards for verification as they nodded their heads in agreement.

"Ok, put out your hands" he replied back. He and another man came closer to me, while the guy with the machine gun stood nearby. They came forward, and proceeded to take all my personal belongings. They took my belt, my wallet, the spare change I had in my pockets, and a folded piece of paper I had in my jacket pocket. All of which, they put in the upper drawer of the metal desk. They then untied my shoes and took the laces out of my shoes.

I smiled inside when they took my shoe laces. A survivalist side of me took over and my mind started to race. I knew that guards would often take a prisoner's belt, so that he couldn't hang himself if he got the opportunity. I also knew that many prisoners had their shoe laces taken away for the same reason. However, I wore dress shoes which had thin laces anyway. Each lace was probably eight inches long, and I didn't expect that I could use my laces to hang myself in the first place.

Well, at that moment, I guessed that I couldn't hang myself. It seemed totally silly thinking about it at the time, and seems more ridiculous after the fact, but strange situations bring strange thoughts.

The border patrol produced a zip-lock bag with the bullets they found in my car and gave them over to the man. He looked at them with interest. I could just imagine him saying, "Oh, these would be great in my gun!" He turned and stashed them away in the drawer too. One of the gang members opened a door at the other end of the room. I could see that it opened up to a small hallway revealing cell bars at the end.

The realization finally came to me: This was a Mexican Jail. It seemed strange for a Mexican Jail, but none-the less, it sure enough was a jail. If this was a jail, that meant these thugs were the jailers? No way.

I turned to face the border patrol guards, took a step forward and looked directly at my English speaking guard. I had fire in my voice and was not too happy. "Wait a minute. You guys told me we would see a judge. You didn't say any thing about turning me over to these guys."

The leader of this new group of guards didn't seem to like my objections. He put a hand on my shoulder, pulling at me to turn back around. Reluctantly I turned to face him. I straightened my shoulders and stared him down.

"You have to spend the night in the jail," he said.

I turned my back to him and faced the border patrol guards. "So, what's the deal?"

The English speaking guard shrugged his shoulders and replied, "Well, that's the way we have to do it, you can probably see a judge tomorrow." Thanks a lot Mr. 'It's no big deal' traitor. It's a bit obvious now that it's past 11 pm that I wouldn't see a judge tonight, but I really didn't want to be in the hands of hoodlums. I didn't want to be in trouble with the Border Patrol in the first place, and it's getting worse now that I have to be turned over to these low life guys.

At one end of the room were the border patrol guards. These four men were in uniform, the light at their backs. They now actually looked organized, fit and proper compared to the other end of the room. At the other end were street punks wearing cowboy boots, whose leader looked younger than I was. I really couldn't think of anything good to say about these guys. Their appearance, demeanor and personalities were as dark as the room. I tried to find some redeeming quality, but these guys were definitely out of the ordinary, almost to the point of outrageous. I didn't like the idea that I was being handed over from the organized Border Patrol guards to a Rat Pack. The outlook seemed grim.

With no other choices, I consented and walked toward the hallway with the cell. The border patrol left the way we came in and I was left to the devices of my new guards. I followed one man into the hallway, the leader followed behind me and headed towards one of two cells.

The cell door was made of large steel bars on large hinges opening into a concrete room. The man in front opened the door and the leader pulled out a set of keys. I was instructed to step inside and turn around. I did so as the leader reached and took a key to my handcuffs. At least I had those things off.

I went into a dark unfamiliar room while the cell door was closed behind me. It was locked with a large padlock the size of my hand. I watched the two men as they finished their job and started to leave.

"Oh, wait," I called to the leader. My voice was calm and I wanted to ask some questions before they left. "The others said I needed to see a judge, what do I have to do to see him?"

The leader looked at me and with good English asked, "Do you know a good lawyer?"

I shook my head in disbelief, now this guy WAS making a big deal out of it. "I don't need a lawyer," I protested, "I was planning on just seeing the judge and getting this cleared...."

The man interrupted me, "You are in jail and you need a lawyer!" I could tell he was feeling good about winning any sort of power struggle we were having. He started to walk away.

You jerk, I thought to myself. You have been watching too many American movies. But rather than trying to ask any more "what's next" questions, I watched him leave the hallway and close the door behind himself. I was left alone, in a concrete cell, the only light coming from a light bulb in the hallway.

Standing in the darkness, I tried to understand what happened. Where did this go wrong? Was it when I was passed over to these guys, was it when I got into the truck? I still couldn't get out of my mind the fact that this was so out of the ordinary for me. 'Somewhere where they won't find your body' didn't seem so funny anymore.

New Surroundings

It looked like I would be here for a while, at least overnight, so I began to assess my situation. I started looking around at my surroundings trying to unwind from my recent experience with the "policemen" in the other room. I took a deep breath, "I can do this," I said to reassure myself.

The room was a square 10 by 10 foot room dimly lit by the light bulb in the hallway I first came through. My eyes quickly adjusted to the darkness. The floor was concrete in addition to the walls around me. The ceiling had a covering of metal bars. About a foot above the cage, a ceiling of drywall patched the top. Other previous prisoners had grabbed pieces of the drywall and had torn some of it down, revealing the trusses that supported the roof. Taking down the drywall here and there didn't do much good either, you couldn't get through the cage of metal bars covering the ceiling.

The light from the hallway poured through, but it was still dark inside the cell. I didn't mind that, if I were to sleep tonight this little amount of light wouldn't keep me up. Besides, I don't think I could call the guys back to ask them to turn the light out just so I could get some sleep.

I reached my hand through the cell door and felt for the lock. I had a hard time inspecting it because my head wouldn't fit through the bars to allow me a good look. Besides, I didn't want to make too much noise with rattling the padlock on the metal door, which might result in the guys coming back. I had thoughts of grandeur, trying to pick the lock. However, it was one of the largest padlocks I had ever seen and I really didn't know how to pick any kind of lock. Besides, if I did know how, I still didn't have anything to pick it with. They even took my shoelaces! I quickly gave up on the idea of escaping by way of lock picking the cell door.

I inspected the other parts of the room. In one corner was a stack of newspapers and several paper plates covered with tin foil. I didn't want to look, but knew there was old food under the tin foil. It probably was midnight by now and I really wasn't hungry for a midnight snack anyway. Besides, there was no way of telling how long these plates of food had been there. I decided to avoid that part of the room for now.

Bunched in a corner near the newspapers, was a stack of 2 blankets and a bed sheet. The blankets looked like they had been there for a long time. One was a grungy yellow, the other was soft faded blue that had seen better days. I figured this would be my bedding, but I didn't want to sleep in them as the blankets scared me a little. I could just imagine what could be crawling in them if I got cold or tired. "It's OK, I can do this," I reassured myself again that I was going to get through the night and decided to figure out my bedding situation later.

After all the thinking about blankets and how to keep warm for the night, I suddenly realized that I was a bit chilly. I zipped my jacket to the top and put my hands in my pockets. It was December and it gets cold in the desert. I was grateful I had a jacket.

As I squatted down to look the blankets, the button on my pants popped off. I could feel the pressure of the waistband of my pants loosen and I immediately knew what happened. I'm not the least bit overweight, but I guessed it was just time for the button to pop off. I reached down and picked up the plastic button from the cold concrete floor. Oh great, I thought. I don't even have a belt to cover my missing button or to keep my pants up.

I stood up again to assess the damage to my pants. It didn't seem so bad. The zipper of my slacks kept my pants up and over my waist. I decided to re-tuck my shirt in to create some more bulk at my hips so my pants could stay up. I pulled my jacket down around my waist so it would help keep it up too. It seemed to work. Despite a missing button, I still had my pants where they should be. "Whew", I thought. "You can take my belt and my button can pop off, but I'll still manage!"

On the wall opposite of the cell door was a toilet. Seeing a toilet in the jail cell with me was quite a surprise. I had always been told of horror stories of jail cells with holes in the ground, but right in front of me was a clean looking, sit down on the pot, toilet!

At first I thought this white throne was a joke, and surely must be broken. After being in the jail cell now for a while, I needed to go to the bathroom again, but was reluctant to use this one provided for me. I would hate the possible fact that it would be broken and I had already used it. Imagine me trying to explain to any of the jailers that I used a broken toilet and there was a gift for them in the morning. So I decided to inspect it before I would use it.

I lifted the seat up. It was sparkling clean. Not a speck of dust or stain mark was on it. It was truly amazing. Like a brand new BMW among a Monster Truck Mud Rally, this toilet was so out of the ordinary!

There was water in the bowl, also clean for that matter. I decided to lift the back cover to see if there was water in the tank. I knew I needed to be very quiet not to disturb the jailers in the next room. I didn't want them to know that I was inspecting the toilet. Amazingly enough, there was water in the tank and all the working components seemed to be in order.

Now to put it to the test. With the porcelain lid in my arms, I worked the handle. Flush! I was so happy, it seemed like I had discovered fire! The tank filled up again and everything seemed to be all right with my newfound porcelain friend.

I quietly placed the top cover back in place, and was overjoyed at the discovery of a working toilet in my jail cell. Since I had just flushed recently, I waited for a while to go to the bathroom. Once again, I thought that multiple flushes would arouse the suspicion of my Mexican jailers. Finally after an ample period of time, I was so happy to have something to sit on and relieve myself.

After finishing using on the toilet, I listened for commotion in the other room. I was really worried that I aroused unneeded suspicion and wanted to hear what the others were doing. Soon enough I knew they were undisturbed by my testing of the toilet.

A television turned on in the main room. Some must have stayed behind to bed down for the night, it seemed a bit weird to be spying on my captors, but hey, they had put me here, and anyone else would have done the same.

I was reminded of what I thought about the guy who put me in here. My accusation was justified when I saw their next activity. I smiled inside when they put on a movie as they fell asleep. I could hear through the sound bouncing off the walls that was an American movie with English words. I imagined that it had Spanish subtitles, but for me I could understand the movie. It was some action movie where there were more gunshots than words spoken. No wonder these guys thought I needed a lawyer. Their heads were filled with enough American images of gunfights to the point that any American that came their way needed a lawyer.

Tired of listening to nothing interesting, I put the toilet seat down and sat for a while and sat, thinking about what had happened. At least by using the toilet lid as a chair, I was sitting off the cold cement floor. This really wasn't what I had expected. How could one possibly expect this anyway? My goal was to come to Mexico for a nice two-day vacation. I wanted to be with dad, have some fun and eat my fill of great Mexican food.

However, I was now stuck here for the night. But it didn't seem that bad as all my plans were not permanently stopped. I would see the judge in the morning and he would give me the rest of tomorrow and the next to be a free tourist in the wonderful country of Mexico. There was no reason for me to think any ill feelings for anything that happened so far. I made up my mind that no matter what happens I decided to keep good spirits about this. Besides, this would be a great story to tell my co-workers when I got back!

I decided to try to get some sleep, despite the uninviting look of the bedding provided. In the corner were two blankets and a bed sheet. That was all there was to the cold concrete floor. I wasn't really looking forward to sleeping as I knew it was going to be a rough night, however I tried to make the best of it.

As I shook out the two blankets, a small cloud of dust filled the cell and faded away. I folded the bed sheet in half and laid it on the hard concrete. I then did the same with the two blankets and sat on top of them for a bit. The bedding now looked a little nicer, and not so slept in.

I was really worried that there still would be creepy crawly things around, so I decided to only lie down on top of my newly made bedding rather than getting in the covers. I figured that it was Mexico, the weather wouldn't get that cold, so I made the resolution to sleep in my jacket on top of the bedding.

It worked for a while until I woke up in the middle of the night shivering. I was wrong about the cold. It became very cold and my jacket alone was not sufficient. I remembered it was the desert in December and it does get chilly in the nighttime.

The guards in the other room had settled down, their snoring competing with the sounds of the television. No matter what I could do, the brisk air was getting to me. I became a little frustrated because I needed to get some sleep while I could but was worried about getting in the covers. My worst fears would be that there would be fleas or some small insects in the unclean blankets that would eat me alive.

I weighed out the choices of laying on top of the covers and being cold and awake, or sleeping under the covers with the possibility of bugs. Frustrated, cold and sleepy, I decided that I needed some sleep. "Ok", I said to myself, "I will make a mental note in my mind to wake up if I feel anything biting me." And with that sense of sleepy logic, I crawled under the covers, got warm and soon fell asleep again.

> I will make a mental note in my mind to wake up if I feel anything biting me.

CHAPTER 2

TUESDAY

All Day in the Jail Cell

Waking Up

I slept better than I thought I would, but woke up anxious to get going. The bugs didn't bother me, or at least I was ignorant to the fact. I now had other things on my mind. If the jailers told me that I must speak with a judge, then I wanted to meet this judge. However, I also realized that there wasn't much I could do about it until someone let me out.

I got up from my blankets and looked around the room. Directly in the middle of the room was a spot of sunlight about the size of a quarter, shining on the floor. I moved over to the sun spot and put my hand in it. The light was coming from a hole at the edge of the room between the ceiling and a wall. It wasn't big enough to be warm to the touch, but it was still nice to waive my hand through it. I put my eye in the sunlight and moved the spot so it danced across my face. I was always taught that looking directly into the sun could be damaging, but somehow I really didn't care at this moment. It was sunshine and it certainly felt good as I needed some kind of contact with the outside light.

In a matter of ten minutes, the sun had moved enough that the spot disappeared. The sunlight was caught in the hole and stopped shining into the room. I smiled, "I have seen the light!" I said to myself. Silently, I counted my blessings for even briefly seeing a ray of sunlight.

It was still early morning and a bit chilly. My jacket kept the desert morning out as much as it could. Of course, being in an empty concrete room didn't help either. But once I got up and moved around a little, I soon began to warm up.

I put my ear up to the wall that separated my cell from the main room. I knew there were several of the police men when I came last night, so there had to be a few who had spent the night as I faintly heard several sets of snoring. I thought for a couple seconds about yelling loud enough to wake them up. Even though it would be fun, it wouldn't be beneficial in the long run. So I decided to let them sleep and let them wake up on their own.

My attention went around the room and rested on a set of newspapers. They were a couple weeks old, but I still had something to read. I picked up the front page and attempted to understand what was printed. The text was in Spanish and I could understand about every other word. The front page had something about President Fox who had recently been elected as President of Mexico. I got the basics of the message, but really didn't get the details. I became a little frustrated with my lack of Spanish vocabulary and finally put the paper down. To get to the newspapers, I had to move some of the plates of food that lay nearby. I really didn't want to lift the tinfoil, fearing what I would see. I just imagined what could be under the tinfoil covered plates and left them, unexamined where they were.

By this time I was getting a little stir crazy, and heard some sounds coming from the front room. I heard the sliding glass door open and then voices at the far end of the entrance room. They were in Spanish and muffled enough that I couldn't understand, followed by footsteps and then a woman's voice too! This seemed strange in an unsophisticated police office, but all of this was strange anyway. The door to the hallway opened. Someone was coming to see me! I tried to remain calm as I continued to sit on my bed of blankets.

A man finally came into view looking through the cell bars. He was a Mexican man who I had not seen before. He had a large mustache and seemed to match his large and tall build. We looked at each other for what seemed a minute, both of us examining each other's situation.

I finally broke the silence. "*Buenos Dias*," I said to him.

"*Buenos Dias*," He replied back, his voice echoing the room. It was so deep; it reminded me of a Mexican Darth Vader as it sent a chill down my spine. This was the first real sound I'd heard that morning and I wasn't prepared to hear such a powerful voice. He caught me off guard enough that I really didn't have much else to say to him. So he looked at me for a couple seconds longer, and with a nod of his head, turned and walked away from my view.

> His voice was so deep; it reminded me of a Mexican Darth Vader as it sent a chill down my spine.

I nicknamed this deep voiced man "The Captain", because his presence was so dominating. He was the first person I saw for the day and as the captain left, I continued to stay on my blankets and thought.

Do You Want to Eat?

For what seemed like another eternity, I sat in my cell on the blankets until another man came to the cell door. This was becoming interesting. I could imagine that the police in the other room were advertising that there was a gringo being held in the cell and they were selling tickets. This particular guy didn't seem official, as he was thin and had dingy clothing. However that didn't mean much, considering those who put me in here in the first place. I stood up and walked over to him as we looked at each other though the bars.

"Wassup!" He said with a grin. Then he started speaking Spanish, talking so fast that I couldn't understand. He touched his mouth and I finally figured the gestures he was making. *"Do you want to eat?"* He asked me.

"Yes please" I replied. I wasn't sure if this guy was teasing but I wanted to be honest.

"OK, you wait here," he replied in a quite Spanish voice and with that, he turned around and walked away. I chuckled to myself. Where else did he think I would go? I guess I could have asked him if there were other options for waiting somewhere else, but he was already gone through the hallway and into the other room.

I really didn't know what to make of my conversation with this new man. It all seemed to go by so fast and I really didn't think that he would help me out anyway. He seemed so out of the ordinary that I really didn't think he was an official and I didn't think that he would be back with food either. Deep down inside I hoped he would. Any type of breakfast would be good.

I went back to my blankets and sat on top of them again. With little else to do, I started to think. What was I going to do after I got out of here today? I wondered what time I would get out and how much time would be left to spend with Dad. I had never been to Rocky Point Mexico before and was excited to go to a new place and experience the culture of Mexico outside of a jail cell.

My mind started to wander back to home in the United States. I thought about work and the fact that I had the next three days off, still counting today. It would be a nice relief to take some time in the middle of the week. However, it was just my luck to get involved with being in jail, just because I forgot a box of bullets in my car. I knew I should have cleaned my car before hand. Sitting there in my situation, I remembered that hindsight is always 20-20.

The Sweeping Lady

Not really being able to solve my problems by sitting, I decided to "walk" around a bit. There really wasn't a lot of room for walking however I had been sitting for a while and needed to stretch my legs. The room was only three paces across and three paces wide. After roaming around this restricted space for a short time, I wandered over and stopped at the cell door.

The light bulb was still shining in the hallway as it continued to be the only source of light. I looked down the hallway and realized that the captain and the guy who asked if I was hungry had left the hallway door open and I had a view of part of the main room. I saw the desk in where my stuff was stashed last night and the tile floor around it.

At that time, a woman came into view. She was an older, heavy set Mexican woman who had her hair in a bun and a broom in her hand. Her voice rebounded in the main room as she talked to the Capitan and started to get busy sweeping the area.

I thought to myself, the police have a cleaning lady? That was something else, however she seemed more like family rather than a subordinate worker. Just then another woman crossed my field of vision and then disappeared out of view. This other woman had a baby in her arms and seemed happy to be there. She said good morning to the sweeping lady and to some of the other men. I guessed this woman with the baby was some policeman's wife.

This seemed especially odd to me. However, I quickly realized that this could be a family operation. Just like a bakery or any other business, the whole Mexican family would somehow all be involved. Wife would bring baby to visit and mother-in-law would sweep.

The sweeping lady kept at the task of sweeping the whole side of the room not letting the arrival of the lady with the baby slow her progress. She was very proficient with her

45

broom and even when she was out of my view, I could tell where she was from the swishing sounds that her broom made.

She finally came around the room again and back into my view. She started sweeping around the desk and then looked up from her work. She hadn't realized that she was being watched and until she looked up now and became aware that I was watching from the cell.

"Buenos Dias, Senora," I finally got the courage to say as she was only about 15 feet away. I don't know if she was more startled to hear my voice or just to see a friendly gringo in jail, but it really surprised her.

She nodded her head, mumbled some greetings back and then quickly continued sweeping. She seemed a bit embarrassed that someone was watching her. My thoughts were that if I was friendly to this old woman, maybe this might prompt someone to come back to my cell and I could start the process of getting out of here.

It didn't work. She wouldn't talk much and I knew she felt uncomfortable with me watching her do her work. I didn't know what else to say as I knew how uneasy she might have felt. She looked around for a moment and reached for the door.

My last look at her was when she closed the hallway door. I guess there are some people who just don't like being watched while sweeping.

I wanted to call out "wait", but of course, didn't. I don't think it would have done much good. She shut the door and now all I could see was the empty hallway. I knew if I yelled and made a total nuisance of myself they would be sure to leave me there. So I decided to stay quiet and let the Mexican Sweeping Lady shut me off from her work.

Well so much for my view. It was actually nice to see out into the main room while it lasted. It gave me something to do and at least I could see what was going on. But now, I was left alone again, thanks to the quick decision of the Sweeping Lady.

The Can of Coke

Time passed and I heard more noises from the other room. The young thin man came back and opened the door in the hallway. I got up and met him at the cell door.

In one hand he had a paper plate, covered with aluminum foil, in the other hand he held a can of Coke. He smiled and offered me what he had in his hands. I was really taken back by this gesture. He was giving me food and I truly felt grateful towards him.

He folded the paper plate like a large taco to pass through the bars. I took a warm plate of food from his hands as he also passed the can of Coke through. After accepting both items I said "*gracias*" and looked at him for a second.

His smile reflected that he was happy with what he had accomplished. It seemed that he was pleased to serve me. I still didn't know who he was or how he was affiliated with the jail. He still didn't seem to be an official policeman, but I guess you never can tell. After all, he was walking around in a police station in the morning giving out breakfast.

> It's true that people turn closer to God in times of turmoil.

The man answered "*De nada,*" and walked out of the hallway. At least he kept the door open. I watched him until he was out of sight and then turned my attention to the food in my hands. It smelled good and I was anxious to see what was under the aluminum foil.

I returned once again to my blankets and sat down. Before I started to eat, I bowed my head and said a prayer. A flood of gratitude filled my heart. I was thankful for the food and the man who brought it to me. I asked a blessing that I would have a strong stomach if there were any problems and that I would learn from this experience. It was a simple prayer, but it was heartfelt. It's true that people turn closer to God in times of turmoil.

I set the can of coke aside and uncovered the foil. Underneath were three corn tortillas, a combination of fried meat and fried bell peppers and a lime slice on the side. I took out one of the tortillas and made a taco of meat and vegetables and squeezed the lime over the top.

I could only finish two of my tacos. I was getting full and didn't feel like finishing the whole plate of food. It was good but it really seemed like a lot of food. I set the rest aside, thinking that I would eat it later. However, I was also concerned about leaving the food out for any period of time without refrigeration. I then looked around and saw the other plates of food covered with tinfoil. Looks like the others before me were fed in similar manner. However, when they left, the leftover food stayed behind. I was glad I had my own food rather than having to scrounge through the leftovers. I figured I wasn't that courageous anyway.

I now reached a dilemma. The guy had given me a can of Coke. I picked it up and looked it over. It was bottled in Mexico and had a picture of Santa printed on the can. He was smiling back at me with a coke bottle in his own hand. All of the text was in Spanish, but a Coke can is still a Coke can.

It looked appealing, but I wasn't particularly thirsty. I really wasn't a big Cola drinker either, and so this seemed like a nice treat for someone else to have given me a Coke. My dilemma was whether I open and enjoy it now, or wait. If I wait, when should I open it?

A thought came to me. I was in a dilemma myself. Why not save the can of Coke until I'm out of this mess? It would be my Victory Coke! I would drink it as a free man. This meant that later this afternoon when I spoke to this judge, I would get out and have a nice refreshing beverage waiting for me.

I set the unopened Coke aside near my own plate of food and sat down to think about my situation. I was really content. I was looking forward to getting out, and seeing dad. In the mean time, I was comfortable on some folded up blankets in a jail cell. At least I was full, happy as much as I could be and comfortable for the time being! What a great experience it is to be in the middle of a bad situation and be content in the present moment.

A Visitor

The next moment of activity came from another man entering the front door of the main room to the jailhouse. I got up close to my cell door and looked down the hallway into the main room. The hallway door was open again, thanks to the man delivering my breakfast and I could see this new man walk around. He seemed to be very comfortable with the fellow officers, but somehow I got the impression that he wasn't a policeman. He actually appeared a little higher class than the police I had seen, especially the ones from last night.

This Mexican man wore a brown suede jacket and his dark hair was slicked back. He smiled and fraternized with the sweeping lady until the Captain came up. They both talked for a moment and then shuffled out of view. I could still hear them talking but couldn't understand the words as the main room had an echo that melted their words together.

I went back to sitting on my blankets again, there wasn't anything else I could see or do about the new visitor in the main room. A couple minutes passed and then I heard steps and voices in the hallway. I got up and went to the cell door and saw the man in the brown suede jacket standing with the Captain. Now the ball is rolling, I thought to myself. I smiled half heartily, and looked at him. I didn't think I was in control of this situation so he finally he spoke up.

"You the one who is at border last night?" His English was broken but I could understand that he was looking for me. "I was at border this morning and they said you are here."

Whoever he was, I was actually happy to see him even f I wasn't sure why. "Are you the Judge I need to speak to?" I didn't know who this guy was, but I hoped he could help me out.

"No, I am Lawyer." He smiled, I smiled too. Apparently he had gone up to the border, spoke to some of the guards there and heard that there was a Gringo in the local jail. So, he saw an opportunity and decided to investigate further to see if I had a need for a lawyer. "I be your lawyer," he said. Well, I guess the guy who put me in last night was right as the words that rang back in my ears: 'You're going to stay here tonight and you need a good lawyer!'

"Fine," I said, wondering if he was a good lawyer or a poor one. "But you have to talk to my dad first." This was one way I could get to my dad. I hadn't even been out to get a phone call, so anything would help. He gave me a puzzled look. He didn't understand what I was saying in English. So I decided to try my best in Spanish: *My dad is in Rocky Point*

The light came on in his head. He repeated it back *"your dad is in Rocky Point?"*

"Yes," I replied, *"on vacation."*

Now we were getting somewhere. If he could call my dad, they then could get me out of here. The lawyer offered to find my Dad, so Dad could hire him and then asked how to find him.

That was a good question. I really didn't know myself. Dad had just told me briefly the name of hotel where he was staying in Rocky Point. 'You can't miss it if you were on the main road', he said. My plan was to be there last night, go to the front desk and ring for him. I didn't even know the phone number of the hotel or his room number. I guess it was a lack of preparation on my part, but it really didn't occur to me that I would get in this much trouble that I would need this kind of information.

"Can you get me out?" I asked. I was really asking this to find out what was next and what was in store for me. I really had no clue how to go about seeing the Judge and expected that something would be done by now. He turned to the Captain and spoke a couple of fast words. I realized I'm not as good with my Spanish as I would like to be. Once again the Mexican Darth Vader voice spoke. His deep voice bounced off the cell walls and gave me a chill.

The lawyer looked back at me and in his poor English said, "I get you out, but first, uh," he paused for a moment trying to find the English equivalent, "I get your dad." It appeared he was really set on finding my dad. That was fine with me, as long as that meant getting out today. I had no sense of time anymore. No watch, no sunshine. I was trying to keep my hopes up, but was getting anxious.

I told the lawyer the name of the hotel and gave my dad's name (Sam). That was all I knew. "Ok, I go get your dad. You wait right here!" With that, he and the Captain left. Well, there's still nothing much else I can do, I thought to myself, and why did everyone tell me to wait here anyway? He seemed nice, but I really felt out of my comfort zone anyway. Without a phone number I supposed that he would travel to Rocky Point and find my dad. I didn't even know how far Rocky Point was from this border town.

I watched the two men leave the hallway and felt some contentment that something was happening. Since I came here, no one had talked to me about how long I'd be staying here or how long the process of getting out takes. I was grateful for the food, but was even happier that I would be getting out soon. I hoped it was relatively fast, but compared to what I was experiencing, I should be grateful that anything was happening at all. Besides what could I accomplish if I made a fuss about it anyway? They probably would just shut the door to the hallway and forget about me.

I started thinking about this Mexican lawyer. He had me over a barrel and both of us knew it. What would he do if I'd said 'no thanks' to his "I be your lawyer" offer? So as long as he was trying to find my dad, at least he was useful. I would let Dad decide what to do with him.

> This Mexican lawyer had me over a barrel and both of us knew it.

That would be an amusing conversation. I could only imagine how this lawyer would go up to the hotel. By now I would be really late, however Dad was patient, but he would now doubt wonder where I am. I could just picture it: There's a knock at the dad's hotel door. He opens it up and there's a Mexican standing there instead of me.

"Mr. Sam, I am lawyer. Your son's in jail," he would say with a big accent and even larger smile. He would then instruct dad that he had to follow him back to the border town to get me out. Would dad believe him? Or would he just let me stay? Only time would tell if he trusted this random stranger, or if I'd be left here like the forgotten foil dinners in the corner of my jail cell.

Taking a Nap

I really didn't know how long the lawyer would be away, for all I knew he could have walked down to the local bar and forgot about me. I hoped the guy would be good for his word. After all, he did say that he would find my dad. I really didn't think that he would forget about me, but this was Mexico, I was in jail and nothing had gone as planned so far. It was weird to think that my time in here was contingent on how fast some guy could find my dad. However, I had faith, mostly because there really wasn't much else I could do anyway.

Time passed, but I really couldn't tell how long. An hour seemed like five minutes, and five minutes seemed to take forever. I lost all interest in tracking time and tried to find other things that I could think about. By this time I was feeling quite frustrated, so I sat on my bedding and started to think.

I leaned on the cell door to hear what my jailers were doing. All was quiet and I figured it was siesta as I continued hearing their movements, but I could never fully tell what was going on. By now, they put a movie on and it seemed that things were quieting down for a while. It was another American movie. Not as many bullet sounds in this movie as the one last night.

I really got a kick out of the idea of Mexican jailers watching American movies on their down time. I never heard of many Mexican movies, so I guess there was a demand for American made ones. I thought of the marketing that it would take to get a movie ready for Mexican promotion. I think the largest hurdle would be to make the movie in the first place. It seemed a smaller task to put Spanish subtitles and find another means of distribution.

I guessed there was a market for these dubbed movies. Even though it's a bit obvious, I suddenly became aware of how much influence Hollywood has on society as well as the development of ideas in other countries. I hoped others would know that Hollywood was much different than that of regular society.

I started thinking about my situation here and what kind of a movie this misadventure might make. I hoped that it would be interesting enough for others to watch, but if my story was a movie, then they would surely take this part out. There was nothing I could do now except wait for my dad to find me. The hard part was all the hurry up and wait environment that I was in. Hollywood would never be like this.

All I could do was think about how I got into this mess and the fact that my jailers were watching American movies.

Slowly, as I lay on my bedding, I felt drowsy. I figured if the others could have a siesta, I should too. When in Rome....I thought to myself. Besides, there wouldn't be much activity if my jailers were down for a nap. I was also running out of things to think about and that was also causing me to grow sleepy. I fell asleep with the thoughts of Hollywood and Dad trying to find me running though my mind. The drowsy combination resulted in some pretty strange dreams. I fell asleep with a smile on my face, it wasn't everyday that I could take a nap in a concrete jail cell. Besides, I wasn't at work anyway, so any nap was nice.

More Visitors

I woke up from my nap to the sounds of the hallway door opening and the shuffling of feet. Someone was coming to see me. Already today, I had been visited by the Capitan, the Mexican who gave me food, and the lawyer who was all about getting hired to find my dad. I could now tell when people were just walking around in the other room or coming to see me. This time the shuffling feet accompanied two male voices.

I got up from my bedding and moved toward the cell bar door trying to rub the sleep from my eyes. Two men were standing before me. It was a very small hallway the narrow-ness of which caused the two of them to appear squished together. I had more room to move around than they did while standing in the narrow hallway.

I recognized the first man, standing the closest to me, from before. He was in the main room this morning, walking around when the Captain left the door open. I also saw him talking with the Sweeping Lady. I though I even saw him last night with the rest of the hoodlums. However, he was a normal looking man, not as scruffy as the others in the main room. He had Levi's jeans with a brown belt and large silver belt buckle. He wore a black wind breaker and cowboy boots. This guy looked like a normal citizen, but I swear I saw him last night.

The other man was one I had never seen before. He too was in blue jeans and wore a brown jacket. He was a bit heavy set and had on thin rimmed glasses and carried a notebook. I didn't know what to make of these two as they came to my cell door, still talking to each other. I smiled trying to be friendly, but waited to say anything until they finished talking to each other. I didn't want to interrupt them even though I couldn't understand what was said.

The one I thought to be the policeman spoke first. He started with a lot of "um's" and "uh's". I guess he was thinking of English words. He finally asked if I was the one who came across the border last night. The question was in half Spanish and half English. I gave him an "A" for his effort anyway.

"Well obviously I was the one here last night", I thought to myself. He should have known as he was one of the guys who put me in here in the first place and there were no other prisoners anywhere. But I just nodded my head politely.

He then started talking really fast in Spanish. He tried to ask me questions but I couldn't make heads or tails of anything he asked. He ended each sentence with the word "*cartuches*". I didn't have a clue what it meant.

"*Cartuches?*" I asked back.

"*Si, Cartuches.*" He replied. We both had puzzled looks. I didn't know what he was asking and he was wondering why I didn't understand.

"*What is Cartuches?*" I asked. At least I knew that much Spanish to ask him in his own language.

With that, he pulled his jacket up over his waist and reached for the gun at his side. First thing that ran through my mind was, "Oh, he has a gun," the second was "Oh, he's reaching for it. I'm in trouble!"

My heart beat a little faster as he fiddled with it for a second and pulled out the magazine clip from the back end. The gun itself was still holstered, but with one hand he held the magazine clip and with the other he pulled out a single bullet from the clip. He held it up and said *"Cartuches"*

> **With that, he pulled his jacket up over his waist and reached for the gun at his side.**

"Oh, bullets, cartridges" I said in English. Now I knew the word.

"Si, Cartuches" he replied back. He was glad that I knew the word, but he was now waiting for an answer.

What was the question? I started to get an idea of what he was asking me. Were they my bullets? Did I own them?

"Yes, they are mine," I answered back in Spanish. I was happier that I understood the question more than why he was asking me.

"Where is the gun?" Was his second question. He was not the only one who asked me that recently. However, under the circumstance I was beginning to understand that it was really weird for the Border Patrol to find bullets and no gun.

"It is back in Arizona, at home." I answered back as we continued our conversation in Spanish.

"Were you going to sell the cartridges? Who was going to buy them from you?" The guy was nice about asking his question, but he wanted answers.

"No, I was not going to sell them to anybody" I knew what he was getting to. He was trying to establish some motive or benefit for me bringing *"cartuches"* or bullets into the country. That was the million-dollar question. I asked myself the same question. Why did I get into this mess?

He finally came out and asked me the next question. *"Why did you bring cartuches into Mexico?"* he asked. This was reasonable, I could understand it. If I didn't have the gun with me and if no one was going to buy them from me then why did I bring them with me?

I was ready for this question. *"It was an accident, I am really sorry. I was going to see my dad on vacation and forgot I had them in my car. I'm really sorry."* I lowered my eyebrows to show my remorse.

They started talking fast again to one another as the second man wearing glasses started writing notes on his clipboard. I paused and looked at my visitors. I got another glimpse of the magazine clip and the bullet in the policeman's hand. Then a humorous thought struck me.

No wonder I was in trouble, I had brought in a higher quality of bullets over the border than even this policeman used. Last night the Border Patrol had found my box of "hydroshock" bullets in my car. The shell casings were nickel and the head or tip was hollow pointed copper. However, rather than normal bullets, the type I had were also used by many US police forces because of the quality. The border Patrol had written in their report that I had a set of "special bullets" that were only used by the Mexican Army and Air Force. I didn't realize that Mexico even had an Air Force, but that was beside the point.

Even though I still was a little unsure *why* I had brought them, I remembered *how* I had them. A week before crossing the Mexican border I went target shooting in the open ranges of Arizona during Thanksgiving weekend with some friends. After the target shooting, I store the Hydroshock bullets with the gun. When I went out with these friends, I put these bullets aside and did target practice with some other cheaper bullets. When I finished for the weekend I put the gun away, but had not put the bullets back with it. So the box of original bullets was left in my car unknown to me.

Growing up as a young man in Arizona included gun ownership within the family and friends that I had. I understand that living in a city on the East Coast of the US probably couldn't accommodate such a privilege. However, there was a mentality within the wide-open spaces of the Southwest that could foster such thought. The friends I grew up with developed a respect for gun safety as well as firearm education. Most of us had also accomplished our Eagle Scout Awards, which also helped influence our actions with prudence and as much wisdom as we could.

I know that the media has mostly endorsed a negative light on gun ownership. There have been many terrible crimes committed with the use of guns. These give reason to question why people do such acts or why anyone is permitted to possess such weapons. Growing up my friends and I conversed several times on the benefits and drawbacks of gun ownership. Our opinion was that of gun ownership and praying we would never have to use one except for recreation. We resolved to use impeccable safety around each other and at target practice with increased courtesy whenever we knew we had firearms in our possession. Crossing the Mexican Border with bullets in the car was negligent on my part. Having a handgun in the first place wasn't.

Still, I was responsible for my own actions and I was stuck behind bars conversing with two strange Mexican men, one of which still held a bullet in his hand. They continued talking back and forth. Finally, they were satisfied and turned back to me.

"*OK, so there is no gun?*" The policeman verified again.

"*No, it was an accident to even have the bullets,*" I replied. I really wanted to stress this point so that I might have some mercy.

Both men thanked me for my time. Well they were most certainly welcome to it. After which, they left by going down the hallway, back into the main room and out of sight.

I really hoped that this conversation would speed up the process. I also wanted to know what was next so I could get out of here. But no one seemed to know, other than the fact that the lawyer I met earlier today went to find my dad. I really hoped that getting my dad wasn't a necessary step to getting out of here or else that would take some time. Who knew how long it would take for the lawyer to even find dad and then come back with him. I guessed that in the meantime, the secretary with glasses had to fill in a report and came with the policeman with the big belt buckle to interview me.

After these two men had left, I was grateful that they had come, at least it was some company with some amusing thoughts about bullet quality. I sat back down on my blankets and began thinking. I mused over the fact that some policeman had my confiscated bullets. He most definitely would sooner or later put them in his own handgun. I wished him good luck with his new bullets. I really didn't mind giving bullets to the Mexican Police. It was obvious that I wouldn't see them again even if I got out today. Had I known I had them in my possession, I would have given them to the US border Patrol as a gift rather than going across the Mexican border with them. But to the one Mexican policeman who was fortunate to get my bullets, I thought he honestly needs them more than I do.

Dad Comes

I thought long and hard for the next hour or more and was still contemplating my current situation when I heard some more commotion from the main room. I didn't seem to mind the commotion, I figured it was more police conversation. But then I heard the distinct voice of the lawyer I had spoken with earlier. Had he come back? I was actually amazed to hear his voice. Then I heard the hallway door open and the lawyer calling out, *"Roberto!"*

I got up and walked to the cell door and could hardly believe that I saw him: my dad. I still remember the look he had on his face. It was a cross between "I can't believe I'm here" and "am I being hoodwinked?" I could understand his predicament. Was dad being led to his grave by some conniving Mexican or was there some truth to the 'your son's in jail' story? Either way, he was right there, standing in front of me.

I smiled really wide and said "Hi!" Well, I really didn't know what else to say or do. I was shocked about the whole situation myself and now very relieved to see him. My dad, Sam is a kind gentleman but getting up there in years. Now past retirement age, the guy can still get around really well. He gave a big sigh of relief when he actually saw me, however it meant that this growing nightmare was true. I was really in Jail and some Mexican Lawyer had knocked on his door. I still couldn't tell what would be worse for dad, the truth or if this all was some kind of hoax.

> Was dad being led to his grave by some conniving Mexican or was there some truth to the 'your son's in jail' story?

The conversation started although I still don't know how. I began telling briefly how I was detained at the border and how I spent the day here waiting for someone to get him. I told dad that I was the one who told the lawyer to go and get him. He seemed to stay quiet and just listened to the things that I spoke. When I finished my story, his first question was if I was OK and was being treated well, in which I responded affirmatively. I mentioned that I had been fed earlier that day and was still doing well.

"I thought you'd be coming last night," he said.

"I thought I was too", I interrupted.

"Well, when you didn't come last night, I waited a couple of hours this morning and then called Christina." Oh, yes. I thought of her and wondered how she was doing. I hoped she wouldn't hear about this yet, but now she knew because Dad called her when I was nowhere to be found. "She didn't take it too well." He continued, "She said you left yesterday and if you didn't show up last night then something's happened. There wasn't anything I could do, just wait. Then the lawyer showed up and that's how I found out".

I cringed at knowing that both Dad and Christina are involved. I knew Christina would get worked up over it too.

Dad asked me again why I was here. Ok, here we go again. I was stopped by the Border Patrol who searched my car. They found bullets in the car and I was detained because I had crossed the border with a box of bullets.

Why were the bullets in the car? This was a tough and direct question. I told him I kept asking this myself, why WERE there bullets in the car? Good question, but I kept thinking that the answer was pretty stupid. I had gone target shooting during Thanksgiving the week before and had left a spare box of bullets in the car. This was all familiar to dad, he knew I had a firearm, and he knew that I was generally responsible, but the combination of a young adult having a gun and now getting in trouble with any part of it was just a bit overwhelming.

He drew a little closer towards the bars and reached an arm inward. I thought he was going to put his hand on my shoulder so I leaned in a bit. Instead he grabbed me by the back of the neck and held on tight. Dad's not an aggressive man, nor abusive in any way, so this act of power startled me a little. His eyes were now laser focused, his grip was strong, his breathing sturdy.

"When you get back, you tell your friends you're having no part of this anymore". He was referring to the three friends I had that usually go shooting with and the fact that we made it a hobby to try to peaceably have guns. I knew dad admired my friends for the length of time we had been together and the friendship and support we had been for each other. But this time, I knew he was mad at me. Very few times have I seen a look as if to say 'I raised you better than this!' Dad truly wanted to shake me and ask 'what were you thinking?'

I took a deep breath. "Dad, if you're going to blame someone, I'm the one in here, not them. I was the one who got in trouble and it's totally my fault." This took him back a bit. Rather than passing blame, I chose to stand up and take responsibility on my shoulders, even though I really still didn't realize the weight. I couldn't blame dad for thinking that my friends were involved in some way or that their actions had influenced me. I guess they did in a way, but I had thought about this long and hard today. The first decision I came to was that I was in this mess because of what I did, not from the influence of others.

Dad looked at me and his countenance changed. It was from a look of stress and upset to deep thought. "Ok," he said, but he still kept a hold of the back of my neck. He was still trying to absorb the whole idea.

"Dad, I'm really sorry," I looked down, it was now hard to see my dad disappointed and distressed because of something I did. However, I knew my dad loved me enough to find me and that's all that mattered to me right now. The bars of the cell door were between us, but it didn't seem to matter. I was glad my dad was finally here and I knew he was glad to see me. He finally loosened his grip and put his hands over mine as I held the cell bars.

By this time, there were two men standing behind Dad. Until now, neither dad nor I cared who was nearby. My attention now turned to these two men as I looked over dad's shoulder. I soon realized they were twin brothers and I had a hard time telling them apart. However, I knew that at least one of them was the lawyer I spoke to this morning. I supposed he had contacted Dad and gave him directions back to the jail.

I looked at them. These two brothers smiled from ear to ear. I didn't know whether it was from the fact that they had brought father and son together, or that they were standing in the hallway, blocking dad's only exit out. "OK" I asked them, "W*hat's next?*"

At first they didn't know what I was talking about. I could tell they were thinking 'What do you mean, we brought your dad right?'
"What's going to happen?" I asked using different Spanish words this time.

"Oh," now they understood my Spanish and answered in English for Dad's benefit. "The police need to, how you say, write a report. We see judge tomorrow". That brought two things to mind. First, at least I had a time frame as to when I would get this situation resolved. And second, I realized that I would spend another night here. I knew it was maybe getting late, but I didn't realize how late in the afternoon it was considering I had no watch. I looked at dad, he gave me an 'oh well' back. We both knew there wasn't much else to do other than wait for tomorrow again.

The lawyers started talking to each other and then turned to us. "Ok, we go and talk to the others to write the report." And with that, they left the hallway, into the main room.

"I don't want to leave you, but there are a couple of things I must do before it gets any later," Dad said reluctantly. I knew he felt bad for leaving me now that he had finally found me. "The lawyers are taking me to your car to get your things if you need them. Can I get you anything to bring back?"

I thought for a moment. "I have a sleeping bag in the trunk of my car." Yes, I randomly carried one around in my car. "It was really cold last night and if it's possible, I think I could use it." Dad nodded OK.

"Oh, yeah" I added, "one more thing. I'm going stir crazy here, if you go to my car, can you bring something to read? I have a book in my overnight bag." Dad thought for a moment and nodded his head again.

We said our goodbyes and dad walked out the hallway and into the main room. I watched him until he turned out of sight, feeling that it was great to see my dad. He was a good man and I felt a deepening pride to be his son, even if I was in trouble.

I sat back down on the blankets, again alone with my thoughts.

Making the Report

After an extra long while, I heard some more commotion coming from the main room. I left my thoughts and headed for the cell door hoping to see something. The door to the hallway was closed, but it didn't take long for it to open. The lawyers came into the hallway and were all smiles again, followed by the captain and another policeman. I wondered what was going on! Could I go now?

One of the lawyers was the first to speak. "Ok, Roberto. We need to write a report. We let you out for a few minutes to help write this report."

That was funny I thought to myself. "We let you out,"I wondered if it really was the ability of the lawyers to let me out in the first place. If they had that ability, why wouldn't they let me out for good? They sure were feeling good about themselves anyway.

I smiled and said "OK," as I watched the captain take a key from his chain and unlock the padlock securing the cell door. It was the first time in about 20 hours that this door was opened. My liberty was soon hindered when the other police man produced his handcuffs. I looked at the lawyers and they shrugged there shoulders in unison with a continued smile. Rather than going through the song and dance like I had last night with the border patrol about putting on handcuffs, I decided just to go along with this. Hey, if I was in a Mexican jail, I guess it would be reasonable to wear handcuffs now and then.

I was led down the hallway back into the main room. There were several people already in the room. Mostly policemen, but I couldn't recognize any of the ones that were there yesterday. Maybe it had something to do with the lights being turned on this time. Looking around the room, I noticed dad was now there too, I guessed he had come back from his errands. In his hands was a plastic grocery bag, I could tell it contained a jug of water and some food. I smiled and was glad to see him again. Near the metal desk was a rolled up sleeping bag I recognized as my own from my car and two blankets I knew were ones from dad's car. "I brought some things for you" he said as he pointed to the items nearby.

What a comfort and reassurance it was to see dad. I knew it was getting late, it was like him to make sure I was taken care of. I knew he had a long drive ahead of him to get back to the hotel tonight, but was grateful he had returned. But the thought then came, what else would he do? I was glad to see him, even if I was just helping with a report.

We all followed the captain and the lawyers into the greeting room behind the sliding glass door. No daylight shown through the windows and I wondered what time it was. I think time was playing tricks on me. In December, the sun goes down early even around six. But it still seemed late, but how late, I still couldn't tell.

The man with glasses I had met this afternoon sat behind a desk typing away on a computer. The lawyers came around back to see what he was writing as the jailers offered me a chair next to this desk.

It didn't take long to discover that the lawyers and the guy in glasses were very comfortable working together.

As the man asked them questions, the lawyers would respond back in Spanish and he would continue typing.

"He needs to ask some questions," one of they lawyers said. I nodded my head and was ready for whatever question came. A brief thought crossed my mind. They said they needed my help in writing a report, but I was relieved that I was wrong about typing the report myself. Now that this guy was behind the computer typing rather than me, a burden seemed to be lifted. I didn't mind talking now that I found it comical to think I could have been typing the report.

First question. How long have I had the gun? My mind raced backwards through time. Although every time someone brings up the "where's the gun" question I smiled inside. They were as much interested in a gun not being in the situation as much as the bullets that were. I had to think about that for a second and replied "three years."

> Besides, US citizen's rights really don't mean much in a different country anyway.

I was interested in what Dad's silent reaction would be. I had been in college and out of the house on my own for the duration of my gun ownership, but it still felt uncomfortable that I had to disclose this information for the first time to him and to these other guys. Dad took it in stride, I was relieved that dad accepted it as comfortably as he did.

Now the lawyers asked "What do you have a gun for?" Well, other than it being an American privilege, I had to think for a brief moment as I didn't dare say that. Besides, US citizen's rights really don't mean much in a different country anyway. I shrugged my shoulders hoping to show that it really wasn't an important topic and said *"for target shooting and for camping"*. Simply put, I was from Arizona. I had the opportunity to live in wide open spaces that accommodated such things as gun ownership, and I still hoped myself an asset to my community rather than a hindrance.

They nodded their head ok. My answer of "target shooting and camping" seemed to be a suitable answer for them to understand as they nodded their heads and continued.

How old was I?

Twenty-five.

Where did I live?

Phoenix Arizona.

The guy's fingers just flew over the keyboard. I was really amazed watching him. He seemed to know what he was doing but didn't mind the extra encouragement and vocabulary the lawyer offered him while typing.

At that moment, the front door opened and in walked a man in a Border Patrol uniform. I immediately recognized him as the same guard who originally stopped me on the Mexican side in the first place and had discovered the bullets.

My first reaction in seeing him was that of anger. I though to myself, "You jerk, why couldn't you just let it go?" My attitude towards him shifted in a matter of moments. He was just doing his job, and at my expense, he was good at it too. There was no way I could be mad at this man. I needed to take full responsibility, no matter how unfair it felt. There was nothing "unfair" about it, I had to take this bull by the horns no matter how rough the ride became.

I was still curious to see what he was doing here. This Border Guard seemed calm as he walked in like he was expecting to see all of us sitting in this office. He didn't pay attention to me as he walked by and shook the hands of the lawyers, the captain and the secretary. He exchanged a few words and the secretary began reading out loud from the computer screen.

I began a mental conversation of what these guys were talking about.

"Ok this is what we have so far," the secretary would then explain what he had written.

"Yes that looks good, that's how it happened," the border guard would say. The discussion went back and forth a couple times.

As the guys were talking, I had an opportunity to look at the computer screen as the guys were typing and talking. The document was written on Microsoft Word. However everything was written in Spanish. I wondered how a computer could recognize Spanish and accomplish a spell check on it. I figured it was the Spanish version from Microsoft and really got a kick out of seeing a Spanish version of a Windows based program.

About this time, I was brought back to reality when the side door opened and more people came in the main room and then into this front office where we were. It was the Sweeping Lady and two women carrying babies. The whole family's here, I thought to myself. I soon learned I was actually right. The sweeping lady stood to the side, over-looking everything as an old mother-in-law would. One of the women came up to the captain and handed her baby to him. The Captain took the baby in his arms and the woman stayed by his side, somewhat snuggling up to him. I hoped that this was his wife, but it still seemed out of place to have wives and babies in a police station. The other woman came close to another man who started playing peek-a-boo games with the giggling child she held in her arms.

This was weird, these guys were mixing business with pleasure, what's the deal? My thoughts answered: because they can. There seemed to be a sense of family when it came to these people. Family came first, even if it meant mingling family in with police business. I started to admire these women now for supporting their husbands by even being here.

I watched as these wives interacted with their men in the front office. They all acted like I really wasn't there. The secretary was busy typing away with the encourage-ment of the lawyers and now the Border Patrol guard and the police men (or the guys with guns) were preoccupied with their women.

I got a better look at the woman cuddling with the Captain. I almost shuddered when I noticed that this girl had really bad teeth. There was a large gap between her two top front teeth and the bottom ones were just going everywhere. What made it worse was that she kept telling jokes that she was the only one laughing at. She had a really big smile and an even bigger laugh. I was really amazed at the confidence she had despite her crooked smile. I guess she knew that she was the Captain's Woman, so she could laugh at just about anything and get away with having terrible looking teeth. I wasn't going to say anything about it, that's for sure, I was already in trouble. The Captain would have thrown away the key if I commented on his wife's gnarly smile.

The infant in the arms of the Captain was picture perfect. I was surprised at this family because all the beauty that the mother didn't have, the baby did. What caught my eye was that this baby had brilliant blue eyes. I guess all newborns have light colored eyes, but this kid still had sparkling topaz eyes. I didn't want to stare, so I studied her for a couple of moments, then lowered my head and looked at my hands so that I wouldn't offend any of the police men by looking at their ugly wives and beautiful babies.

The secretary finally stopped typing and the lawyers and the border patrol guard nodded in agreement. Looks like whatever they were typing seemed worthy of their approval. They looked at the jailers, then at me and said that they were finished with the report. The lawyer told me the synopsis. The report stated that I was vacationing down here, that I had gone target shooting a week before and forgot that I had bullets in my car. I had no intention of bringing them over the border and would like to get this resolved as simply as possible.

Well yeah, I thought to myself that's what I've been trying to tell everyone. That's my story and I'm sticking to it. However, it seemed that the secretary had to have a big stretch of imagination to come up with this story for me tonight. I found it humorous that the lawyer and the secretary felt it took a huge effort with this report. I then reminded myself that I have to be a bit more humble and let them have their glory.

I knew there are times when you let others think that it was their idea and just let it go. This was a time like that, I said to myself. So, I continued to play the game as I thanked them for their help and their method of explaining what happened. They nodded their heads with a *"you're welcome."*

So, that was the report for the night. I stood up and was escorted back to the cell. I knew it was getting late and I could tell that the others were getting tired too.

We passed the metal desk in the large room and went into the hallway leading to the cells. Dad followed me, picking up the sleeping bag, the extra blanket from his car and the bag of food while the lawyers followed behind. The provisions were put inside the cell and once again I was locked away after the handcuffs were removed. The policemen were getting restless and wanted dad and the lawyers to go away, but I took a few moments to see Dad before he left.

"You going to be alright?" he asked.

"Yep," I replied. "Thanks for the food and the sleeping bag". I told him about sleeping in my jacket last night and the dirty blankets. He shuttered at the thought of bugs and was happy now that he had made my life and circumstances a little more bearable. I didn't mind the jail so much any more. I had spent 24 hours in this place and it was getting cozier (if a concrete box can be considered cozy).

I thanked him again for coming. I told him that I was glad that he believed some lawyer knocking on his door of his hotel earlier this afternoon. He smiled and told me good-night. He'd see me in the morning as he turned to leave. There wasn't much else to say.

I watched him as he walked into the main room and the door shut behind him. I was left to myself with the light in the hallway once again shining through the cell bars. I looked around, everything was the same. My bed of blankets on the bare floor, the trough of newspapers and old plates of tinfoil wrapped food, the white toilet, and the cell bars.

I started to get situated for the night. I pulled out the sleeping bag from its bag and laid it on top of my small mattress of blankets. It looked like dad and the lawyers had already left the building, so I examined the contents of the plastic bag before I crawled into my new bed.

Sure enough, there was a gallon jug of water and some food. I was more thirsty than hungry, so a long swig of water satisfied me. I guess if I didn't have what Dad brought me and I became thirsty enough, I would have eventually opened the can of Coke. But after that, would I have resorted to the toilet water? I was glad I didn't have to find out.

Reading Myself to Sleep

I put my legs in the sleeping bag and sat upright for a while. I thought of this past day and all that was involved. What a mess I had gotten myself into. This really wasn't the ideal trip I had in mind, however it had been eventful. Not every day I get to spend in a Mexican jail. Not every day did I want to either.

I thought about tomorrow. It wasn't a bad dream, so I expected to be waking up in the morning in the same place and circumstances that I was in now, however I had the chance to finally get this reviewed by a judge. He would understand the situation and then I would be out of it. I would still have the rest of tomorrow to spend with dad and have a great dinner and be able to be back to work on Thursday.

In order to build a little more faith about my near future, I pulled out the book dad left with the bag of food. "Mere Christianity" by CS Lewis. I started it a couple of days earlier, and was only a couple pages into it. I really questioned why I would read the book. It was a challenge from my girlfriend, but thought that it would be good reading anyway.

As I started reading for the night, I asked myself the same question the book asked: "Why am I a Christian?" What was the point when I had gotten into so much trouble? Why was I having so many problems when I really didn't mean to do anything wrong? Why was everyone making such a big deal about what I thought was such a small one? Did a belief in a Savior also benefit me now, here in physical imprisonment?

> Why was I having so many problems when I really didn't mean to do anything wrong?

I knew deep down inside the answer to this last question was yes. If a belief in a Savior could give hope for a better spiritual life, then surely I could also have a hope in my temporal condition. I resolved to make the best of my situations despite how grim it looked. Still deep in contemplation, I had not read long before I drifted asleep.

CHAPTER 3

WEDNESDAY

Hot Water and New Surroundings

Waking Up

Wednesday morning, I woke up again to the same surroundings I was getting more and more accustomed to. I kept hoping that this was a dream rather than reality. This was too bizarre to be reality, but no matter how much I tried to pinch myself, I just couldn't change my surroundings. I was in a jail cell in Mexico. As much as I wanted to dream this away, it was reality.

This morning I was much cozier than yesterday morning and I thanked the Lord and my dad for the opportunity to be in a sleeping bag for the night. I decided to stay in my bag for a while. It was nice to "sleep in", besides it didn't seem important that I bounce out of bed first thing in the morning.

I put my hands behind my head looked up at the graffiti studded ceiling and started to think. It was now Wednesday. With any luck, I would get out of here, have dinner with dad before having just enough time to get back to Phoenix for work tomorrow. It would be a busy day, but with enough blessings from above I could pull this off. All this excitement would also be one great story to tell my co-workers tomorrow.

I got up and put my pants on. The button was still missing, but I didn't seem to miss it yesterday. I was actually happy with myself that I could still manage to keep my pants up even without a button. It felt a bit strange, but with my shirt tucked in and my jacket pulled below my waist, I was still able to stay dressed and move around. It was now day three that I had been wearing the same clothes, and the same underwear. I figured I smelled pretty ripe and not too pleasing. But the honest fact was that I wasn't out to please any of the ladies. The only ones I had seen were the sweeping lady and the wives of those that were with the police last night.

The thought of last night's women made me shiver. The image of the woman with crooked teeth with the wide smile stuck in my mind. However, it felt a little more comfortable seeing families last night rather than just tough policemen. I yawned and then lifted up the toilet seat. I still had to smile every time I looked at this shining white toilet in the middle of the dirty cell. My morning gratitude extended to a working toilet too.

I sat on the toilet seat for a couple minutes. No one was going to bother me, so I started to ponder a little longer than necessary. Once again, as the sun arched in the sky, a spot of light came through the ceiling and onto the concrete floor in front of my feet. As I stood up, I put my hand out and let the light dance up my arm. What satisfaction from a simple pleasure.

After a few minutes, the sun moved and the light faded until the spot was gone. I went over to my food, grabbed my book and a sandwich dad had made. The sleeping bag made more comfortable seat than the blankets. So I sat down and with one hand holding a sandwich, and the other holding my book, I started to eat and read.

Dad in a Tie

I finished my tuna sandwich, and took a break from my book. Normally, I really don't eat many sandwiches, not at least any that I make. It seemed really strange to be eating sandwiches in jail. For some reason the sandwich was really good as food that is made with the TLC of others always taste better than food you make for yourself. With the combination of the chips and the jug of water Dad provided, the sandwiches seemed like a feast.

I looked in my bag of goodies and saw that there was one more sandwich rapped in cellophane. I decided not to open it and leave it for later. It would be good with the Coke and my freedom. I grabbed a small bag of Doritos and opened them.

I continued to realize that dad was the greatest, especially for bringing me food. Oddly enough, this was one of the first times dad gave me Doritos. Our family really didn't eat much junk food, so chips were actually a rarity while growing up. I guess it takes going to jail to get special chips.

As I sat pondering the few times when I've had chips and Coke, the commotion from the other room started up again for the morning. Chatter from the policemen filled the air. I could hear the Sweeping lady too. I guess she was a regular here just like the rest of them.

And then came the voices. The unmistakable sounds of the shrill, *"Hey, how you doing today my friend"* coming from one of the lawyer brothers. I guess they were chummy with the police men even before I ever came here. The voices came closer and I hopped up from my position on the bed in the corner and came toward the doorway.

The hallway door opened and the lawyers came in, dad tagged close behind. I was happy to see him, but something about him looked strange. I then realized he was wearing a tie. I was familiar with dad in a tie, because before he retired, he always went to work in a tie and would stay in one after he got home. He also wore ties for Sunday and any other dress up occasion. He was a proper sort of man, but the guy was on vacation in Mexico. Who packs a tie to go on vacation in Mexico? I guess my dad does, nevertheless, there he was before me in button up shirt and tie.

"*Buenos Dias,*" I called out to the three of them.

The lawyers were still smiles "Buenos Dias Roberto, how you sleep?" They asked. "Today's the big day," they cheerfully reminded. I didn't want to tell them that everyday so far had been an abnormal day. But I guess today, a judge would review this and send me on my way out of here. They left leaving Dad and me alone.

I nodded and looked at dad, "You look nice." He smiled, and commented that the lawyers asked him to come with them to plead my case if perhaps judge asked him some questions. He looked impressive and I was honored that dad would dress up for me. I knew he would dress up for any occasion, but getting your son out of jail in Mexico was definitely a new one for him.

"How was last night?" he asked.

"Thanks again for the food and sleeping bag. Last night was great. I even read for a while."

Dad nodded and I could see he was pleased that he was able do something in order to help out. "OK, wish me luck," he said as he motioned goodbye. "We'll know more when I come back." I said goodbye and watched him as he once again walked out the hallway to join the lawyers in the main room. In just a few more hours, I would be a free man again.

I decided to sit back down and think some more. I had been reading for a good part of the morning and I really didn't know what time it was. I figured it was still morning, but specifically when, I couldn't guess. Besides, who really cares when you have to wait anyway?

I started to make some plans. I assumed I would get out later today and spend what time I could with Dad before I had to travel about four hours north back into Phoenix. Tomorrow would be my first day back at work. I would have some bragging rights and I was anxious to get back into my world and make accomplishments. It also meant being back in the society I was used to.

My mind was running a million miles an hour. It seemed that I had so much to do, so much good I could do, so many ways I could help out. All these thoughts flooded in until I realize that there was not a thing I could do at the present time. I was stuck in a jail cell at the border town in Mexico. It became a little frustrating as I desperately wanted to do more, but was confined to the limits that the cell bars created.

At that moment I realized two profound ideas. First, that I didn't realize how much I had going for me and how much I was involved in life until I'm physically prevented from doing so. The second idea was that I could still dream. Physical incarceration could not stop my mind from working. I still could plan and I could still think and I knew that I was a valid part of whatever community I was in. There were people that needed me and I felt I was important to them. What a powerful lesson came to me as I sat in the jail cell contemplating my life. I knew I was worth something still, and didn't realize how much I could achieve until I was taken away from the circumstances and prevented from accomplishing anything.

After a few more moments I decided to read again. I now needed time away from my thoughts and needed to learn other things. I turned again to "Mere Christianity". It didn't seem so "mere" anymore.

Hot Water

I finally heard the voices again of the lawyers and knew dad would be close by too. I figured it was only about an hour and a half, but really didn't know specifically. I was still on a "whenever" timeframe. I got up and walked towards the cell door.

By this time dad was through the door to the hallway. "Hello again" I called out. Dad was especially somber and deep in thought.

"Are you ready for this?" he asked flatly.

Ready for what, I thought. I nodded my head.

"Robert, we didn't win the case. I don't think you realize how bad this is. The bullets you brought over are only used by the military. Because of this, it's really a serious situation."

Dad continued on, "The local judge didn't want to discuss it because he said it was out of his jurisdiction. This is something higher than even he wants to handle." All this was coming to me too fast and all I could understand was I was in hotter water than I expected.

The perfect world I dreamed of was crashing down around me. This morning Dad and the lawyers went to see

> The perfect world I dreamed of was crashing down around me.

a judge who would hear the case and let me out. I guess the judge saw it a different way and didn't want to make a decision. "So, what does this mean?" I asked, not sure I really wanted to know the answer.

Dad explained that there was a possibility that I would need to have the case heard from a different judge on the county level in Rocky Point, Mexico. There was also talk about me being transported to a bigger jail in Rocky Point. Dad smiled, "at least you would be closer to my hotel room!"

We began discussing the current situation and the predicament I was in. "Robert, the lawyers are charging me a lot of money to get you out of here". My stomach grumbled. It really hurts when you start trying to act like an independent adult and you get pulled back by the reality that sometimes, your parents still pay for things.

"How much?" I asked. I didn't think I was ready for the answer, but I needed it anyway.

Five thousand dollars was the reply. However, dad had a worried smirk on his face. "I'm not going to give it all to them up front" he said. I thought this was a wise idea. Stories ran through my head of where you pre-pay for things and then are expected to pay more later. I was amazed on how much thought Dad had given this on such a short notice. He then proceeded to say that the agreement was that he would pay half up front and then the other half later. Later than what, I still didn't know.

The Phone Call

While talking to dad, I heard my name being called from the other room. A couple of the guards came dashing in and unlocked the cell door. They motioned for me to quickly come out. I had a phone call waiting for me in the office.

Who in the world was calling me? Who in the world knew that I was in jail in Mexico other than my dad standing in front of me? Who in the world would want to call me in jail and why should I take the call? I really didn't think asking the guards to take a message would be appropriate, so I followed them out the cell door so I could answer the phone. At least they were in too big of a hurry to remember the handcuffs.

They led me again to the front office where the receiver of a phone was off the hook. One of them motioned that it was for me. As I crossed the room and picked up the phone, I didn't know what to say. I finally mustered the words, "This is Robert."

The call turned out to be from the US consulate in Nogales, Arizona. They had just heard that I had been detained and understood from the guards that answered the phone that I was to be transferred to Rocky Point.

"Yes, I have heard that we can't fix this here and that I'm going to a bigger jail deeper in the country. Is there anything that you guys can do to help me out?" I asked.

I quickly became informed that there really wasn't anything they could do. I was technically on my own and in the hands of the Mexican authorities. Inside, I became a little frustrated. So, they were calling me to wish me a good time rotting away somewhere else. Thanks guys as the sarcasm turned to slight resentment.

The guy on the phone was nice enough. He sounded of Latino decent and just couldn't do much about my situation. However, he did help prepare me for what was coming next. This was welcomed as I was trying to get this information from the lawyers and guards since I arrived here. He told me that I would be transported down to Rocky Point, and that a judge there would interview me. He said that usually most of the time, Americans in this case would pay a fine and then be released to cross back into the United States. Well, I was hoping to get out of jail, let alone anything else.

He then said that he could help manage the relationships back in the US and asked some questions. For example, was this OK to inform the media if they ask questions? I thought about this for a minute from the view point of my work and said that I thought it would be better if the media didn't know.

Was it OK for the consulate to inform relatives about my situation if they called in? Dad was all that mattered right now and Mom was in London. So I really didn't have any reason for other family members like aunts and uncles, cousins and siblings to know right now. So I asked him not to disclose information.

Was it OK for friends to get information from the Consulate? I thought about this. There might be a benefit for people to know that I was here, but since I said "No" to family members being given information, I said no to friends as well.

He thanked me for the information and we ended the phone call. As soon as I hung up, there was a flood of questions I had for him, but I didn't think about them until it was too late. Dad had come up and listened to the last half of the conversation, and as soon as I got off he mentioned that he was aware they would call sooner or later. Great, my only contact with any form of US government and I let them go.

I looked at dad, gave him a thumbs-up and said, "Ok, it looks like I'm going to Rocky Point after all."

Getting Ready for Transport

After the call from the consulate, I didn't want to go back in the cell. I found that my time out of the cell was precious, so I savored every moment. Dad was there, I could see outside the windows to a brighter day and I now had the thoughts of going somewhere else, wherever that was.

At that moment, the lawyers came in through the side door. They were all smiles. I walked through the sliding glass door of the office and back into the main room.

"Hola, Roberto" They said. "You know you go to Rocky Point?" One thing about them was that they seemed always happy. At least they kept a good attitude even if they were a little slow in giving me the news. I didn't know the difference between what I was doing here and what was ahead of me in Rocky Point. It would be a new experience and more of the adventure, but to be honest I was a little scared of the idea of a new situation.

I nodded my head and said that Dad had told me I was going there. "So, what will happen in Rocky Point?" Other than staying in another jail, I wanted to hear some good news of things yet to come.

"Uh," said one of them, "We will see, how you say, a judge and he will say what to do." He smiled again, he was beaming with pride about his English vocabulary and the fact that he could now practice with a gringo. "You need to get ready to go."

I looked at dad for any kind of validation. He nodded and I figured I had to go back in the cell to get my sleeping bag, blanket and my bag of food. Well at least I had some direction. At least I knew what to do for the next couple of hours or so. But then it struck me, this also meant that I would not be free today.

I gave a smile to my dad as he followed me back through the hallway while the Captain waited for me with keys. He motioned me for me to step in. I looked up at him and actually said, *"Thank you for holding the door."* It seemed really silly that I thanked my jailer for locking me back in, but at least I was out for a couple minutes and was grateful to him for letting me out. He locked the cell and walked away with a grunt and a *"De Nada."*

The lawyers followed and were in now with us in the hallway. "Who's going to take me to Rocky point?" I asked them. The brothers looked at each other and then back to me. The reply was a shrug of the shoulders and a response that the jailers had the responsibility. I wasn't surprised, but wanted to ask just for the fun of it. I figured if perhaps anybody could drive me to Rocky Point, then let my dad take me. Then we could turn the other way and cross back into the USA! But no such luck. Besides, there's nothing wrong with asking anyway.

"Ok", I said, knowing this meant whenever the jailers got around to it. Maybe after siesta again. I thanked the lawyers for working on my case today and for all they've done so far.

Their eyes lit up and said *Gracias*. "We see you later at Rocky Point jail. No worries Roberto, we get you out." They said in reassurance as they started to leave.

I looked back to dad. He seemed relieved that the lawyers maintained a positive attitude and were still helping us out. "At least you will be closer to Rocky Point," he joked. "It's just so long of a drive back and forth from the hotel to this jail," he was trying to make light of the situation.

I smiled. "I always wanted to see Rocky Point. I guess it just took a couple more days to get there than what I expected." It was good to see dad smile. I knew this was really taking a toll on him. He had the weight of the world on his shoulders, at least the weight of a son in jail. I was glad that he could still bear it.

"Listen," I said to him. "There's nothing more that you can do. I will get ready and these jailers will take me down to Rocky Point. Why don't you take a break from this whole situation and go back to the hotel?"

Both of us could see my suggestion made sense and he was trying to justify the fact that he would leave me. Now that we knew what was going to happen, should he take a break, or should he stay by the side of his son who was still in trouble? I could tell he was struggling with the decision as he finally nodded his head. "OK," he replied. I tried to talk myself into it too. It was sure nice to have him around even if we were partitioned by iron bars. It didn't matter. Dad would still be dad.

We said our good-byes and good luck for the day and I watched dad leave the hallway. Once again, I was left to myself and my jail cell. I looked around at my sleeping bag on the floor, the plastic bag of food to the side and the white toilet on the wall. Boy this was starting to feel cozy. I halfway felt like I was going to miss this place. Well, no not really, I changed my mind on the thought. This had been an interesting stay, I will be glad to say "Goodbye jail cell, it's been fun."

I wondered when the Jailers would take me to Rocky Point. I also wondered how they would take me. I figured I should prepare my stuff so I went to work stuffing my sleeping bag into its sack and folding my blankets. I even folded the worn blankets and bed sheet that was here the first night. I started getting some hunger pains and wondered if I should have the last half sandwich from my food bag. Would I need it for the trip or should I eat it now?

At the risk of loosing it, I thought it would be best if I ate now rather than think about it later. So, while seated on a stack of blankets, I had my sandwich and the rest of the chips and drank from the jug of water. But I decided to still keep my can of Coke. Keeping the can was more a matter of principle as I would drink it tomorrow when I got out. I would pack it away for now and hold off on opening it.

I smiled at the thought that maybe the jailers would come in right now, while I was eating. I would just politely tell them that they would have to wait as I was having my meal. There are always priorities in life. At the time, eating was the priority, no matter who wanted to take me away.

Writing on the Wall

I started to read the graffiti written on the wall. Any scratches or writing on the white walls created darker lines and provided good opportunity to leave messages. By the look of the room and the number of messages, it seemed that this room had plenty of visitors. Most of the text was in Spanish and I couldn't make out the messages other than some names.

One message caught my eye. It was in English:

"Vacation from Hell
Two Gringo's down for the weekend,
Spent a night here, June 2000"

Well, at least they got out after one night, I thought to myself. I get to go to the Jail in Rocky Point. However, it had been relatively interesting enough staying here. At least the toilet worked.

I continued to look around at the messages on the walls. Next to me near the newspapers was a house key. I picked it up and looked at it. I wondered who had left it and how long it had been there.

I smiled as I imagined that it had been left behind by the two gringos that left the message. "Oh no!" One would say to the other, "We have to go back, the house is locked and I left the keys in jail!" I guess they didn't come back for it.

I decided to leave my own message. With the key in hand, I scratched on the wall:

"Crossed the border with bullets in my car,
spent two nights here and have to go to Rocky Point Jail,
Dec 2000"

With my claim to fame on the wall of a Mexican Jail, I put the key back in its place and reviewed my message. It really wasn't an earth shattering declaration, but at least I left my mark. So, for any one who goes to the corner cell in Sonoyta, Mexico, you can see my message in the corner about a foot and a half off the floor near the wall of the fireplace. I don't recommend anyone going just to see my message, but it's there anyway. You too can leave a message, but only if you do something stupid, like carry bullets across the border.

> You too can leave a message, but only if you do something stupid, like carry bullets across the border.

The Extra Blanket

After finishing my own graffiti, I sat down again on the folded blankets and read. C.S Lewis was now writing about the benefits of faith and I started to think how this applied in my life. The book stated that faith was something you still believed in, even though you don't know the specific outcome or reality. Believing in God was really natural for me. I had been raised up in a home that taught that faith was a necessity. But how much did I really believe? And if I believed, did I rely on this to get me through difficult situations? There's a big difference between believing something and living it.

I decided to put my new dedication to the test. I was in a transitionary state. I was familiar and starting to get comfortable with my current jail cell, and I was feeling a bit of anxiety over going somewhere unfamiliar, given the circumstances. I guess you can get casual in your thinking, even about being in trouble.

So, rather than worry about my situation, I made a choice to turn this around. I said a short prayer. If I was going to a place even tougher than this, I would put my faith to the test and trust that I would be alright.

After a while, the Captain opened the door to the hallway and another guard came in and worked the lock of the jail cell. *"Come out, we'll get your stuff,"* the guard said.

I followed the Captain and walked out of the jail cell and into the main room. Waiting for me were a half dozen guys. Still no uniforms, just rag-tag individuals you would imagine on the other side of the law had they been in the US. This seemed unreal, everything felt backwards. Even the first guy who put me in Monday night was there. I looked at him but he didn't seem to have much authority or interest in me today.

One of the policemen came to me with handcuffs and also leg cuffs. I guess I was traveling with accessories today. He put the handcuffs on first and knelt down to ad the cuffs to my legs. It felt awkward, because had I wanted to, I could have laid him out flat with a nice strong kick to the face. I decided not to, considering it wouldn't get me far, but grinned because I knew my potential.

By this time the Captain came out with the sleeping bag and the plastic bag carrying my water, Coke and my book. I looked for the blankets but he hadn't brought it with him.

"Hey, please get my blankets?" I said turning half around trying to look over my shoulder to communicate with the Captain. This seemed to frustrate the guy bent down in front of me as he was having a hard time with my leg cuffs.

The Captain couldn't understand my English and I didn't know the Spanish word for *blanket*. So I said *"one more"* in Spanish and motioned my head back towards the cell. The captain grumbled some swear words and went back. Half a second later he was with the green blanket that dad brought. I nodded my head and said *"the other one too"*. With that, the Captain went back again and got the grey blanket that dad had brought and the worn blue one that was in the cell when I arrived.

Rather than explaining that I wanted was the two blankets dad brought me, not three, I just said *"gracias"* and let it be. I knew we were taking an extra blanket which meant only the yellow one remained in the cell. But I figured the jailers knew what's best and decided not to push the issue. By this time, my leg cuffs were on and I was still their prisoner.

I thought it ironic that the guards would help me to steal a blanket from their own jail cell! I immediately eased my conscious by quickly making a plan to leave this extra blanket behind in the next jail.

The Drive to the Jail

The trip from the border town to the jail in Rocky Point was a very memorable experience. I really can't say it was enjoyable, but memorable. Handcuffed, I was put into the back seat on the driver's side of an older Jeep Cherokee SUV parked next to the building. It was actually nice being outside, even if I was destined to go to another jail. Still, it was a brief moment where I didn't care if I was handcuffed. I could still breathe clean air. I was quickly pulled back into reality when the door to the Cherokee opened and I was motioned to get in.

Two police officers who escorted me sat in the two front seats. One of the men was part of the rough looking group. I remembered being turned over to them during my first night there. Both were scruffy looking, had moustaches, and un-kept hair. They were also both in almost worn out plain clothes. The only way you could tell these guys were official was the clip-on red and blue lights on the sun visor and the fact that they were carrying handguns.

The only thing I could do was pay attention to details. After all, I was handcuffed, and ankle-cuffed, guarded by two Mexican men, being transported to another jail. The only freedom I had left was to think, watch, observe and analyze. I analyzed the stuff in the back, there was a bag of tools in the seat next to me, my door was unlocked, and both of my escorts smoked. My mind raced as fast as we went down the road.

The Jeep started picking up speed as we rolled along the highway connecting Sonoyta to Rock Point. It was a barren land, full of bushes and sand. The two up front started talking in Spanish, I couldn't make out what they were saying. The driver had rolled down his window part way to accommodate his smoking, the other just let his smoke fill the car as he used the ash tray.

At some point I noticed that the land was going by really fast, I decided to look over the drivers shoulder at the dashboard. One hundred miles an hour and pushing it. I guess they really wanted to get rid of me soon, or maybe they simply liked being speeding policemen. Besides, no one would pull them over.

The road started to gradually turn this way and that. We took some turns much faster than I would normally want to go. I started to think, what happens if this car rolls over? At this speed, it would be pretty fatal. My mind started to race again until I stopped and laughed inside. I mapped out how the car would tip over going around a tight curve. The two would get thrown out because they weren't wearing seatbelts. I would find the keys to my cuffs from a dead policeman, better yet, I would find a paperclip and lock pick my way to freedom. There would be a gun thrown under the seat if I really needed it.

Well, at least I still had a good imagination! The crash never happened, but I decided to play it safe and wear my seatbelt still.

We finally reached some civilization again and continued into the heart of the city of Rocky Point, Mexico. Puerto Penasco is the correct name, but everyone calls it Rocky Point. Driving in, I didn't get to see the beach as the road we were on didn't accommodate a view of the ocean, but I guessed that we were close to it as it was a coastal city and the temperature dropped again.

We finally pulled up to a set of concrete block buildings. After thinking about it, I realize that describing the buildings as concrete really doesn't help. All buildings in Mexico have concrete block as a major material. The driver spoke quickly to the other policeman and got out. The passenger policeman stayed and continued to smoke.

"We are here?" I asked in Spanish?

"Si, this is the jail and we will drop you off." He turned around and smiled. He was missing teeth and the ones he had were severely stained.

"Do you live in Rocky Point, or back in Sonoyta?" I asked trying to make small talk. I didn't know how long it would be until the driver got back, so I decided to make the

most of it. I had never talked to this police guard before, he was never around when I left the cell.

"I live in Sonoyta but have family in Rocky Point," was his reply. We spent a couple of minutes talking. He was actually nice and I was glad I could pick up a conversation with someone. The discussion flowed into understanding that he had been a policeman for the past 15 years, and that most of his family was part of the police force in the area.

I then became aware of something. As part of survival in a developing country, his family chose to embrace law enforcement. Each group of people tries to survive the best way they knew how. Because gun ownership is so rare in Mexico, you can either be a criminal, or a policeman. This family had chosen to stay on the side that the law favored. Sure, compared to the United States, this police system looked like a legalized mob, but it still was legal. I found a new respect for my captor. He was trying his best to support a family and make a difference in whatever ways he could.

My train of thought was interrupted when the first policeman came back to the car. He opened my door and motioned for me to get out. I did so, along with my smoking buddy from the front seat. He got out and helped me with my sleeping bag, my bag of food and blankets.

We walked into an open archway, where I received my first impression of my next area of confinement, the Rocky Point Jail. I figured this had to be the jail because of the large gate closer across the entrance. We walked in and I found myself in a large room with a ceiling over 20 feet high.

The receiving room was 15 feet wide by 30 feet long. To the right was a desk with an older man with a mustache sitting behind it. He had on a brown button-up shirt and I guessed he was a guard. He looked up from his papers and looked at me, then to the policemen. As he spoke a few words, I knew he was surprised to see this gringo.

I guess he was expecting someone a little more hardened over. I knew it and he knew it: I felt like a cream-puff. Me, going to the Rocky Point Jail. I still had dress shoes and slacks on. What was I doing here, that's what he'd like to know too. He reviewed a clipboard provided by the transport policeman and saw that things seemed to be in order. Sure enough, I was the prisoner he would be taking off their hands.

> I guess he was expecting someone a little more hardened over.
> I felt like a cream-puff.

In front of me was a large metal gate made up of thick metal bars with a wire mesh welded to it. Through the entrance, I could see into a long dark hallway. There was another gate at the end of the hallway, some forty feet long.

Because the other end of the tunnel was bright, it made the hallway darker and I couldn't adjust my eyes yet to see what awaited me. I could see figures of people walking around, but I still couldn't tell who they were.

Sitting in the guard room at the entrance to the gate in front of me was a very fat man. He was in good spirits, waiting for the gate to open up. I figured he was waiting to go in, but really couldn't tell why. He had on jeans and a regular shirt and I didn't know if he was a prisoner or a guard too. Either way it seemed a bit strange. As heavy set as this guy was, it didn't make sense that he was a jailer, but it didn't seem like he was being incarcerated either. He exchanged words with my two transport guards, as well as the older guy with the mustache and seemed to be enjoying this game of "Pass the Prisoner".

Going In

"Ok Roberto, lets go" said the fat man. I guessed that was my queue to go in.

"What about my stuff?" I asked.

"They will pass it in after they check it. You will get it soon enough," he replied. His accent was heavy, but he knew the English vocabulary. He sure seemed to know a lot about what was going on. So, I followed him towards the gate. It took a great effort to go near it. The darkness made my skin crawl. I still couldn't make out much, other than silhouettes of people walking past the light at the end of the hallway.

I looked at the guard and the fellow policemen who had escorted me. They seemed in agreement with this fat guy. The guard was already at the gate unlocking it. He swung it open, just enough for us to go through one at a time. I followed my big leader into my new home.

Everyone hears of horror stories about going to prison. Eyebrows rise when you mention Mexico and prison in the same sentence. As soon as I walked in, I knew I was in a whole new world like nothing I had ever experienced before. It was a good thing that this was my first time, but it created a sense of worried curiosity.

I took a few paces in and found myself in a hallway. It was about 6 feet wide and what I figured 40 feet long. As I stopped and let my eyes adjust as the big man left me and went a couple steps farther on.

At that moment, I heard the metal gate crash shut behind me. The sound of the iron gate closing behind me rang through the hallway and in my head. With that sound, I knew I had reached my darkest hour. No longer was I taking a joy ride down to Mexico. No longer was I in a cell by myself waiting to get let out. I was now in an official Mexican Jail, and part of a justice system I knew absolutely nothing about.

I shook myself out of my despair and made a resolution to figure this out. I decided to first figure my surroundings. The wall to my right was actually a wall of metal bars, revealing a large room even darker than the hallway I was in. This dark room was all cement, no beds, no windows, just a large dim lighted room. My eyes adjusted and I saw a few men in there. They were scattered around, leaning on the walls. They looked really destitute and I immediately counted my blessings that at least I was on this side of the wall of iron bars. I didn't know what the difference was between this side of the jail compared to that side, but the feeling that came from the countenance of those in there were as bleak as the darkness.

On the left side of the long hallway were two cells, one closest to the gate near me and one farther down the hallway. The doorways of iron bars to these cells were open as you could come in and go as you pleased. I looked in the cell closest to me. It was rather dark, but I could make out two sets of bunk beds, stacked three high. There was also a small table at the far end of the cell with a TV sitting on it.

The hallway was illuminated by two light bulbs hanging five feet down from the ceiling by power cords. The ceiling of the hallway was at least 20 feet high, but the low watt bulbs were ineffective at lighting such a massive area. To the far end of the hallway was another metal gate. This was closed but revealed a courtyard with concrete walls. The sun was shining in the courtyard still and the dull brilliance from the light colored concrete partially illuminated the hallway.

I decided to walk down the hallway to follow the fat man as he seemed to know what was going on. As I took a couple more paces towards the end of the hallway, the he man immerged from the far cell.

"Hey Roberto!" He said with a smile. "How you like?" This struck me as a strange question, but he seemed to get a kick out of it. Several others were around him and I heard the words "Gringo", and "Americano" spoken to each other. I looked around and found that there weren't any Caucasians inside this jail, I was the only one. With dark-red hair and fair colored skin, I stood out. But a weird sense of security as I was now near the fat man and figured either he would look out for me or I somehow would handle anything that would come.

My new friend introduced me to a couple of the others around, but I couldn't remember their names as fast as he making the introduction. Rocco, Ivan, Pablo, who these guys were I couldn't keep straight. I figured that I would soon find out since the jail only held about 25 people.

I looked around at the guys. All Mexicans and most of them looked like they were callused over from hard times. My mind raced on what the others were in jail for. Who knows? I knew that could be a touchy subject, so I figured that such information come out soon enough. As I looked around I met the eyes of those looking back at me. With a nod of the head we silently said our 'hellos'.

I could just hear the thoughts in their mind. What in the world is this Gringo doing here? He must have screwed up really bad. We don't get Gringo's here very often and when we do, they really don't last long. This guy should break down in a few hours or so! What's he in here for anyway? What in the world has HE done to get here?

That's right guys, I thought to myself. I carried 32 bullets across the border, I just wanted to go on vacation and didn't make it through. I wasn't about to tell them, but what a conversation I had in my head.

My concentration was interrupted by a voice from the cell. Another guy had walked out into the hallway and leaned against the open cell doorway. All eyes were now on him. He had a presence to him that commanded our attention. He asked the fat guy a question and everyone laughed. I smiled too, but knew whatever humor was at my expense. I didn't mind because what I don't know can't hurt me anyway.

"This is Eddie" the Fat Man said to me. "He speaks English too, so you should be fine." Well at least it was good to have others to communicate with.

I looked at him and said "Hi."

"What's-up?" He said with a nod. This guy was a cool cat. Eddie seemed to be in cahoots with the fat guy and if there was seniority, Eddie was certainly at the top.

So far things seemed to be going rather well. Despite I was in a Mexican Jail with what I could count as 20-25 other Mexicans, I wasn't doing to bad. At least I had made "friends" and had a fat man looking out for me.

"Ok, well that's it, I have to go," the fat guy said. Go where? I thought to myself, where was there to go? We are in Jail with a hallway and two large cells. Where's this guy going, can I go too? I decided to find out what he was talking about.

I followed a couple paces behind as he went back to the main gate. He knew that I was following him, it didn't seem to matter. Looks like his "got to go" was out the main gate. The other guard who let us in was waiting for the fat man. As soon as he approached, the gate was opened and he was let out. What in the world? Who was this guy? I watched him from a distance through the metal gate. The fat guy and the guard grabbed my stuff and headed back to the gate.

"Here you go Roberto." I guess it was time to have my stuff passed through. Rather than opening the gate, there was a small door inside the gate. This small door was 2 feet by 2 feet locked by a padlock. Rather than opening the whole door, they could open this smaller opening and pass my items through. I said thank you as I received my goods. I guessed that the other guard looked through my things while I came through. With that finished, the two of them went about their business.

Then it struck me. The fat guy I thought was a prisoner like me was actually a guard. Boy, was I wrong about this guy. I don't think it's a compliment if I thought him to be a prisoner, but he sure seemed out of place as a guard. Whether or not he was a guard or a prisoner, I was glad he was friendly. At least I was in good hands either way.

I turned my attention back to the hallway full of real prisoners. They had split up and were now doing their own things. I really didn't know what to do, so I slowly moved my stuff down the hall closer to the courtyard door and the farther cell. I made it to the far end of the hallway and was wondering what to do next. Sooner or later I had to find a safe place to stash the stuff until I needed it.

We Are All Friends Here

At that moment, I found myself in unfamiliar circumstances and uneasy surroundings, with a bunch of belongings consisting of the only possessions I had to my name at the time. I felt like a cat swimming in a pool of sharks. You don't like the hot water you're in and sooner or later you know you're going to get eaten alive. What was I going to do?

I didn't know where to go or what to do with my belongings. I didn't know who was friendly or who would knife me as soon as I turn around. By this time my back was to a wall, literally. I was at one end of the hallway looking at a bunch of prisoners swimming around me, waiting for the right time for them to get their next victim.

> I didn't know who was friendly or who would knife me as soon as I turn around. By this time my back was to a wall, literally.

One of them made a move. He was a man about 10 years older than me and had a proud stance. I looked around for Eddie, but he had already gone into the cell. As the guy came closer, I clenched my fist waiting for whatever would come.

"Hey," he said in broken English. "What's your name?" It seemed like he wanted the names of those he killed, maybe he had a plaque with all the names of those who had "gone" before. My mind ran wild, but I tried to remain calm as sharks can always smell fresh blood.

With that I motioned my head in a "how's it going" and said, "My name is Roberto, what's yours?" If we were going to have a short conversation, I might as well prolong it as much as I could.

"I'm Rocco. It's going to be ok, we are all friends here," He smiled a bit, trying to be friendlier. "This is Joey," he said, pointing to another prisoner now nearby. He was a young man about my age and had a bit of cockiness to his walk.

I looked into Rocco's eyes and found a sincerity that couldn't be false. He was saying the truth and I started looking around. Rather than a look of anger, all of them had a look of curiosity. I was just seeing this wrong and now there was a sudden shift in my attitude towards those around me. I began to realize that I didn't need my back to the wall. Rather than a look of intent to do harm, these guys just looked callused over by their past experiences. I looked back at Rocco, trying to understand more.

"We're all in here together, some for a long time," Joey added, "some of us for a short time, who knows? So rather than giving up, we try to make it OK for each other." Joey started noticing I was losing my worry. He continued onward. "We're all friends here," he repeated.

"The church brings us food. It's good to eat and we share." He pointed into the cell. At the other end of the cell was a low table with a TV showing some program. Near the table was a box of food. I could see tinfoil and some paper plates. There was a large 5 gallon water jug and a set of plastic cups nearby.

"Later on, the guards lock us in the cell for the night, half of us in one cell and half in the other, so you should find a place to put your blankets in the cell for later tonight." Joey could tell I was beginning to catch onto how life worked here and I started breathing easier again.

I nodded my head OK. I grabbed my sleeping bag and my bag of food and slowly headed for the cell. "Thanks" I said to Joey. It was nice to have someone to let me know how to handle this. Joey picked up my set of blankets and followed after me. Rocco stayed outside the cell, there were already a couple people in the small cell and he didn't want to add another person to the already small room by coming with us.

I set my bag of food down next to the community food box. Under the tinfoil, I smelled some kind of beef, beans and tortillas. By this time Joey found some room under a set of bunk beds where he stashed my blankets. I joined him and stuffed my sleeping bag under the head of the bunk bed near the corner.

Eddie was lying on the bottom bunk not paying any attention to what was going on around him. He was focused on the program on TV and tuned out all other distractions. As I entered the room, there were a couple of others sitting on bunk beds or on the floor watching Joey and me move my stuff out of the way for others. I nodded to them and some smiled back. They too were curious as to why this gringo had joined them.

I thanked Joey again, now that I had my stuff stashed away and out of my hands. He said *'no problem'* and left the cell room.

I took quick inventory of my surroundings again and of what just happened. I then remembered I had a can of coke in the bag and it was now in the community section. Realizing that the Coke was sacred, I placed the can of Coke in my inner jacked pocket and took out my book. It was also passed through with the bag of food. I decided to put that away too and slid the book and the can of Coke in a plastic bag and stashed them between a fold of my blankets under the bed. I was all set now and felt better about my situation.

I decided to explore a bit. I walked out of the cell and through the hallway. For the first little while, everyone seemed to be interested in me. I guess I was the new guy and a gringo at that. Everyone talks about what's new. Now that I had a new outlook on the jail, it didn't look so gloomy for the first time. At least I was a fellow comrade, rather than somebody's dinner.

Meeting the Secretary

I continued walking up and down the hallway. There wasn't much to do other than observe the other guys and what they were doing. Since I was to be here for the evening I wanted to know what the other guys do to pass the time. Besides, walking helped settle my nerves and it wasn't long until most of them lost interest in me. Most of them had gone into the cell rooms and were watching TV for the late afternoon. Others walked around, others sat, a few read and some played cards. Looked like most of them kept to themselves. But compared to the amount of time they had been here, I guess you start to find various things to do and get into routines.

Just then I heard my name spoken from the main gate. Some of the guys at the gate called me "Roberto!" I realized they wanted me to come to the gate. I thought dad came to visit, but I couldn't see anyone from where I was. I walked up to the gate and found an unfamiliar face waiting for me. A Mexican man was in the front room waiting with the heavy-set guard. He came forward as soon as he saw me. I guess he recognized me as I was the only gringo in this jail.

He wanted to ask me some questions and started speaking in Spanish. There were echoes in the cell rooms and hallway and I couldn't clearly hear what he said. I put my finger up asking him to wait a minute and looked around for Eddie. He was nearby and I called him over. The look on his face reflected that I had burdened him by just calling his name. Reluctantly he came over to the gate, still perturbed I asked him to come over.

Eddie started talking to this man. I asked Eddie who this new man was. He looked annoyed and said "he's the Secretary working for the judge. He wants to know if you own the gun."

I was grateful that Eddie was a translator, but wondered if I would pay for his translation services later. I hadn't told any of the guys why I was here, but now Eddie knew. I guess sooner or later it would come out. So, Eddie was now in the middle of it.

"Yes, I own a gun" I replied.

Eddie spoke again to the Secretary, and then back to me, "Do you have a permit for it and where is it?" I guess the secretary was doing a report too.

I replied back that the gun was back in Phoenix, I didn't bring it down. Eddie replied back to the Secretary and then back to me. Eddie's demeanor calmed down a bit. And I could tell he was starting to have fun as the middle man.

"He still wants to know where you have your permit" he spoke back to me.

I looked at the secretary and spoke in my best Spanish, *"It's not necessary."* The secretary looked at me for a bit and then back to Eddie. Eddie spoke again. Eddie tried to explain to the secretary that you didn't have to have a "permit" in the United States to have possession of a gun. The secretary nodded and then said good-bye.

I thanked Eddie for his time. "Yeah," he replied "but next time don't play games with the Secretary, if he asks you something just tell him."

What? I was really confused. I guess Eddie had to explain to the Secretary that I didn't need a permit, rather than telling someone in authority that it wasn't necessary for me to answer. "Thanks for helping explain that, I couldn't get the right words".

"So, what's this anyway?" Asked Eddie, I knew he was curious about this conversation. "You had bullets?"

"Yes," I replied. "I came down for vacation and forgot I had a box of bullets in my car. The border patrol found them and I got in trouble. I didn't have the gun, just the bullets."

The corners of Eddie mouth turned in a sneering smile. It still sounded stupid to me too. Eddie smiled because some gringo was now here because a box of bullets. The truth was out already. He turned and walked away to go back to whatever he was doing. "Good luck" he called over his shoulder.

Locking Down

Soon after the Secretary left, the gate opened once again, letting the fat man back inside. "Hey Roberto, How's it going?" I finally discovered his name was Francis. Some name for a 300 pound guard. He carried two large padlocks in his hands. I nodded my head that I was alright and doing OK in here.

"OK, it's lock down time." He informed me, "Pick a cell." The others already knew what that meant. Within a couple of moments the guys filed into the two cell rooms. I decided to go into a cell where my possessions were.

I was the last one in the cell and it was already cramped. Within a 12 by 15 foot room, there were twelve guys. Six of them were on the bunk beds out of the way, the rest were either walking around the others, who were sitting on the floor. There was very little room to move around, so I stood in the corner waiting for Francis the guard's next move. Francis slid the cell door shut, locking us in the room for the night with one of the large padlocks. It seemed that during the day, we had the option to roam around the hallway, or maybe the outside courtyard would get opened now and then. But for tonight, we were in the cell.

"OK, Robert Deniro! Maybe you'll go home tomorrow, but tonight, sleep well, see you tomorrow!" That was a new one, I was never called Robert Deniro before. Maybe, that was the only Robert that Francis knew of before me. Or maybe Denero was the Spanish sound for Money and that I was being set up as an American in prison who's going to pay some heavy prices later. At least Francis was positive with the idea that I would go home tomorrow.

I looked around. Most in the room were settling down by watching the TV. Eddie sat up from his bunk bed and pulled a set of slippers from the floor "OK Robert, pick a spot and stay there, it's not good for everyone to be moving around after we get locked in." I was near my rolled up sleeping bag and pulled it out and sat on it like a cushion. No sense wandering and I didn't have any where else to go.

I sat on the floor near Eddie's bunk bed. This seemed a good corner, the side of my body leaning against the bed, and my back resting upon the bars of the cell door. I stuffed my jacket behind me as a cushion from the hard iron bars. Joey was next to me on the floor. He had pulled out his folded blanket as many of the others on the floor had done the same. Rocco, who was the first to speak to me and help ease my fears, had the bottom bunk of the other set of beds. I didn't know many names to other faces around me. Many said hello, but faces and names seemed a blur.

Eddie got up and went to the community table and started working with the box of food which had been passed in earlier that afternoon. On the floor next to the TV was an electric skillet. He and another man started preparing food. I kept watching this other guy. For a Mexican he was really tall. I didn't mean to stereotype anybody, but this guy appeared different from the rest. I thought I'd call him the Tall Guy.

However tall he was, he was really good in the makeshift kitchen. They took the meat and wrapped them in small individual corn tortillas, then fried them in a little bit of cooking oil in the electric skillet. With the appliances and tools they had, both men seemed to know how to cope with their meager kitchen. Within a couple of minutes they had fried about two dozen "mini tacos".

As soon as Eddie had a few made, he would say something in Spanish and the nearest guy would come close and grab a paper towel into which Eddie would place two tacos. I didn't know the rules to the eating procedure, so I just watched what went on. The other guys from the bunk beds jumped down and would take a turn getting their share of the cooked food.

"Robert," Eddie called out. "If you want some food, come here," he said sternly. I guess it was my turn. I got up from my seat and walked closer. Eddie wasn't finished my share yet, so I stood close by, trying not to block the view of the TV. A man lying on his stomach was on the next bunk bed above Eddie. As I got up, he looked over. He has a younger man, compared to the rest of them, about my age. He had the starting of a mustache, but he still needed to grow it out. He gave me a nod and I asked, *"What's your name?"*

"Ivan", he replied. I told him it was nice to meet him, and he nodded again. He didn't seem to talk much. My mind raced as I tried to recall of all the Ivan's I could remember. They all seemed very powerful in history. Thoughts about Ivan the Terrible or Ivan the Conqueror, but this guy didn't fit the part. He was pretty much laid back, not the conquering type, but it was now nice to have a name to his face.

Eddie handed me a paper towel with two tacos and a slice of lime. With a literal handful of food, I said thanks and walked back to my spot. The mini tacos looked pretty good actually, but were screaming hot for the first few moments. I held the paper towel by the edges until my food cooled down. It gave me time to say a silent prayer of gratitude for coming to Rocky Point safely, helping me keep the sleeping bag for the night, making some friends and even for Eddie making food.

I finished and squeezed the lime over the tacos and started to eat. Not bad. I sat there, eating my tacos and watching a TV program that I couldn't understand. The TV program was a Novella (Mexican soap opera) and I didn't quite know the stories or subplots to what was going on. Still it was noise for us as well as something to watch while eating. With a full belly, a finished prayer and the mesmerizing affect of a TV I could listen to but not understand, I slowly drifted off into the comfort of satisfaction for the moment.

I followed the example of the others by throwing away my used lime and paper towel in a small trash can at the other corner of the room. Trying to step over legs and find an unoccupied place to safely plant my foot was a chore. Like stepping on rocks in a creek to avoid getting your feet wet, I had to be extra cautious where I was stepping. There were people all over the place. While I was up, I decided to see if I could go to the bathroom for the night.

The Toilet

I wasn't as fortunate in this jail as I was in my personal cell in Sonoyta when it came to bathroom facilities. At one end of the cell, there was a small closet with a shower curtain for a door. Inside the closet was a cement floor with a 6 inch hole in the ground. Just a hole, no toilet to sit on, no toilet seat, no flush, just a hole in the ground.

> Just a hole, no toilet to sit on, no toilet seat, no flush, just a hole in the ground.

Once inside, you would drop your pants, squat and do your business. Fortunately, the open hole led into the city sewers. There was a faucet in the closet with a white five gallon bucket nearby. The idea was to finish, then fill the bucket with water and flush by dumping the water into the hole yourself. This would rinse the pipes and wash everything away. The faucet had a switch valve where you could switch between the faucet near the hole, or the pipe leading up to the shower. Whichever way you switched, it was one temperature: cold. Still it worked and was efficient as well.

I was surprised that it didn't smell too bad for an open sewer. I knew it could have been worse, but I missed my personal sparkling clean sit down toilet from the first jail. Now I had to work a little harder to make sure my aim was a little better.

I finished up by dumping the five gallon bucket into the hole. I thought back to where some US city and state governments required new toilets that would only require 1 gallon on the flush. I realized that pouring five gallons down a hole into open sewers was way out of the norm for me, but if that's how it's done here, might as well go with the flow!

I filled the bucket back up as I had found to leave it for the next person and began my journey back through the maze of legs back to my spot for the night.

The Razor

It became dark outside as we continued to watch TV until there was a commotion from the other cell and the main gate. A few moments later, Francis the fat guard, came up to our cell gate with my two lawyers. I was quite surprised as I stood up and greeted them as they had been led down the hallway. I figured that was ok, all of us were locked in the cell anyway.

As usual the Lawyers were all smiles. In the hallway light they looked similar to each other more than any time before. *"Buenas Noches Roberto!"* one of them called out.

I replied back with a 'hi guys!' They asked me how I was doing and if I was going to be warm enough. This was a thoughtful gesture of them as they seemed to care and I really welcomed it.

I was OK in my surroundings, but it was nice to know that these guys on the other side of the bars cared.

"Tomorrow's a big day," one of them told me. *"We have an appointment with the 'how you say' judge and he wants to meet you."* Me? That was interesting. I thought for a moment and said OK. At least we are getting on with this.

"Oh yes," he continued. He then reached in his pocket and pulled out a handful of items. "Here take these". He handed me a folded up piece of paper first. It was a half sheet of white paper with text printed on it.

I opened up the folded page and glanced over the text. It read: "I didn't remember I had them cartridges. I am very sorry, I didn't want to cause trouble...." What was this? Oh yeah, these were words I could use while I was in the interview tomorrow. I read the words again, this time more carefully. The words were really out of order and the sentence structure was terrible. I figured that he had written the words in Spanish on a computer and had a program to translate into English. However, the translation was really bad.

In Spanish, describing words are listed after the subject while English has the adjectives before the noun. The Spanish would say *"I was a boy bad"* while English will write it as "I was a bad boy". Needless to say I got the vocabulary anyway. I smiled inside when I read the note. I wondered if I could take the note and pull it out when the judge would ask me a question. I figured that wouldn't look so good so I made a mental note to myself to review it later. I thanked the brothers and told them I would read the words over.

They passed me their second item. A *BIC* razor. This was rather interesting. I took it and looked at it for a bit then looked up, ready for an explanation.

"You need to clean up and look good for tomorrow" explained one of them. Well that made sense, however, this had created a problem. I had never used a safety blade razor before. At home I used an electric shaver. Nevertheless, I decided to figure this out later.

The third item was a toothbrush. Oh, I was really happy to see a new simple toothbrush still in the plastic container! I had not brushed my teeth in two days and was starting to feel it. Boy, I thought to myself, you guys think of everything. It is interesting that small things like a toothbrush and a BIC razor meant so much. Right then, all my possessions laid in a plastic bag under Eddie's bed. I was grateful that I could add a razor and a toothbrush to my can of Coke and my book.

I thanked them for the items and said that I would be ready for tomorrow. I looked forward to meeting the judge so I could get on with a normal life. The lawyers left and I sat down again to watch the Novellas for the rest of the evening. For now, I had all my needs met and tomorrow would be a new day.

Bedding Down

I finally settled down again some time after the lawyers left, but I kept thinking of all that was going on. Tomorrow was going to be a big day for me as I would see the judge and get out of here. I'd get this cleared up so that I could have dinner with dad and head back to the United States. I figured I would go to work on Friday and was excited about tomorrow. Just for the fact that I would be on the other side of the law again and back into my comfort zone. However, it would be a busy day with seeing the judge, getting out of jail and out of Mexico. I determined that I would maintain the energy, attitude and confidence that would permit me to continue onward.

The guys were winding down also. Everyone was now either in bed or sitting down. I wondered how long we were going to be awake. Eddie was in the bottom bunk next to me on my right. Ivan was above him and the Tall Guy was on the top bunk. I figured that they had been there for some time and that there was some sort of seniority to having a bunk bed. Eddie had a shoe box taped on the wall and had some of his personal items stored there. It was his personal apartment wrapped in a bunk bed space. Ivan didn't have much stuff and I couldn't see what items the tall guy had on the top bunk. This top third bunk was about 6 feet off the ground. It seemed like double that height especially when he looked over the edge and me sitting on the floor looking up at him.

It was the same thing on the other side of the room. Three bunk beds stacked on top of each other. Rocco had the bottom bunk and seemed to have a bit more stuff than Eddie. But Rocco was organized. He seemed more sophisticated than the others, almost as out of the ordinary as I was here. He too had a shoebox and had stashed his toothbrush, a box of playing cards, along with some other things.

On top of Rocco, in the middle bunk was another guy who really didn't say much. In fact, other than at dinner, I really didn't know he was here. During dinner he smiled, revealing that he had no front teeth. It seemed a bit strange. He was a middle aged man that looked like he had gotten into a fight he didn't win.

This guy who was missing teeth didn't stop him from smiling. He also had one of the best set-ups for his bunk bed. He hung two bath towels in front making a curtain for his bed. He stayed most of the time behind his curtain, and by this time, he seemed to have gone to bed already. Hey, I wouldn't blame him. If I had my own bed that I could shut out the rest of the world (or the cell for that mater) I would stay in there too. I didn't know what his name was, so I called him 'the hermit with no teeth.'

On the top bunk was another guy who I hadn't met yet. He had a buzzed haircut. It seemed that whoever cut his hair only had one length of trimmer, so this guy had it all the same length. This guy seemed nice too, but didn't talk much either.

There were five additional guys with me on the floor, three propped against the cell door close to me, and two closer to the TV. By now they had blankets out and sat on them, folded up like a cushion, rather than sitting on the concrete floor. As I looked around, I felt content. Even though I wasn't in a bunk bed, I didn't feel I needed to be. I was comfortable enough. I figured we would go to bed, but it seemed that there wasn't enough floor space for the six of us to sleep. But I guessed these guys had done this before last night, so I would just follow what they did when the time came.

The guys on the floor seemed a bit young. I guess they were lower in seniority and therefore got the floor for a bed. Joey was next to me and seemed only 16 years old, the others were about the same age. One had a mustache on that seemed like peach fuzz, but you could tell he was proud to have at least that. I called these guys "The Kids." I would figure soon enough why they were in here, but for now, I felt sorry for them that they were starting their adult lives getting in trouble. I wondered what row they had plowed in life to cause them to get here and found myself feeling grateful for the blessings I had.

Even though I was in trouble and in jail along with these kids on the floor next to me, I once again realize how great my life actually was. I had a good income (considering I had a job left when I got back), and had friends who supported the noble things I did. I even had a Dad that supported me even when I dumb made mistakes like trying to cross the Mexican border with bullets in my car.

It took a while to count my blessings as my mind wandered through my life. I was even grateful I had a sleeping bag. I felt out of the ordinary with a sleeping bag full of a room with guys with only blankets. I pulled the sleeping bag out of its stuff bag and laid it out along side of Eddie's bed. He didn't seem to mind how close I was, he was accustomed to others sleeping on the floor around him. I pulled out the blankets from under the bed and looked around.

The Kids came prepared with blankets, but Joey's seemed to be a bit small, it only covered his legs. I tossed him the blue blanket which startled him out of his focus on the TV. He looked at me as I said in Spanish "*I don't need it*". He nodded his head with a thank you and went back to watching TV.

I slipped my shoes and socks off, and slipped into the sleeping bag, zipping it up to my neck. Now was the trick. I knew from boy scouts that it's best not to sleep with your clothes on. Your body can't breathe nor get the warmth back from the sleeping bag. So under the cover of my sleeping bag, I took my shirt and pants off. I wadded them nicely and slid them down to the end of the bag at my feet. I also slipped the extra blanket in and wrapped it around me to keep warm. With the blanket inside my sleeping bag, I was warmly content. I wrapped my jacket around the green army blanket Dad gave me and used it for a pillow.

I knew I wouldn't be going anywhere for the rest of the night, besides I had my clothes off, so there really wasn't anywhere I really wanted to go. I would fall asleep and when I woke in the morning I would put my pants and shirt back on, before I got out of the sleeping bag. I had this all planned out, just as long as there was no fire and the others didn't go running and screaming and I had to follow them without my clothes.

Finally the TV program finished on the hour and the Tall Guy on the top bunk on Eddie's side hopped down and turned it off. He then jumped back on his bunk and reached for the light bulb

He unscrewed the bulb a half turn and the light went out. There was some dim light coming from the hallway, but the guys had weaved cardboard between the iron bars of the cell door to keep most of it out. They had made quite a home for themselves here with what supplies they had. I guess when there's a need, you find a solution to make life more bearable whenever you can and wherever you are.

The voices from the other cell faded off and soon it was quiet in the Rocky Point Jail. I could feel my heart beating as I laid there on the concrete floor. I slowly relaxed myself and drifted to sleep.

CHAPTER 4

THURSDAY

Hurry Up and Wait

Shaving

I woke up on Thursday to an aroma I didn't recognize at first. The smell of the cigarette smoke the night before had faded away into the morning air and was now replaced by the smell of the open sewers. It was very nauseating at first, but after smelling it for a while, I could bear the odor. I just thought to myself that is was only a strong outhouse type smell and got over my irritation.

The rest of my fellow inmates had not awoken yet. Eddie had told me the night before that because there were so many in the cell, we all should get up at the same time. This also meant that if I was the first one awake, I should stay where I was until everyone else was ready to get up too. I sat up in my blankets and started to think. It was very quiet, and I could hear the distant sounds of cars and the chirp of a nearby bird. It was actually peaceful and gave me some time to ponder.

I reached my hand my in the grocery bag and pulled out the BIC razor. Previously in my life, I had always used an electric shaver, which suited me just fine. I took the razor out of the package and looked at it curiously. Ok, here goes, I thought. So I started dry shaving while still sitting in "bed" as I didn't know what else to do.

Eddie was the first one to get up. He gracefully walked over and around the sleeping bodies on the floor, I watched him as he got up and went around the corner and thought to myself that he's had some practice walking around those who are sleeping. He went into the bathroom where he proceeded to cough up a lung from last night's smoking. I knew sooner or later everyone would wake up if he continued the racket from the bathroom.

He finished in the bathroom and came around the corner again. I was trying to feel my face and the whiskers I had missed. I was complete with about half of the right side of my face as dry shaving was harder than I thought it would be. I remembered I would always know which men shaved with a razor because of the toilet paper they would stick to their faces from of their cuts. I tried to be careful to not cut myself. I really didn't want to have cut marks on my face when I saw the judge. I almost chuckled out loud at the thought of pieces of toilet paper hanging from my face as I met him! I also laughed inside about the worst-case scenario. It was in the form of a news story: Young man cuts his throat while shaving for the first time: dies in Mexican Jail!

Eddie interrupted me from my private humor. "Hey", he whispered, "There's shaving cream here if you need it." I got up and went to him as he showed me a small box of toiletry items that was part of the community property near the bathroom. I thanked him and started to shave properly.

Someone had taken a gallon milk jug and cut part of the top and side out. This way you could still grip the handle and use it like a washbasin. I filled the jug up with water, lathered my face with the community shaving cream and used a six inch mirror hanging near the toilet closet for reference. It was really weird shaving for the first time. While doing so, I thought to myself that when I would teach my future sons to shave, I would tell them about their dad's first time shaving while a prisoner in a Mexican jail!

I finished up and couldn't help feeling proud of myself for successfully shaving with a safety razor. My lesson for the moment was that I hoped next

> I hoped next time it wouldn't take going to jail to try something new.

time it wouldn't take going to jail to try something new.

Breakfast

By this time, most everyone on the floor had awakened and were starting to roll up their blankets. I went back to my sleeping bag, and stuffed it back into its carrying bag. After everyone finished shuffling in blankets, I also heard noises from the main gate. Francis the fat guard unlocked the big large gate and started walking down the hallway. He then looked into our cell. I could tell from his point of view, we must have looked like a bunch of sardines. At least I felt like one. He looked for a couple more seconds then noticed me from the night before. His size filled the whole doorway of the locked cell.

Francis the guard seemed really happy and on a first name basis with most of the other prisoners, even me. "Good Morning Roberto!" He had a big smile on his face. "Did you sleep well?" I was gullible enough to not know if he was making fun of me or if he really cared how well I really slept. I nodded my head and said yes thank-you.

"Maybe you get out today, no?" he cheerfully replied back.

With that, he unlocked the large padlock of our cell and opened the door. The last of the prisoners mulled around a bit, and all of them finally got up. The guard also unlocked the door to the courtyard and the door of the other cell. Finally he went back to the large gate where another guard was standing to let him back outside. The fat man then walked through the gate and disappeared in the room further on.

We now had a little more space as we started filtering out of the cell. I was really appreciative that Francis had opened the courtyard. I was beginning to wonder if we could use it, and now knew it was open for the day. Those of us who slept on the floor finally stacked our blankets under the bunk beds and started to meander out of the cell door.

The other 10-12 guys from the other cell started to drift out as well. With *good mornings* and *Hola's*, I met the guys all over again. Once again, all of them seemed pretty nice, or at least they were still sleepy enough not to appear to hate me.

I ventured down the hall and out to the courtyard. It was a large cement area without a ceiling with concrete walls 20 feet high. The floor space wasn't so big, maybe 25 to 30 feet wide and long. But there was still room to walk around more than the hallway. The center of the concrete floor had a storm drain, which was also the link between the bathrooms in the jail and the sewers.

The ceiling was made of a chain link fence that covered the whole top of the courtyard. This served the purpose of keeping us in, while still allowing the courtyard to be in the open air, which also allowed in sunlight. I walked around and then just stood there basking in the sun. It was good to feel the sun again. Mexico was relatively cold during the December months, but the sun felt especially good. Many of the guys from both cells came out to the court-yard. They were beginning to stretch their legs and walk around, working the kinks out from sleeping on hard beds or concrete floors.

Within a moment of walking in the open air, there was a call from back inside, "Breakfast!" What in the world could that mean? I couldn't imagine breakfast, let alone food for that matter. I knew that there was food in the cell for community use, but I didn't know there was enough for the whole cell to be called to breakfast. So, I went back inside the hallway to investigate.

Breakfast consisted of two box tops containing food, being passed through the main gate. One box was filled with Styrofoam cups with lids on, the other was filled with bananas and bread. Each prisoner bunched around to take a banana, a bread roll and a covered cup.

I stuffed my banana in my jacket pocket, took a cup in one hand and a roll in the other. With food in each hand, I went back to the courtyard and sat on the ground, happy to have some breakfast. I wasn't really hungry yet, but knew that I should eat when food was available.

The bread actually looked like a large dinner roll, but it had a taste of honey. I ripped off little bite sized pieces and ate them. I tried to spread the process out rather than just quickly eating the whole roll. I guess it was the idea of savoring my food for as long as I could.

I pulled the banana out of my pocket. It had been a long time since I'd had a banana, I thought to myself. Well, I guess it takes going to jail to start eating banana's again. After I finished, I pulled the lid off the Styrofoam cup. It was a soupy cross between grits and cream of wheat. It was still warm and I looked at it for a while.

Right then one of the guys sat down next to me. *"Good morning Roberto, how you doing?"* He was one of the guys that slept in the other cell room last night, but I had met him in the hallway yesterday. He always had a good humor about him and was one of the first people that made me feel welcome here. I named him "Joker". I replied that I was doing pretty well, now that I was eating breakfast.

As he sat with me, he peeled and sliced his banana and then put it in between his roll making it into a banana sandwich. I figured he was pretty familiar with this routine and that he had banana sandwiches before.

Joker's English was good enough for him to tell me how the guys here in jail would get food on a daily basis. He thought that the food came from the local Church. It always was bananas, rolls and the hot cereal drink for breakfast. Then for dinner we would get corn tortillas, meat and some fried peppers and onions. I remembered this from last night, but was glad to know that food came on a regular basis. He also mentioned that family members would visit us here in jail and would pass through soda, sweets and other food as often as they visited.

He started on his hot cereal. I still couldn't get excited about what was in my Styrofoam cup. I was grateful for it, but it really didn't look very appealing. I took a swallow. Sure enough, it was neither grits nor Cream of Wheat. I couldn't quite figure what it was other than some sort of weird hot cereal. I managed to finish about half of the gruel in the cup before I had to stop.

I knew this cup of stuff would fill you up, but I wasn't comfortable with finishing the rest of it. I offered the rest of it to Joker. He looked at my half finished cup as I tried not to show much disgust. He had finished his and looked at me.

"Ok, one is usually enough for me, but I think I want some more today." He thanked me and took the cup out of my hands. I was actually glad I could get rid of it. I could not finish it, and certainly didn't want to throw it away either. I didn't know who was watching and figured that someone, would be mad at me if I threw away any part of my first breakfast.

I sat with Joker for a while longer. I asked him where he was from. He answered that he was from here in Rocky Point and he had been here a month and had worked construction before. He really didn't look like he was capable of construction as he had a small frame. He had tattoos on his arm and had hair that looked like it had been un-kept forever. He said that this jail isn't so bad. He went on to spin a story of spending seven years in the state prison in Caborca, Mexico, a neighboring state away.

"Seven years? No!" I was surprised.

"Si," he said. He was one of the only guys here that had been to prison before. Most of the others had come here for the first time or had not yet been in a State prison. I asked what a state was like.

He started weaving a story together of prison life and how he got there. Apparently, many of the guys who come here to the Rocky Point Jail eventually end up going to the state prison in Caborca. I shuddered at the possibility for me too! The state prison is much bigger with obviously a lot more people. There, you share a cell with one other person. There is TV and you get some channels (not like the antenna TV we get here). There are courtyards and extra stuff to do. He made it sound like a nice place to stay.

Still, I figured that I really didn't want to experience it, Rocky Point Jail was quite enough for me. However, I started to realize going to a State Prison that really wasn't my decision to make anyway. However, it was my hope to get out of here rather than go somewhere else. Who knew, considering my luck?

He pulled out a cigarette and offered me one. "No thanks" I said.

"You don't smoke?" He asked somewhat amazed as he lit up. I guess in his eyes everyone smoked, which made me feel out of place. I told him that I never had before and really didn't have a desire to start now. He was pretty surprised, but glad for me. "That's a good idea. Maybe I quit too?" Then he paused and replied with a smile, "No, I like it too much!" He had a thoughtful look on his face and began feeling his chin, which hadn't been shaved in a week.

I was amused at his humorous commitment to his habits and started to get up. I said goodbye, and that it was nice talking to him. With a cigarette in one hand, he raised his other hand in cheers still holding onto the hot cereal I gave him. He thanked me for the cup of cereal and said, "See you later."

The Blanket Party

After everyone had gotten up and had breakfast, some of the guys started quickly talking. Others gathered

119

around them and started to agree to something I couldn't understand. As far as I knew, they were planning on 'stringing up the new guy'.

A few of the conspiring guys started for the cell and began taking blankets out from under the bunk beds and then carried them out to the courtyard. I had heard of a blanket party before, where a victim is wrapped in a blanket and the others beat the tar out of him. However, I had never been the victim yet, and had only talked about doing it to others a few times. I stood there helpless and watched for a couple moments.

The guys started tossing the blankets to others who grabbed a partner and began opening each blanket up. Each guy grabbed an end and started shaking their blanket. Immediately, a cloud of dust filled the courtyard. I was greatly relieved to figure it out, they were cleaning.

I was actually surprised how many blankets there were in the cell. Other guys joined in and blankets from the other cell came out too. I grabbed an end of a blanket and helped Ivan with one he was working on. *"Do you do this every day?"* I asked.

He looked at me with the strangest look. *"No, this is the first time we have cleaned this good."* I now knew there was international body language for "what, are you crazy?"

I saw my blankets taken out of their spot and dragged into the courtyard. I didn't mind, it felt good that we were all helping each other. For the first time, I thought that being in jail wasn't so bad after all! Besides, no one knew who owned which blanket anyway. My blue blanket was really dusty, and needed a good shaking out. Well at least I was glad that there was no possibility of bugs in it anymore.

> I now knew there was international body language for "what, are you crazy?"

The other blanket didn't make it so well. The two guys got carried away doing such a good job that they pulled at the same time and RIP. Right down the middle, the blanket tore in half! The two of them looked at each other in astonishment, not knowing what to do with someone else's shredded blanket.

"That's OK," I called out to the two inmates each holding half a blanket in their hands. *"It's old anyway."* My words echoed the courtyard, breaking the seriousness of the blanket's misfortune. The silence turned to laughter as everyone chuckled. In the midst of all the humor, the sobering thought then crossed my mind: that was Mom's old blanket that she used for everything, what was I going to tell her? 'Um, Mom, I ripped your green blanket in jail, sorry.'

All the blankets were folded and placed back in the cells. Just from the simple cleaning, the place looked much better that it did before. By this time, we had the entire group in the courtyard, helping out. Once everything was off the floors, two inmates grabbed brooms and swept the cells and hallway and courtyard. They didn't have a dust pan, so they used a sheet of paper to sweep dust on. The paper was then picked up and the dust slid in the trash with the floors was mopped afterward.

I started to wonder about other times where I had damaged something by accident. By circumstance, I was a steward over mom's old blanket. How much time would be needed for mom to forgive me and get over the loss of an old blanket? I was glad she wasn't too haughty over her worldly possessions. However, it still didn't lessen the fact that I ruined her blanket and would have to seek some small pardon for it.

Dad Comes to See Me

Later that morning Dad came to see me, but still no lawyers or judge yet. It was weird looking at dad through the metal grid of the gate. He asked me how I was doing. I replied that I had slept on the floor, and that the air smelled of sewer when I got up, but other than that I was doing pretty well. My spirits were up, I had been making good friends, and had a good breakfast.

"How are you doing, Dad?" I asked

He looked somberly at me through the iron grid of the gate, "I have been beside myself, trying to figure out what happened and how to get you out of this."

I could see the worry in his eyes. We both knew my situation was bleak. I stuck my fingers through the grid holes and he stepped forward to hold my fingers in his hands. Tears started to swell up in his eyes.

For one of the few times in my life, I saw my dad cry.

> For one of the few times in my life, I saw my dad cry.

I could tell it was the paternal instinct to worry about a son and there was not much this father could do. This fact started to overwhelm him as his eyes turned red and watery. I felt terrible. I was the cause of his pain. It's not really a good feeling knowing you've made your dad cry.

It got worse. Dad took a couple of steps back and sat on a nearby chair in the guardroom. He bent over, putting his head between his knees and started to breath slow and deeply. I knew what was happening. Several years before, Dad had heart problems. Under stress, his heart would start racing and risk greater complications if he didn't do something to calm his heart down. Now I felt helpless.

I really hated to see this. My first thought was "Oh no, I'm going to kill my dad with a heart attack." Great, I thought. This is worse than any prison smell. Tears started to swell up in my eyes too as I watched my father, bent over trying to get control of his heart beat.

His mind started focusing on calming down. He had learned some breathing techniques and would use them to get his heart back on rhythm. His tears stopped as he closed his eyes and continued breathing thoughtfully. After a couple of minutes, what seemed like eternity, he opened his eyes, and got up. It was over. Dad was back to normal as he returned to the gate.

"I took a long walk on the beach this morning," he began. "I kept thinking of what I could do and what we needed to do. I didn't realize until then how bad the situation is." He finally smiled and said, "If these lawyers don't get it right, it's mortgage the house time!" I knew he was trying to make light of the subject, but deep down there was truth to his statement.

Dad laughed to himself. "I finally called Christy last night!" I forgot that she knew. He called her on Tuesday to ask if she knew where I was, and she got worried when I didn't show up. Dad was so busy on Tuesday night and Wednesday that it was finally Wednesday night before he had a chance to call her back in Arizona. "Oh, you're going to wish you were still in jail when you see her again! She is livid!" Both dad and I had a good chuckle.

He informed me that she would call my manager to tell him that I wouldn't be coming back to work yet. Oh yeah, I needed to be at work this morning, I totally forgot that too! I told dad that I hoped my vacation hours were enough to last through the time I'd be gone.

This brought me to an idea to help the situation. I started talking to dad about what we could do. There were many people of influence back in Arizona that knew me. My idea was to ask them for letters of recommendation. We then figured that our church leaders could write letters as there was bound to be more credibility that I am a good person. We also thought about my manager who could write about how great of an employee I am, and also the city attorney of where dad lived. He knew our family and could also write a letter. Dad was in favor of the idea and said he would get on it when he talked to Christina again.

Dad hung around for a little while longer after we finished compiling our list of contacts. After finding that there was nothing more to do for me, he said he had to run some errands to get the plan in motion. He was also going to the store. He asked if I needed anything.

Gum. I asked for a couple of packs of gum if it wasn't too much trouble. He looked at me strangely, as he knew I didn't chew gum and asked me why I wanted some now? I came up with the idea last night when I saw some of the other prisoners exchanging "stuff" for cigarettes. A couple of years before, I had the opportunity to visit a friend in jail. I learned that there is a practice of bartering stuff for stuff, as there's not much currency anyway.

Since I didn't smoke cigarettes, then gum would be the next best thing to barter and to "make" friends with. He understood and said that he would see me later. With gratitude that dad fought off a potential heart attach, I watched as he walked out the door and I returned back to the courtyard.

The Interview

I waited around all day hanging onto the piece of paper the lawyers had given me. I put it in my pocket and would periodically take it out to read it again. It also helped pass the time. I was getting a bit anxious to meet this "judge", I knew he was my ticket to freedom and I wanted to get out of here, hopefully today.

I thought of how I would plead my case. It was basically spelled out in the contents of the note. I came down for vacation, and was too excited to be meeting up with dad that I forgot to take the bullets out of my car. I had simply forgotten that I had them in my car and had no deliberate intention of crossing the border with them. I am really sorry that this happened and didn't want to cause problems. That's my story and I'm sticking to it. As stupid as it sounded, it was the truth and it was negligence on my part for not cleaning my car before I left home. Explaining that clearly to the judge would be another challenge.

Finally that afternoon, my name was called. *"Roberto,"* it was from the now familiar voice of the fat guard. I looked toward the main gate and recognized the two-brother lawyers waiting for me. They had big smiles pasted on their faces. I hoped that was a good thing.

"Good morning" I said, as I came up to the gate.

"No, its good afternoon" one replied back to me. Oh yeah, by now, it was afternoon, I thought we were going to meet in the morning, but I kept forgetting about the Mexican "hurry up and wait" time standard.

Francis looked at me and started to unlock the gate "Roberto, maybe you go home today, no?" He had a smile on his face too. This seemed encouraging, but I couldn't make out if he was serious, teasing or just always jovial.

The gate opened and I was invited to come out as I stepped around the partially opened gate. I had been in this jail since yesterday and a good part of today. It was Thursday, my fourth calendar day in jail. It was mentally good to walk free, even for a psychological minute. However, this feeling of freedom was short lived when the second guard came towards me with a pair of handcuffs. By this time I was used to being constrained while traveling.

The handcuffs were put on and thank goodness no leg cuffs were added. I was instructed to follow the lawyers and the guard across the street. We started out the door as I had a couple of *"goodbye Roberto"* call outs from my new found friends back on the other side. I looked back with a smile, hoping that the next time I see them would be only to get my stuff. Either way, I would be back, but it was still nice to walk away from it for a while.

We walked out the door into the bright afternoon sunlight. My eyes had not adjusted yet, so I squinted as I took in the open air. It was still crisp December air and I recognized the smell of saltwater nearby. After all it was a coastal town, but from where the jail was, you couldn't see the ocean.

After leaving the jail, we crossed the street to the next building, it was another municipal building. I felt a bit awkward in handcuffs walking in the open air. The guard was right behind the lawyers and me. I thought to myself I could make a sprint for it, but where would I go and how would I get these handcuffs off? In an instant, my mind raced with an escape of grandeur, but decided that at this point I was too lazy and would just go with the flow.

We entered into the other building. It was another tiled floor building that had seen better days. A lady at a desk looked up, and spoke a few words to the guards and the lawyers. One of the brothers responded back. It didn't seem like official conversation, but more like he was picking up on her. I could only imagine what was being said. They talked a bit faster than I could understand, but I imagined my own story from their conversation

She would ask "are you here for the interview?"

Then he would reply "yes, it should last about an hour, but we will pick you up for a date later!" I think my mind got carried away with this, but it was amusing anyway.

A door opened up in a hallway and the "Secretary" that I met yesterday motioned for us to come in. The other brother lawyer looked at me and whispered, "Do you remember your words Roberto?" I nodded that I was ready.

We went in. There were about five chairs in the room, with a desk and a computer. The Secretary I met last night sat at the computer and typed away. This was my interview? I was not expecting that I would talk to this guy again. He scared me last night when I talked to him and I wanted to talk to somebody else. This guy was intimidating enough, now it looked like he had the power to make decisions too? I swallowed whatever pride I had left and sat down.

I later found out from dad and the lawyers that the Judge had already gone on Christmas vacation and left this Secretary to make the decisions while he was away. This was getting really weird, however I did the best I could to sit there and remained silent. I kept thinking to myself, just shut up and let the lawyers do the talking for me.

I could see the Secretary had on his computer a copy of the text that the first secretary created when I was at the border town the night before last. He looked it over and started typing additional notes and paragraphs. Periodically he stopped and asked a lawyer a question. One of the brothers took an interest to what he was writing and walked around so that he could have a view of the monitor too. The Secretary didn't seem to mind.

This lawyer and Secretary began a dialog that continued for what I thought was an extra long time, probably ten minutes, but my track of time was already way off. So I decided not to guess. The lawyer interjected a couple of comments that complimented the Secretary. "Of course, yes that's good, exactly" and so on. It really seemed like this brother was helping the Secretary write his part of the report. It became interesting that the lawyer had the privilege both times to assist the secretaries in writing their reports.

I realized that that lawyer was trying to help out, but couldn't help wonder who's side was he on? I still couldn't figure that one out. Finally he turned to me. "OK Roberto, he is almost done. The report says that he has interviewed you, that you have been 'how you say' cooperative. Now do you have anything that you want to say to him?"

I looked over at the other brother who was to the side watching from a distance. His face beamed and motioned a couple times for me to do something. This was my queue, I was waiting for this moment and now this was my chance. I smiled at the idea that this was my interview. It's a good think I was at least, "how you say" cooperative.

"Thank you," I began speaking softly, *"I am very sorry. I didn't know I had bullets in my car. I was excited to go on vacation."* Well this was going smoothly. I said everything in Spanish so far and the brothers looked pretty happy I could

127

do this. Then I started to fumble with some vocabulary and looked at the lawyer next to the Secretary.

"You say it in English, and I will tell him." He responded to me. This was my out. Plead ignorance again and let them help me out of this. Wink Wink.

I continued in English. I basically told them that I didn't remember I had the bullets, I would have taken them out and hadn't planned on getting in trouble in the first place. The brother listened and then started to speak in Spanish again to the Secretary.

By this time, I knew the Secretary didn't know English, however the lawyer didn't know much either. But that was OK, he told me basically what to say anyway and he could repeat it to the Secretary too.

The Secretary had some more questions for me. This was going to be the routine questions probably to fill in the blanks on his report. So, here goes. He looked at me, then down at his computer. Where was I born? I listed the town in Arizona. Where was I currently living? I recited my address in Phoenix Arizona.

What was my religion? I paused for a moment then said in Spanish *"Church of Jesus Christ of Latter-day Saints."* I was glad I still knew how to say the title in Spanish.

The Secretary looked up from the computer and asked me to explain *"Are you Catholic or Protestant?"*

"I am Mormon," I replied. I thought they would get it. The Secretary looked at the lawyers and shook his head in frustration.

One of the brothers had a light bulb turn on in his head and started rattling words out faster than I could understand them all. I caught the words "young men missionaries, white shirts and ties, and bicycles." I guessed that he was trying to explain what a Mormon was to the secretary and how they differed from other religions.

I smiled and thought to myself that this man has not run into many Mormons, hopefully due to the fact that there shouldn't be too many Mormons in Mexican jails in the first place!

The lawyer satisfied the Secretary's question and the interview continued. What do I do for a living? I really had to think for a minute. I was really happy I had what I thought was a great job. But how much of a great job do I need to explain to the Mexican authorities. Especially when it came to relating my financial situations.

"*I work in investments*" I replied. I didn't want to say much. Once again the Secretary looked up at me and then to the lawyers.

"*A bank?*" he asked. The lawyers shook their heads and tried to think of the words. I had no clue how to describe what I did in Spanish. I had a hard enough time talking about it in English. The lawyers finally answered that I worked with people in a stock exchange (*bolsa*). The Secretary nodded his head again and started typing.

> Ah, the money question. I was expecting this.

The next question was the ringer: How much money do I make? Ah, the money question. I was expecting this. I looked at the Secretary who had stopped typing and was waiting for an answer. I probably thought more into the situation than there was, but I had interpreted the question to be: "tell us how much you make, so we can determine how much of a fine we can charge you with and get away with it".

I pretended to think a minute and answered "20 thousand". The secretary started to type again and I pondered for a bit. My answer was pretty much correct, after taxes. Hey, you can interpret the question more than one way.

That about wrapped up the questions. The Secretary had a few more words with the lawyers and he started to finish by closing some folders on his desk.

"*Ok Roberto! We should go back,*" spoke the brother closest to me. Wait a minute! I didn't want to go back just yet. I had some questions that needed answering too! Don't they mean I would go back to get my stuff because I would be free to go?

"Ok, what's next?" I asked. I really tried to keep emotions at a minimum even though I felt very animated inside.

"Oh, yes," replied the other Lawyer. He then started to explain that the Secretary had some things to do and that it would be reviewed on Saturday.

Saturday! What about today or even tomorrow!!? By this time, I was getting flustered and I really tried to not show it. I felt like asking for some definite answers. He then started to explain that they would take the Secretary up to Sonoyta so that he could interview the original border guard that found the bullets. They would also look over the car and then come back and review it again on Saturday. I guessed that the task of going up to the border town, an hour's drive away and messing around, would take all day so that this wouldn't get reviewed until Saturday. Or at least there was so much to review that it would take until Saturday to go through all this mess. I really didn't have a leg to stand on to support any objection and I knew it. I had to go with this. Rocking the boat and fighting with the lawyers in front of the Secretary was not a good strategy. I kept saying to myself: "Shut up and just go along with this, you're already in enough trouble".

"OK," I said. I thanked the Secretary and followed the lawyers out the room. The guard was nearby to escort us back to the jail.

The trip back was depressing, although it was nice again to be in the sunshine. Once back at the jail entrance, the guard un-handcuffed me. I said good-bye to the lawyers and then joined my friends again in the concrete container I temporarily would call home for a couple more days.

A flood of emotions came over me. First, judgment of others around me came up. Then anger. Why in the world would anyone take so long to make a decision about me getting out? This was way out of control and there would be some changes if I was in charge. Well, obviously I'm not, so what do I do now? I'm missing work, stuck in jail, dependant on some power hungry secretary to get off his duff and deal with working with two sleazy ambulance chasing lawyers who always want their cut. How could I create something different than what I'm feeling? Do I have a choice in how to feel about this?

I was internally reminded of others before me who were incarcerated. Thoughts came to mind of Paul of the New Testament, Joseph Smith, the founder of the Church of Jesus Christ of Latter-day Saints, even the stories of the Jewish Holocaust. What could I learn from these examples? Deep down inside I knew that the strength those people drew from came from knowing who they were, despite their physical circumstances.

So, to create a different experience, I had to move past placing blame on others and keep the fact that I was still responsible for my circumstances. The lawyers, the Secretary, the system were just all part of the factors and I couldn't forget that. But deep down inside, I knew that my reactions to them held more power than anything else. The meanings I create around the facts and events made a world of difference.

I decided to adjust my attitude and see if I could make my experience any better. We'll see, I thought to myself. Now comes the real test.

Locking the Courtyard

I took my mind off the interview by joining The Kids in a game of dominos. However, we were soon interrupted when we saw Francis the fat guard enter the courtyard. It was time for his afternoon rounds. Smiling as always, he walked through the hallway until he found most of us in the courtyard. "Hey Robert Deniro!" he called out. I guess that was my nick-name was catching on. "You play games? Just don't let them take your money!" The others laughed. Knowing that I was poorly out numbered and out smarted in a domino game, I quietly agreed with him.

It didn't seem that they played with money, I don't think they had much with them anyway. Still gambling in a small environment when you can't walk away from where you won or lost your money didn't seem like good sense. My mind raced with the thoughts about the economics of a jail. Money didn't have much power over these guys here and now. If no one had much money, it wouldn't be fluid enough to be used properly.

Other items seemed to have a bit more power. I even thought of my own personal things and how important they were for me. If someone didn't have a toothbrush, what would they do to get one? There were certain habits that maintained, even in a prison. Most everyone smoked and whoever had cigarettes had power over those that were without. Cigarettes were passed around, probably in exchange for other things. Some could get creative when it came to bartering. Cigarettes were such a used commodity, that there was always a high demand for them.

I noticed today that there were several family members visiting us in jail. They would pass in food and I would imagine that cigarettes are passed in when inmates requested. This way, there was always an inflow of cigarettes and other useful things that had inherent value.

There were also a couple of Mexican comic books being read this morning. When someone was finished, they would pass it to the next guy who wanted some reading. Books were valuable here, I guess because they were rare. There really wasn't a scarcity mentality as everything was usable. I wondered if it would be the same if we were all on a deserted island. If money wasn't an option, would we work together, let others use games and read books? It's not everyday when you can say you're a lot better off without the mention of money.

Francis the guard interrupted my train of thought. It was now lock down time and we had to go inside, out of the courtyard. I guessed I entered the jail after this same time yesterday as the courtyard was already closed when I entered.

Without the inmates having any awareness of time, the guards still kept watch on a somewhat tight schedule. I wondered why the courtyard needed to be closed right now, but figured that the darker it got the more secure the guards wanted it to be. Most of the courtyard couldn't be seen from the front gate looking down the hallway. Rather than push the issue of wanting more time outside, I decided to comply with the Francis' request and move into the hallway. This had been my first time in the courtyard and didn't want to loose any privileges if I protested. Besides, I would be here tomorrow and would have a chance to walk the courtyard and bask in the sun again.

I thanked "the kids" as we put the dominoes back in the clear plastic bag and smiled at Francis as he rounded the last of us from the courtyard. He locked the gate to the courtyard with a large deadbolt and walked out the front entrance.

So now we were in the hallways and the cells. I knew that later on, we would get locked up in the cells, so I didn't want to be in the cell rooms while I had the chance to be out in the hallway. I meandered through the hallway and wondered what everyone did now. By this time, I was a familiar face to the inmates and most of them were cordial with me. The men watched TV, some talked and horsed around, there was also a few still at the front gate talking to family.

There was plenty of time for me to think as I walked up and down the 40 foot hallway. While absorbing all the sights and sounds around me, I took personal inventory of my situation. I had just met with the lawyers and the secretary. They were still "working things out", which meant I would be here for the next couple days. I might as well continue to make the best of it and keep myself positive and productive.

Being positive was no problem, but how could I be productive in a jail? What usefulness could I be while here in the Rocky Point Jail, when I knew that I would be here until Saturday? My mind thought about the younger prisoners here. They invited me to join them in a game of dominoes. That simple gesture was so welcoming, I was glad that they were friendly, especially to me as a gringo. Everyone made themselves into an all inclusive group of friends and seemed better off for it. I decided that I would find ways to help the others have a better time here too. I resolved that I would stay happy, stay friendly, and get to know the others.

> I decided that I would find ways to help the others have a better time here too.

It also meant keeping my integrity and honor. It meant shaving while here. Even though I was at the mercy of a Secretary who only focused on what happened on Monday night, I would still give him reason to believe that I was a good person over all. Not that appearance meant everything, but I would strive to help everyone see that I cared about myself and about others.

With that resolution, I wandered into my cell room to see what was going on. Not too much, most were just watching the TV, so I decided to join them and just be with my new companions. The words spoken to me yesterday rang in my head with deepened meaning, "We are all friends here." I was now part of the inmates at Rocky Point.

Gum and Shoelaces

Time passed until I heard my name called. *"Roberto!"* Joey peeked his head around the corner and called for me. I followed him and in an instant, I could see Dad, his hand on the gate trying to look into the dark hallway. Remembering my first time looking in, I always wonder what thoughts go through the mind of others when they look into the dear hallway from the free side of the jail.

When I was within five feet of Dad, he smiled as he finally could pick me out from the silhouettes of others. "Hi", he called out. He seemed to be in good spirits, at least he was happier than the first time he came this morning. I no longer worried that I was going to kill him with a heart attack earlier today.

"I went to the drugstore and got some things for you," he said as he held a plastic grocery bag.

I called out to the guard to come over and he quickly got up. By this time, Dad was a regular here and the guards were familiar with him too. They had been very nice to him as he was the only gringo visiting the only gringo locked away here in the Rocky Point Jail. It almost felt like being a celebrity, but in a negative sort of way.

Dad handed the bag over to the guard who quickly inspected the contents. The guard then proceeded to unlock the port hole of the gate and pass the bag through to me. I said *"Gracias"* as I received my new package. Like a kid on Christmas I was wondering what I was getting, but when it comes down to a couple of personal items as your only possession, anything received was a treat.

The guard locked the portal back up as I opened the bag. Several packs of chewing gum and my shoelaces! I guess that the guards here didn't mind the fact that I had shoelaces to hang myself now. I looked up and saw that Dad was really happy that he could help accommodate my situation. You don't realize how important shoelaces are until you start walking in shoes without them!

The gum consisted of seven packs of "Juicy Fruit" and "Spearmint" gum. Dad remembered our conversation this morning and remembered my request. I grabbed the packs and stuck them in my pocket. I thanked Dad and told him this would provide me with something to give out to the others as needed for the next couple of days.

Speaking of which, I told him about my interview with the Secretary. It went Ok, I told him, but they want to keep me here until Saturday. "I guess he's still thinking about what to do."

Dad shook his head. "I expected this would happen but didn't want to say anything to jinks the situation. It's a hurry up and wait mentality," he commented. I agreed.

Dad seemed to keep positive about the delay, and then he changed the subject. "I called Christy again and told her about the situation. She said that you were taken care of at work until you got back." Dad started to explain his conversations with her in detail. She was planning on coordinating others to write letters on my behalf. Dad also called his local church leaders in his home town and the city attorney. They were happy to help us out and were very surprised at the situation in the first place. I grew up with these men as mentors and they did a double take when dad told them I was in prison in Mexico. Nevertheless, they offered to help with anything they could and would contact Christina later.

Now that Dad had direction on where to go, and something to do, he had a different countenance. He was more aware of his surroundings, more sensitive to what was going on and now more able to get things done. Only yesterday it seemed like he was in a fog. It was because yesterday he didn't know what to do. We were at the mercy of Mexican authorities with no understanding on what to do next. Even though we were still at the whim of Mexican authorities and their system, we felt we could now work on a solution that would satisfy their demands for justice.

What a lesson I was learning. The scripture in Proverbs came to mind where it says "A people without a vision shall perish". In my case, dad now had an understanding on what to do, and with that, he now had the process and a way to accomplish what he needed to. I started to realize that despair was seeing your goal but giving up because you don't see a way to accomplish what you really want.

I smiled at dad, as he looked into my eyes and we connected for just a moment. "Thanks for your help, Dad." It really makes me feel more comfortable. From the shoelaces to the gum, to letters written on my behalf, to just visiting, all I could do was thank to thank him for what he was doing. He nodded his head.

"Well, I guess I'm here for a bit. It's a good thing my hotel booked me until Saturday, but this wasn't how I expected to spend my vacation," he chuckled.

"Yeah, this wasn't the ideal trip I had in mind either, but hey, at least it's something different," I joked back.

By this time Francis had made his way closer to the entrance were we were. "Ok Robert Deniro! Time to say goodbye. Time for lockdown". This ended my visit with Dad. I said goodbye to him and he waved back with a "see you in the morning." The large guard unlocked the main gate and slipped through, this time to lock us in our cells for the night.

Lockdown

Francis walked to the end of the hallway and checked the gate, giving us time to pick a cell. I chose the cell I was in last night, considering that was where my stuff was stashed. The others went into their same cells too. No one changed cells, especially for the guys who lived on the bunks as this was their home. Joey and "the kids" I met yesterday were in the same cell too. I guess, once you stash your blanket, you stay in that cell.

As soon as we scurried in, Francis was right behind us to lock up. He was on a first name basis with the inmates and was a pleasure to be around, even though he held the keys to my freedom. I guess we all became chummy with him hoping that it would help get us out sooner, but who knew?

"Ok Robert Deniro! Maybe you go home tomorrow, no?" He was as usual, all smiles. I guess nobody had told him that I wasn't. It didn't matter, he was being friendly. I smiled at him, shook my head and said Saturday, *"OK Robert Deniro! Good night"*. He passed out of view to lock the other cell.

I pulled out my folded blankets and sat in my corner near Joey. I stuck my hand into my pocket and grabbed a pack of gum. I opened the pack of gum and pulled a piece for Joey, "Thanks for calling me to the gate just now," I said. He looked at the wrapped piece of gum and took it from me with a simple *"gracias."* It was a quiet moment. No one saw this, nor did I want them too. It was just between Joey and me, as I thanked him for getting me.

By this time, Ivan and Rocco were at the hotplate fixing food while trying not to block anyone's view of the television. The scents of sizzling meet and fried bell peppers filled the cell and almost covered the scent of today's cigarette smoke. Within a few minutes, we had mini taco's that once again were satisfying. Everyone in the States comments when they go to Mexican restaurants about "authentic" Mexican food. What makes Mexican food "authentic" or not? I couldn't quite get the definition, but I figured getting small taco's with meat and cooked bell peppers made by a couple of Mexican prisoners in a Jail in Rocky Point Mexico would be as authentic as I could ever get.

Watching TV

For the time being, we just sat there eating and watching television. For dinner it was the evening news in Spanish and then the Novellas afterwards. Even though these Mexican Soap Opera's were all in Spanish, the plots are relatively the same. Never in a million years would I watch soap operas back home, but I guess when that is your only form of entertainment until bedtime, then that's what you watch.

I found it rather interesting that these hardened guys were really into watching this stuff! When a commercial came on, Eddie would curse to himself as he went to the bathroom. *"How could he do that?"* He mumbled, *"What was she thinking?!"* I guessed that watching TV day in and day out, you could get ridiculously tangled up with the story line.

My friends on the concrete floor around me were mesmerized by it too. Joey was really into it. At one point I got confused and asked him what was gong on. He pointed to a girl on screen and commented, "She slept with that guy a while ago. Afterwards, he said he had AIDS and now she is upset because she might have them too. But he really doesn't have them, he's just getting back at her because he hates her family." It seemed so natural for Joey to understand all that's going on, like they were members of his own family. After he told me the whole story, it still didn't make a lick of sense, but I guess I was out of the Novella mentality tonight. I figured I had my own drama today and wasn't into anyone else's.

Writing a Love Note

I pulled out the piece of paper the lawyers gave me last night. I read the jumbled set of words and smiled again. I started to get restless and wanted to do something other than thinking of these words I spoke to the secretary and what effect they might have had today.

My mind turned to Christina. Hopefully by now she was aware of more details than yesterday, thanks to Dad calling her. I hoped she was OK. This seemed kind of silly, I'm in a Mexican prison and I'm hoping that my girlfriend is alright.

"Hey Eddie," I called out, breaking his concentration. He grunted something of a "what" and I asked if he had a pencil I could use.

"Why do you need a pencil?" he asked, not looking away from the TV.

I really wanted to say 'to stab you with it', but instead said something nicer. "I have some thoughts I need to write down." I figured he would have a pencil in his stash of nick-knacks.

He looked over to me and verified that I had some paper. It would have been double the effort for him to provide that too. Knowing that I was serious about using a pencil, he reached to the corner of his bed and pulled out a yellow wooden pencil from his stash box.

I said thanks as he gave it to me and turned my attention back to my own thoughts. Christina was still on my mind and I decided to write her a note.

"My dear Christina," I paused and pondered the relationship I had with her. She was a wonderful girl I met at work. I realized that having a relationship at work might be difficult, however we were in different departments and didn't think much of it.

As I penned a few lines, I felt that tonight, I was really happy even though I was now in trouble in Mexico. She was a great diversion from thinking about my surroundings.

A commercial started on TV and Eddie caught a glimpse that I was in my own little world, writing away. "Hey what are you writing?" he interrupted.

I didn't really feel like telling anyone that I was writing a love letter to my girlfriend, but what else could I say?

"Just a note," I replied. I really didn't want to get into many details.

"Well," he added. "You know you shouldn't write notes about what goes on here. There are some of us who don't want information going outside the jail. If you start writing things down, we don't know what you're writing." He had a semi-stern look on his face, as if he had a private agenda.

"Look," I shot back, "it's a letter to my girlfriend."

"Well, you either rip it up, or you let somebody else read it," he ordered. Oh, this took the cake. This was the second time since I'd been detained that I thought someone was a jerk. It seemed that it was the first jailer I ran into on Monday and now Eddie had the same controlling type personalities, even though they were on different sides of the law.

I was in quite a predicament. However, I felt really calm about it. I decided I had nothing to loose, so I folded up the paper again and tossed it to him. "OK," I said, "then read it."

He looked at me a bit surprised. He took the paper from his lap and started to unfold it. Would I actually let Eddie read a love note? I wasn't flinching on this, as my attitude reflected the works: go right ahead Eddie, be my guest. I figured even though Eddie could speak English, I was betting that he was less capable of reading. It felt a bit weird having a love letter read, but I knew that Eddie was trying to have some sort of control over me. I knew that if I didn't resist, he couldn't push my buttons and this would let the wind out of his sails.

> I decided I had nothing to loose, so I folded up the paper again and tossed it to him. "OK," I said, "then read it."

He started reading my note. I only had written four lines. I could tell he was straining to read the words and this act actually amused me a bit. After a couple moments he looked up from his reading "This is a note to your girl?" He asked. I nodded back as he handed me the paper. I picked up the pencil to begin again and Eddie started to fuss once more, "I don't want to read a note to your girl, and I don't want you to write about stuff here."

Fine, I thought and chuckled inside on how hard this guy was trying to gain control over me. I silently handed the pencil back to Eddie, folded the paper back up and put it in my pocket. I resolved that I wasn't going to rip it up, but that I would just finish the note another time in better circumstances. Rather than have a dictator inmate look over my shoulder as I attempt to write a love letter, I would just find another way to write privately at another time.

Going to Bed

It was getting late, so I followed the others as they laid out their blankets for the night. I began my ritual of rolling out my sleeping bag on the cold concrete floor. I slipped in and proceeded to undress for bedtime. It seemed like a good system. Sleeping on the floor still didn't seem so bad. At least it was flat. I kept telling myself to remember the campouts I've done where you sleep on a big rock right in the middle of your back. With this mental image in my head, the concrete floor didn't seem as hard and uneven as what I would be used to if I was camping elsewhere.

My green army blanket which ripped this morning was now used under my head as a pillow. The other blanket was slipped around me and my clothes were tucked in the foot of the sleeping bag. Joey still had the third blanket.

I said a silent prayer again, thanking God for all my blessings. I was still alive, I was well fed, I still had a dad who loved me and now I had gum in my pockets to give away as needed. I finished my prayer and laid there, listening to the sounds of the night as the TV was finally turned off and the light bulb was unscrewed. This was an eventful day, but I soon found myself dozing off while dreaming of shoelaces and chewing gum.

CHAPTER 5

FRIDAY

A Day in the Life of a Mexican Prisoner

Giving Breakfast Away

I woke up on Friday after a couple others started stirring. My body ached from sleeping on the floor but I was still warm. Once again Eddie was the first one to get up and woke most of the others with his coughing in the bathroom. I soon got up and everyone began stirring. All except the sleeping guy with no teeth above Rocco. He had only come out yesterday to eat and go to the bathroom. He still had his towel curtains drawn and you could still hear snoring. This guy wouldn't wake for anything.

While cleaning up my bedding, I heard the front gate open. This meant that Francis would soon let us out for the day. I was actually looking forward to getting out of the cell, even if I wasn't getting out of the jail today. Being cramped with ten others in the cell seemed ok when we were sleeping, but now that we were up, we were getting a bit stir-crazy.

"Buenos Dias," Francis shouted out as he opened the courtyard gate. He then methodically proceeded with our cell door and slid it open. We were now free to roam around the jail again.

What a relief. I left the cell and followed one of the Kids to the courtyard. The sun was shining over the high wall of the courtyard and through the chain link ceiling. It was nice to walk in the sun and stretch a bit. Several others came out and yawned and stretched, their hair still messed from last nights sleep. I guess many of us didn't have combs, besides who cared what our hair looked like.

The call for breakfast was heard throughout the jail. That meant that the boxes of food were passed through the main gate and was ready for everyone. I went back into the cell to pick up my banana and bread. This time, I left the cup of "oatmeal" in the box with the other cups. Maybe someone else would want it. With food in hand I walked back into the courtyard and sat on a wall next to Joey. We sat there in silence. There really wasn't much to talk about right now and it didn't make sense to get between a man and his food with idle conversation.

I finished breakfast in silence and decided to walk back into the hallway and see what the others were up to in the cell. Walking into the hallway always felt like a strange transition. When in the courtyard, there was at least have some air flowing through the top opening. Even though there was a chain link ceiling above this 20 foot high concrete courtyard, it didn't seem so bad. Somehow, it didn't seem like much of a jail in the courtyard.

However you get a taste of reality when you walk back into the hallway. On the opposite end of the courtyard door is the entrance, which constantly reminded you that Francis and the other guard, along with family members who visit were on the free side. On one side of the hallway were the two cells, on the other side was the wall of iron bars revealing the large room I called the drunk tank.

The large room on the other side of the wall of bars was not as clean compared to the side I was on. It was just a very large room rather than a combination of hallway and livable cell rooms. This room usually had three or four people walking around and I had been told that it was a holding tank for drunks or others who only stayed in jail for one or two days.

Today, there were a few more men in the room than had been there before. However, today there was one man in particular that caught my attention. A young Mexican man crouched near the wall of bars looking through to our side. His back was to one of the large pillars and squatting so close to the ground that his whole frame was less the two feet high. His hands and face were dirty and he would only look at my feet as I passed. His hand clasped the iron bars for balance.

I approached the bars that separated us and squatted down near him. Through the bars I asked, *"Are you hungry?"* It looked like he hadn't eaten for a couple days, and he watched all of us walk around with our bananas and rolls.

He looked at me and nodded his head, still not looking up. I didn't know what he was in jail for, but he certainly was not happy to be there. I didn't blame him. Most of the guys I saw on his side didn't have coats and had stayed the night with no beds, blankets or comfort, just concrete and metal bars. He was reluctant to admit his hunger, but there comes a point where, if asked, you won't turn down an offer for food.

I put up a finger and motioned him to wait a moment. I got up and headed for the cell, which by this time was relatively empty. The guy with no teeth was still sleeping, someone was using the shower, Ivan was on his bed reading and the others seemed to be out roaming around elsewhere in the courtyard or talking in the other cell.

I walked to the table where the breakfast food box had been left. Sure enough, there were three or four more cups of oatmeal, two bananas and a roll. I knew that the bananas and the roll were a favorite for everyone. There were always just enough for each person. From the looks of it, the hermit with no teeth had not gotten up yet to get his food.

I reached for a cup of oatmeal, confident it was mine to take and headed towards the cell door again. I figured I could get by with giving away a cup of oatmeal. No one would care if I gave my share anyway. Yet I still held the cup close to my chest with both hands, out of sight and out of mind to the others.

Ivan lowered his book as I walked passed. *"Hi,"* I said. He gave me a cool half smile and nodded his head once in reply. I stepped out of the cell back into the hallway and the wall of metal bars where the squatting young man was still waiting.

I came up to him and squatted down to his level. I presented my treasure of a Styrofoam cup and passed it through the wall of bars. The cup was barely the right size to pass through. The oatmeal still felt warm through the white cup as the man took the cup from me. He quickly got up and moved to the darker side of the large room to consume his meal. No words were spoken, none were needed. Although I didn't really like the oatmeal, I knew that one man's trash is another man's treasure, at least when it came to food for a starving man.

> He quickly got up and moved to the darker side of the large room to consume his meal. No words were spoken, none were needed.

I got up and headed outside to the courtyard again. No one seemed to notice or mind my little act of food smuggling. It seemed like a small gesture, but the small act of service made a great start to the morning.

Marijuana

I decided to join some of the other inmates and take my morning walk. Walking the courtyard had become a common ritual for many of the guys. This meant walking in a large circle on the edges of the courtyard. The 40 by 40 feet area didn't permit much room for walking very far, so most of the inmates walked a counter clockwise circle around the edges of the courtyard. I called this "walking the circle".

It seemed like the more seasoned inmates dedicated the time and felt the necessity to walking the circle. Without fail each morning, Rocco would walk around for 15 minutes after breakfast. Others would join in like Ivan and the tall guy. In one corner of the courtyard, the Kids got a bag of dominoes out again and started to play allowing the rest of guys the opportunity to still walk by them.

At least walking the circle was something to do and I would get a little exercise from it too. I fell in behind Ivan. I knew he would be OK with me following him rather than me following the other two. It seemed weird, but I even thought about my place in the circle and took the others into consideration before I fell in.

It was actually a great day. The sun was now at an angle and shining on the North and West walls. It was still morning and the air was crisp. Gradually the smell of the air changed from sewers back into that of cigarette smoke. However today, I got a whiff of something else. It was a smoky smell, but I could only describe it as sweeter than regular cigarette smoke.

I looked around to find where the smell was coming from. Ivan and the tall guy were smoking cigarettes while walking (oh the irony, smoking and exercising). I then saw Eddie and another man named Pablo sitting with their backs up against the West wall. They too were smoking, but something looked a bit strange.

It then clicked: This was one of my first experiences around Marijuana. Oh, so that's what it smells like! As I passed Eddie and Pablo on the West end of the circle, the strange smell was strong, and as I rounded to the east end closest to the hallway door, the sweet aroma faded. Within a couple of minutes it infiltrated the entire courtyard and it didn't matter what end you were on. It wasn't really strong, just noticeable. I instantly realized how inexperienced I was at a lot of things within the criminal world.

I didn't want to make a spectacle out of myself, but I really was curious about what they were doing. As I came around the circle, I could watch them more closely as I passed them. It didn't seem to care who was watching. It seemed Eddie and Pablo were comfortable with smoking a joint around others and that they had done it before.

Seeing them smoke the stuff was also rather interesting. Since there was no such thing as cigarette paper, they used scraps of any kind of paper they could get. Today it was newspaper.

It seemed that this homemade stogie was more paper than anything else. I really didn't think that smoking newspaper would be good for them, but who was I to judge what was good about it anyway? This was totally new to me. However seeing the two of these guys was almost humorous.

Each circle that I walked would bring new images of Eddie and Pablo sharing a joint. One would take a puff while the other one tried to hold in the smoke of the previous drag. Every so often they would uncontrollably cough, and I thought it was because they were smoking more newspaper than marijuana. The coughing really sounded bad.

I thought for a moment about the whole idea of Marijuana in a Mexican Jail. How did they get the stuff in here? I guessed where there's a demand, there's a supply. But was it worth it? Seeing this from an outsiders view seemed a lot different than maybe if I was the one smoking. I had never been around anyone who had ever done this before, especially in broad daylight, even though these two were out of view from the main gate.

I then thought to myself I'm not even a smoker, so this was really left field to my ways of thinking. However, their activity didn't seem to bother me. It wasn't that I supported it, but their activities didn't affect me either. In a way, I understood what they were doing, while still not knowing why.

In that moment I realized two important things in my life. One, that I had lived a life that never provided interaction with drugs. The second was that I was actually grateful that I had lived a life that involved not having that opportunity. Have I live a sheltered life? I think the question's relative. My life had been full, it just wasn't occupied with these kinds of things.

A flood of memories filled my mind as I continued walking around the circle. I remembered high school friends. I had acquaintances who I cannot vouch had been abstinent from drugs, but my inner circle of friends had shared my views and didn't join in these activities. I also realize that everyone walks to the beat of a different drum. That is what makes all of us so special. I guess it took me getting arrested in Mexico to finally interact with guys who smoked weed.

The Haircut

My mind had its fill of new smells, so I decided to stop walking the circle as I had all the second hand smoke I could take. It seemed like I had walked miles already (or at least past some of life's milestones) and needed to experience something else. So I went to see what the guys in the other cells were doing.

Stepping into the hallway again was a large contrast from the light of the courtyard. I had to stand in the doorway to wait for my eyes to adjust. After a few moments, I could find out what was going on in the other parts of the jail. I walked the length of the hallway, past the cell I had slept in for the night and into the doorway of the other cell.

Every time I looked in the cell closest to the main gate, I was always grateful I chose to sleep in the other one. Like night and day, this cell was far more un-kept than the one I stayed the night in. By the influence of the first people who helped me on Wednesday or by grace alone, the cell I had been led to was as close to orderly as anything could get in a Mexican Prison.

The cell I was now visiting was in shambles, but some still called it home. There were two sets of bunk beds three beds to a set, same as the cell I occupied, but these bunk beds had totally messed up blankets or none at all, revealing the dingy mattresses.

On the far end of the cell, near the bathroom was another single bed frame with a thin mattress, at the end was a small TV facing outward. The picture was on (TV's always stay on throughout the day) but no one seemed to be watching.

There were four other guys in the room and the attention seemed to be on the inmate named Tito.

Tito was short, but had a much bigger build than the rest of us. He had to have been a weight lifter before coming here. He wore a "wife beater" tank top exposing muscular arms. He seemed friendly, but still powerful.

Some of the guys looked at me and called for me to come in. They were all smiles and laughing at Tito. He had a mirror in his hand and was trying to look at the back of his head with it. He seemed to have some trouble getting a clear view. He looked at me and called out, *"Hola Roberto! Come in"*

"Hi guys, what's going on?" I asked. They were still smiling and chattering up a storm around whatever was going on with him. Tito would curse responses back in Spanish but still seemed to be in good spirits.

I entered the room. The smiles were contagious and I soon found out what was so funny. Tito had allowed another guy to shave the word "SONORA" into the hair on the back of his head with some sort of razor or shaver. He motioned for me to come over and inspect it. I motioned for him to turn around so I could get a better look.

Sure enough, the word SONORA was inscribed in his hair. Tito's hair was short in the first place, but the words were shaved to the scalp. "What do you think?" He asked.

"Very good," I said looking at the others and the one who had done the shaving. The others giggled as it really didn't matter what I thought, it was in there already and it couldn't be fixed it now. I looked at the others, we all knew it really looked a bit silly.

Actually, the letters were out of alignment. The first three, "SON" were really large on the left side compared to the "ORA" wrapping around to the right. They looked as if the guy had to fit it all in and was starting to run out of room, so he made the rest of the letters smaller.

I thought Tito was a good sport. I was impressed that he allowed someone else carve words into his head. He could have had the word LOSER in his head and he still wouldn't see it.

Some of the guys had now left the room and I had a chance to be with Tito while things wound down. He flopped on the single bed near the TV and motioned for me to sit also. I obliged and was happy that I could share in this experience. I didn't really know Tito and I had the chance to talk to him personally as he kept struggling to get a proper view of the back of his head by using just one mirror.

We started up a conversation, I first asked why he would allow SONORA to be shaved in the back of his head. "It's where I'm from," he said. Well I guessed that already, but now I could tell this guy was loyal. Sonora was the state of Mexico that Rocky Point was in. His English was rather good. As we talked, I came to find out he was originally from Rocky Point and lived in the area before he was put in jail.

"So, what's the deal? You had bullets?" He asked me. By this time I figured many of the others knew about my situation or at least part of it. I didn't seem to mind. The jail was a small world and news travels fast.

"Yes," I replied "I brought them with me when I crossed the border. I forgot I had them." It was the same story I told everyone. It was true on Monday night, it certainly remained true now. There really was no elaboration, it's a pretty simple straight forward story, I was a bonehead flat out and I admit it. Now if I could only get the secretary to see that it was harmless as well.

> I must have sounded pretty convincing as Tito cursed under his breath on my behalf.

I must have sounded pretty convincing as Tito cursed under his breath on my behalf. His response was something along the lines of how stupid is this for me to stay here when it was purely an accident. At least I had this guy on my side. "And you weren't' going to sell them!" He could see that I wasn't the master mind hardened criminal type.

I shrugged my shoulders, "No, I didn't even want them." Tito smiled and shook his head while still adjusting his mirror to get a better view of his head.

I knew Tito had been here for a while as he pulled out a cigarette. He had plowed a hard row and it was showing. He was very muscular and had a tattoo of an old girlfriend's name on his arm. In honesty, he was only a guy about my age. I realized that this guy could be a great friend, or could kick the stuffing out of you if you got on his bad side. I was especially glad I was getting to know him. I tried to be as innocent as possible and asked my next question.

"Tito, what will happen? How long do most of us stay here?" If he knew anything, I was really curious about the process.

He squinted his eyes in thought and took another drag on his cigarette. "Well it depends on how well the jailers and the secretary like you." he nodded his head towards the front gate. "Most only stay for a week. You are either let out or if the week comes up, they have to ship you to the State Prison." He mentioned Caborca, Mexico the state prison spoke of before by the Joker. "Sometimes, they think they can resolve it here, so you stay here a while." I guessed that was his situation along with Eddie and some of the others. "Or they forget about you!"

I looked up at him, relieved to see that he was smiling. We both hoped deep down inside that it wouldn't come to this unlikely ending, but it was still fun for him to razz me about it.

"Thanks," I added. I heard my name 'Roberto!' being called and decided I needed to end the conversation. Ivan got up and finished his cigarette by throwing it down the toilet hole of the bathroom closet. I reached in my pocket and pulled out a stick of gum.

"You want some gum?" I asked. He coolly nodded his head and took the piece from me as I walked out of the cell.

Dad Goes Away

I walked out of the cell and back into the hallway as Tito still inspected the back of his head. Dad was standing at the gate waiting for me.

"Good morning," I said as I approached. Dad seemed to be in good spirits today and also had something on his mind. I reached my fingers through the holes of the grate and Dad took a hold of them.

"How's it going in there?" he asked.

"Not too bad" I replied. "Thanks again for the gum. I think its working. The guys know that I don't smoke and it's giving me brownie points when I give it out." He smiled at the thought. He was glad to be of service and happy that something so small would go such a long way.

"Listen," he interrupted, "I have to go back across the border for a bit. Are you going to be OK while I'm gone?"

I guessed that he had some errands to run. I knew that deep down inside Dad was reluctant to be leaving me behind and going back into Arizona. I could tell it was a struggle for him needing to go away, while feeling like he should stay to make sure I was alright. It also showed a father's love that I had not directly seen that many times before.

I smiled and said "Well, I don't think I'm going anywhere soon! So, I think I'll be ok for a while. Besides what could you do about it anyway?" Dad smiled and chuckled too. He could see that I was making light of the subject so it would be easier for him to go and leave me behind. "What are you going to do?" I was interested to know what was in Arizona today.

"Oh, I have to go to a US bank. The lawyers want their money," he said solemnly. "I haven't paid them and they want payment before they continue." Well isn't that nice I thought. I guess it was the lawyers right to ask for payment. Besides, as soon as I get out of here, I'm crossing the border too. So rather than us just leaving them hang out to dry, the lawyers wanted to make sure that they would be paid. I wasn't upset at them for their request. I could actually understand it, but it also created a hurdle for dad to jump over. He had to get back to the US in time to do business at a bank. For some reason, they wanted US money, rather than Mexican Pesos. I guess there's just no beating the dollar bill.

I nodded my head as Dad continued. "Oh, I promised I would call Christina today. She said that she may come down this weekend, so I need to check with her about what her plans are. And I need to make some other phone calls too."

"Hey, I have an idea. If Christina is coming down, then she can bring down the letters of recommendation" I got excited about the idea. We talked about this yesterday morning and now we had a way to get the letters down to us. Dad nodded in agreement.

"There's something else," He said half sheepishly, half smiling. "I still haven't told your mother!"

We both knew what this meant. Mom was still in England on business and still had no clue what was going on here in Mexico. While they were away from each other, mom and dad talked maybe every third day. It was about time for dad to call again and I knew he was dreading having to tell her the news.

> "There's something else," He said half sheepishly, half smiling. "I still haven't told your mother!"

My first through was of what she would do. "Oh man, good luck!" I started to laugh, snorting through my nose. Dad and I had a good chuckle over the task at hand to inform mom. "Well, to tell you the truth Dad, I think that not telling her was ok. What could she do anyway other than worry a couple more days than if you tell her now? However, I think she'd be more upset if she didn't find out sooner than later, it's best if you don't put this off any longer."

"You are probably right. I'm just a little nervous telling her." He replied. Dad's face turned grim. "You know, if you don't get out soon, I need to cancel my trip!"

I had totally forgotten that part. Dad was to fly out to England to visit Mom in the next couple of days. Mom was scheduled to be back after January, but dad was to fly and spend Christmas and New Years with her. He would be there a few weeks and then come home.

"Oh don't say that," I replied with worry. "First, I've got to get out before you leave. Second, you can't cancel your trip just because of me."

"Well, do you think I'm leaving when you are still in here?" He asked seriously. I knew he was right. There was no way a father of his caliber would ever leave his son like that (as much as I deserved to stay in jail and rot).

I shrugged my shoulders "No, but it's not going to come to that. You'll see." For a brief moment, I asked myself why I was keeping faith in this. For all practical purposes, I was no closer to getting out of jail than when I came Monday night. I was still in a deep mess then, and I was still in it now. I still had no definite answer when I would get out. It could be tomorrow, it could be past Christmas for all that mattered. But somehow, I still kept faith that I would be free sooner than later.

Dad caressed my fingers through the grate. "I know," he said. I nodded my head in agreement. For a while we stood looking at each other. I was thinking of ways to remember the glass half full.

The mood lightened up, dad remembered that he had something with him. "Oh, I almost forgot..." He turned around and picked up a plastic bag on the floor near him. "I got some extra clothes from your overnight bag. Here you go."

Dad looked over to the guard who was sitting nearby. Francis had inspected the goods before I came and opened the small door to the gate. Dad slipped the bag though as I thanked him.

"Ok, I need to go." He said. "I'll be back hopefully in a few hours," he said. I thanked him again as he turned to go and walked out of the guard room and out of my view.

Taking a Shower

After Dad left, I walked back to my cell with my bag of goodies. It seemed strange that even a bag of stuff seemed like a great newly discovered treasure. When you now have your whole life in a couple of grocery bags, it changes the way you view your possessions and what is really of importance

I finally got a chance to sit down on the floor of the cell. Most of the guys were in the courtyard or walking around, all except for someone in the bathroom closet and the sleeping guy with no teeth who was still in his bed. I opened the bag to find what dad passed through.

My bag contained a change of clothes. Oh what a relief! I realized I had been wearing the same set of clothing for close to five days now. Had it been that long already?

Instead of my black slacks with the button missing, I now had a pair of blue jeans to wear. They were a favorite pair and I knew that they would fit comfortably and also stay on without a belt!

I also received a nice T-shirt. I could finally get out of the button up collared shirt that I had been wearing.

Then in the bag, there were also shoes and socks. While I received my shoelaces back, my black dress socks were getting really bad. When I took them off at night, they smelled really ripe. In the mornings when I put them back on, they would be dried and stiff. So I was really happy that I got a new pair of white tube socks. The shoes were a pair of blue deck/tennis shoes that were more comfortable than my dress shoes. With these new items, I was so grateful for the new change of clothes.

After inspecting my new inventory, I decided to change clothes. Oh, what a relief it would be. After thinking for a bit, I also realized that I had not taken a shower in quite a few days either. With the combination of no shower and no change of clothes, I knew I was beginning to smell a bit ripe.

At this time, one of the Kids came out of the shower room, and was finished with his turn in the bathroom. He said hello as he left to go out to the courtyard. That left everyone except the sleeping guy away from the cell for a brief moment. It could now be my turn to use the bathroom closet.

Everyone tells horror stories about taking showers in prison. However, for some reason such tales didn't faze me. I felt confident that I would be safe as the shower was in the same closet as the toilet hole, so I knew I could have some privacy.

Then I realized my first problem. I didn't have a towel. How could I take a shower without one? I looked around the cell. No one was around. Had Ivan or one of the Kids been in the room, I would have felt comfortable asking them if I could borrow their towel. Oh, the dilemma of being "towel-less"! What could I do?

Just as I was contemplating my problem, the answer came. Nearby hanging up on a two foot clothes line between Eddie's bedpost and the cell bars was a small no one had touched it since I first came several days ago.

I reached for the towel and pulled it off the line. Hanging up, it seemed like a normal sized bath towel, but now in my hands, the truth came out. It was only a hand towel, 1 x 2 feet square. But as small as it was, it was still a towel. "It will do," I thought reassuring myself.

Now all I had to do was to get myself and Eddie's towel in the closet/bathroom, take a shower, use the towel to dry off, put it back when I finished and all before Eddie noticed. If I could put the towel back before he knew it was missing, then none would be the wiser. Piece of cake I thought. What would Eddie do anyway if he found out I used his towel? I knew Eddie would let me use it, after a while of grumbling about it. I just didn't want him to hang this over me too.

Ok I thought, it's either get up and do this, or get another strategy. Ok let's go! I got up, taking my plastic bag of clean clothes and the towel with me as I quickly headed for the shower. Once in the bathroom, I put the plastic bag in the doorway and pulled the curtain closed. I kept a crack open, so I could keep an eye on the clothes bag while I was in there. I took off my clothes in lightning speed, and dumped them outside on top of the bag.

I reached for the handle and turned on the water and turned the valve to change the water flow from the bottom faucet to the top one. There was no shower head, just an opening on the end of the pipe so the water poured out. I stood in the far corner of the closet and reached my hand out to feel for the temperature change.

Suddenly, new thoughts came. First, there was no water heater, and second, this was the middle of December. Here in Northern Mexico, I had no hope of a warm shower. Here I was, trying to take a "shower", bare-naked in a closet, frigid cold water is pouring out of a pipe onto the floor, draining back into the

> First, there was no water heater, and second, this was the middle of December.

hole we use for a toilet, and my feet on cold wet concrete. Needless to say, if I wanted to get the towel quickly back in its place, I had plenty more reasons to take a very brief shower.

Well, I was here, might as well do it. I was still trying to work up my courage. No turning back now. Besides, I can write this off as an adventure of sorts! So I stepped right into the falling water and immediately went into double time speed! I reached for the bar of soap, lathered my freezing body, and rinsed off as fast as I could. I stuck my head under the water and it was all I could do to keep from yelling out loud as I just about freaked out. I then made the decision to just "wet" my hair rather than washing it. Oh well, no shampoo this time.

Despite what seemed to be an eternity, I finished up in just over a minute or so. Considering the size of my towel, I brushed all the water off I could with my hands and reached outside for the towel (which was fortunately still there). My body started to shiver. As quickly as I could, I dried my body and reached inside the bag for my new clean clothes.

I first pulled from the bag a new set of underwear. Oh, what a joy it is to just have a clean pair of underwear. Reaching for my clothing gave me a chance to reflect on my life for an instantly brief moment. Many times in my life I felt dirty. Today I was physically dirty and felt clean even through I took as quick of a shower as I could. At other times in my life, I knew I had felt spiritually un-kept as well. Just as a shower washes away dirt and grime from the body, there is also opportunity for all of us to clean ourselves spiritually as well.

By no means have I ever been perfect, I also knew I would often fall short of who I wanted to be. But this time, I understood that there was hope and ability for me to always improve and live a better life. I was thankful for the lessons learned even if it came from taking a cold shower. I reached for my pants and shirt and was even grateful for just plain clean clothes.

I finished up by putting my old clothes in the bag and headed around the corner. Now for the next part of my task. This next step was to put the towel back. I looked around to see if anyone was in the room. The Toothless Sleeper was still on his bed, body in a fetal position, his back to the room. Ivan was now also in the room, but he was on his bed looking at some papers. He looked up at me as I walked into the room.

"Hola Ivan," I said trying to sound casual as I walked towards him. He nodded his head once in reply, and went back to his papers. I don't know if he saw the towel in my hand or not, but it didn't seem to matter. I started to realize that Ivan was a "keep to yourself" kind of guy. He was also friendly and I knew that he looked out for me. It was good to have him as a friend.

I sat down in my corner and put the towel back in its place. In a few minutes the air would get to it and hopefully dry it out so no one would know that it had been used. Whew, I did it. I silently thanked Eddie for the use of his towel.

Now that the towel was back in its place, I realized that I hadn't dried off as well as I should have. My shirt and pants had absorbed water in some places. Well, it was too late now. I was clothed and not about to retrieve the towel to dry some more in the middle of the cell. Fortunately there was no humidity and I would eventually dry underneath in this climate soon enough even if I became cold in the process.

I sat down and put my new shoes and socks on. I stuffed the bag of old clothes under the bed near the plastic bag with my toothbrush, razor and my can of coke. My current life in two plastic bags.

I grabbed my book and walked out the cell door. Mission accomplished. I proudly marched into the courtyard with my head held high. I had pulled off taking a shower and it felt good to be clean again.

Eddie Finds the Coke Can

Today, I had brought my book out to the courtyard and read. I was almost done with it and only had a third of the way to go. I couldn't think of a better book to read while in jail than "Mere Christianity". It well reflected my circumstances as I was physically prohibited, but my mind and spirit were still free. Reading a book about Christianity was liberating in a sense. When you start understanding that there is more to this life, you begin to realize that you are part of something bigger than just yourself. Reading the book made me relax, take a step back and realize that sooner or later I would be OK, both with my physical situation as well as my spiritual one.

After a while, I became tired and decided to put my book away back in the cell. Eddie walked up behind me while I was looking through my bag. I really didn't expect any problems. Besides, the grocery bag was under his bed along with half the other group's stuff.

"Hey is that a Coke can?" He asked in a demanding tone.

"Yes, I've been saving it," was my reply, not looking up. I knew his tone of voice and didn't have a good feeling about his next comments.

"Well, you can't have it, we are not supposed to have metal like that. You need to either drink it, or put it on the food table so somebody else can have it." I knew what he was getting at. He wanted it and one way to get it from me was to let me know that I couldn't save it for later.

Now I was in a dilemma. I saved my treasured Coke this long. I still remembered the guy who gave it to me in the first jail. I'd given a lot of thought to drinking it when I got out of jail as a free man. But how could I if Eddie knew I had it stashed under his bed? Should I just let my goal go and drink the Coke now? Was it such a big deal to save a Coke as a victory celebration or was I making too much out of a mere can of soda? Should I let Eddie have his way and just give up? I decided I wouldn't go that far. The can had been relatively safe in my grocery bags, but the bag was clear plastic compared to the white ones in the States. The red Coke printing was easily seen through the clear bag. I wanted to let the can stay, but knew I couldn't now.

I thanked Eddie for sharing the information, put the can in my jacket pocket and put my bag of belongings back under the bed. I walked back into the courtyard with the coke can in my jacket pocket to watch the other guys play in the courtyard. I was still thinking about what to do about having a can in jail.

I really wasn't mad at Eddie, I could even understand where he was coming from. In these kinds of situations, possessions are important, and you are free if you can get another's possessions by legitimate means. More power to Eddie, I just didn't want to give away my Coke and had to think of something else to do differently. Besides, my things were inspected before I was allowed to bring them in.

A couple of minutes later, Eddie left our cell and headed into the other cell room. I went back into the room and got my bag from under the bed again. Within a couple of movements, I took the can out of my jacket and slipped it into one of the black dress socks. With the can in the sock, it didn't look like a red can of Coke, but just a dark bulge of clothing.

I put my concealed package into the bag and slid it back under the bed. Sure enough, it just looked like part of my clothing, no red and white lettering showing through the clear plastic bag anymore. The soda was concealed, and I felt that I shouldn't have any more trouble about keeping an aluminum can. What can?

I walked back to the courtyard to watch the others again but was interrupted by Francis, the guard. He was now in the hallway and calling for us to get inside for lock-down. Where had the time gone?

The hallway wasn't too bad. The long corridor allowed you to walk for several strides, before you had to turn around and go in the other direction. Several of the guys would walk the corridor for exercise too. However, I didn't want to walk right now. I watched as Francis locked the iron gate of the courtyard and meandered through the hallway. He seemed like a jovial kind of guy. I still think that if I had-n't known better, he should be on this side of the jail with us. However, he had the "Get Out of Jail Free" card and came and went as he pleased. This time he stepped inside the each of the cells and looked around as if to make sure everything was in order. I wondered if Eddie told Francis about the Coke can and now he was looking for it too. However, he did-n't seem to be looking for anything really, just wandering around. None of the inmates seemed bothered by this. They knew him personally and didn't consider him as a threat if he appeared snooping.

Soon he passed me by with a *"Hey Robert Deniro! How's it going?"* and walked on his way towards the front gate. So that was his rounds for the day. Must be nice, watching a bunch of inmates' day in and day out. I admired

Francis for being a jail guard. He didn't seem like the stiff upper lip kind of guy, but really was actually down to earth. You could tell he liked his job and didn't seem to have many cares in the world either.

A couple of hours passed of walking the hallway and watching the others as they watched TV or talked. Finally Francis came through again. This meant that it was time for us to get locked in the cell. I didn't complain about it. I had a good day and knew that I had lived the best I could, given the incarcerated situation.

Francis slid the large door to the cell closed as we watched from inside. "Good night Robert Deniro," he called out, "maybe you go home tomorrow!"

I had heard this before, but I knew he was right this time. I nodded my head and said *"Si"* to which the others chuckled. Ok, I was staying optimistic, even though the others knew how slow things were going for them. I didn't mind. I was different, and would get out tomorrow, I just knew it. Frances nodded his head, said good night to the others and went out of sight, leaving us alone for the night.

The food box had been passed through again and Eddie and the tall guy were preparing food. They cooked the meat, and peppers. However, this time there was some shredded cheese too. Like icing on a cake, this hit the spot. Again, I was truly grateful happy for what food I had.

I wondered how I was getting so full with the two small meals of breakfast and dinner? At home, I would normally eat about twice as much as this. I figured my lack of hunger was because I wasn't exerting much energy during the day and perhaps because I was in a strange place, my metabolism was changing to accommodate.

Chess Games

As I sat on my bedroll, Rocco called my name. *"Hey Roberto, you play whiese?"*

I looked over at him, I'd not had the opportunity to talk with him much before now, so I was surprised that he would ask me a question. I wanted to answer, but I didn't understand his question.

"*What is whiese?*" I asked him. I needed some more information before I answered if I played *whiese* or not.

He smiled, trying to find the English equivalent. He called to Joey who was also on the floor finishing up his meal.

Joey leaned over to me, "Chess" he responded. Oh chess, yes now I got it.

"*Si,*" replied Rocco, "*whiese.*"

"*Yes, I love to play chess.*" I replied, "*You have a chess board?*"

"*Si, of course*" He replied as if I had asked a dumb question. Well, silly me, I thought to myself. I guess all jail cells should come with a chess board!

Rocco motioned for me to come over to him, so I got up and moved over to his bed. This was a great opportunity for me just to sit on a bed, let alone play chess. I definitely felt privileged. Rocco pulled out a small wood box which opened up to a chess board, allowing all the pieces to gently fall onto his bed.

Chess seemed sacred to Rocco. He certainly seemed more dignified than a common criminal as he started to set up the pieces. During his time here he had managed to maintain impeccable cleanliness. His clothes were clean, his hair and beard were never messed nor out of place. You would almost imagine him as the upper class in Mexico if you met him on the outside. I didn't know what Rocco was in jail for, but he seemed too fit and proper to be here.

Now I had a chess opponent and was looking forward to this game. We started to play an ordinary game, however one thing impressed me during the opening moves. I was playing an international game with a man I could barely communicate with. However, if there was a "language of chess", we were speaking it now. It didn't seem like we were in jail so much as we were two individuals coming together for a good game of chess. For a brief moment I forgot the fact that we were prisoners of the Rocky Point Jail. I would have played this man given the opportunity on the free side, and that made us free inside.

Others started to take notice of our game. Even the Kids on the floor were interested and Eddie sat up from his bunk bed on the other side of the room and watched us more than the TV. Our game seemed more impressive than the TV anyway. While it was Rocco's move, I looked over at one of the kids and asked if they knew how to play. They shook their heads no, no one had ever taught him.

The hermit on Rocco's side looked down on us and made a comment to Rocco. It was my move and I was too focused to try and understand. He said something with "Gringo" in the sentence and I knew they were talking about me. Rocco looked up, smiled and made a comment back.

I was in my game enough not to want to hear, but I knew the conversation was about this American and Rocco. In no way did I feel offended, but I knew some pride was on the line for Rocco, and me as well. I decided to buckle down and step up to the challenge. I felt I was a worthy opponent for him and it seemed it had been a while since someone could play him. Neither of us were Bobby Fisher, but it was a chess game none the less. I looked at Rocco and we both made a friendly Cheshire Cat smile at each other.

> At times, it seems like my life was a big chess game. Sometimes, I had control of the board, sometimes I didn't.

The game lasted a reasonable time and Rocco's pieces finally dwindled down to where I could get him in checkmate. He smiled at me "Good game" he said, and offered a handshake.

The one thing different about Chess than any other sport or game is there is no need for rubbing it in. Good chess players win with dignity and loose with even more. I shook Rocco's hand and thanked him for letting me play chess with him.

"One more?" he asked. I readily agreed and we set the pieces up again. If it meant sitting on his bed for a longer time, I was glad to play one more time.

This time Rocco won. He gained an advantage early in the game and seemed to hold onto it to the end. Once again we exchanged a handshake and said "good game". I excused myself from sitting on his bed. I returned to my bedroll and decided to roll it out for the night. Everyone had settled down and no one was walking around anymore.

Thoughts of the chess game came to my mind. At times, it seems like my life was a big chess game. Sometimes, I had control of the board, sometimes I didn't. Sometimes I would be a knight or a bishop. This week, I felt like a pawn.

I had crossed the line and was now in trouble here in Mexico. I was still on the board, in danger of being captured for good. My freedom was at risk, hopefully not yet at checkmate. However, with any piece at risk, you can either move or have it protected by other pieces.

I was grateful to have my dad and the lawyers as pieces on my side in life. Soon, I would have letters from those of influence that could vouch on my behalf. I also had heard that Christina might come down and see me. Soon we would see how many pieces the other side had. Who would win and how long this game would last was dependent on the Secretary.

There was one more piece on my side. This was again a point in time where I was glad I had been raised with religion in my life. The knowledge of God meant that I could always ask for help. This also meant that I knew I was just a small piece and that someone higher than me was moving all of them around.

Instantly I felt relieved about my current situation. Even though I was in a bad predicament, I had faith enough to know that I would be ok. I could be captured, protected, moved, saved or sacrificed and it would work out to the higher advantage in the end. Deep down inside I was thankful for the opportunity to learn these life lessons, even from the chess games I had played with Rocco.

Arrested Bar Fighters

It was time to watch the Novellas until we fell asleep. However, this night was different as I settled down in my sleeping bag, not really paying attention to the TV. I started to dose off when suddenly there was a commotion in the large empty room across the way. Voices bounced off the concrete walls and echoed into the rooms around. There was some shouting, some scuffling sounds, and a lot of other noises in general.

I turned over and peered over to the other side through our cell gate bars. Weaved within the cell bars were pieces of cardboard and cloth. This created some privacy for us when we were locked in for the night. I looked through one edge of a cardboard piece to see what the commotion was from the other side. Within a couple minutes, the drunk tank became relatively filled with men whom I hadn't seen before. I looked over at Joey who seemed not to notice. *"What's going on?"* I asked.

"Drunk people have been arrested," was his reply. He then explained that every weekend, the room gets filled up with men who have been arrested mainly from the bars fights or other disorderly conduct. They would spend a night or two in jail and then be released. They stay there in the

empty room with the others until they sobered up or paid a fine to get out.

I rolled back towards the TV and thought for a minute. Why can't I be on that side? At least there is some hope that you will get out! But it also meant that I had to be drunk or rowdy. I wondered if it was better to be in trouble for being drunk or having bullets. I really didn't want to be in trouble either way, so neither side looked pleasant.

These new arrivals really weren't even ready to stay overnight. No bedding and few had coats for the night. I counted my blessing for even having something to sleep on. Tomorrow I will get out of here any way, so I didn't mind being on this side for one more night.

After a while, our TV was turned off and the light bulb was unscrewed. I looked again through the bars and into the other room. It had gotten relatively full with around 30-40 men. I finally knew I was glad to be over here when I heard the sounds of someone throwing up from the other side. Now I was truly grateful that I wasn't over there. Men were standing around or sitting against the walls. Most of them looked un-kept and were unruly. Most of all, they were talking and making more noise than I was used to, especially compared to the other nights I had been here.

Our side started to quiet down, but we were all aware of the commotion from across the way. A couple times Eddie yelled out, "*Shut up*" in Spanish. His demands didn't seem to work on these newcomers. It was long into the night before the noise died down slightly. Slowly, I fell asleep despite the commotion and racket of the arrested bar fighters from the other room.

CHAPTER 6

SATURDAY

Girlfriends but Still Not Getting Out

Watching Eyes from the Other Side

I woke up Saturday due to the fact that my ears and nose were cold. I had my head out of the sleeping bag and the morning air was pretty chilly. I could see my breath rising in the air. I raised my head and found the others were sleeping in fetal positions so they could keep their body heat close.

I laid there in the bedroll for a while thinking. It was Saturday. This was now my sixth day and it would all finally be over today. The Lawyers and the Secretary would work things out, and I should get home free sometime later tonight. This really wasn't the way that I thought I would spend a Saturday, especially so near Christmas. For most people, this time of year was spent shopping before Christmas and Saturdays were very valuable shopping days. Not that I shopped a whole bunch, but time before Christmas was far more important than time after Christmas.

However, instead of doing anything for Christmas, I was laying in my sleeping bag on a concrete floor in a Mexican prison. For some strange reason, I didn't mind. This was an adventure and I was happy to be here just as much as I would be by going Christmas shopping.

My thoughts turned to Christina, she would be down here sometime today I guessed. I wondered how she would take walking into a jail to see me. I didn't want to see her like this, but another part of me did. I guess I didn't have much of a choice: if she came, she came. In this situation, there really wasn't much I could say about her coming down. So I really shouldn't stress about it.

By this time, Eddie got up as well as did the Kids on the floor. I sat up and looked at one of the Kids as he stretched and yawned. It was that "I don't want to wake up" look that didn't have to be spoken. We said our good morning's and started rolling up our bed rolls. By now, we were into a routine as to what we did for the morning.

Just on queue, clanging sounds came from the front gate and Francis appeared in the hallway. As usual, he opened the gate to the courtyard and then worked on the cell gate. Soon it was open and he was in front with a smile and a "Buenos Dias!" to all of us. He seemed to be happy today, but wait, I couldn't remember a time where he wasn't. He was now the happy-go-lucky guard. As the cell door was opened, it reminded me of sand pouring out of an hourglass, one man at a time until the cell was empty.

The call for breakfast came from the hallway and those of us who were in the courtyard wandered back inside. Francis was at the main gate with the port hole opened, stuffing the boxes of food through the portal gate.

While waiting in the hallway, I realized I was being watched. I turned to the wall of cell bars and looked into the "drunk tank". I had almost forgotten about the new occupants in the large room. There was a lot of commotion last night, but I didn't realize how many people were on the other side. The room contained at least forty men all standing around, sitting or leaning on the walls with a few sprawled out on the floor. It was amazing, in a short period of one night the other room was filled to capacity with men who were in trouble. The drunk tank was still dark, cold, and damp as always, but now it was also crowded!

It amazed me to see how many people could get in trouble on a Friday night, too many beers I guess. The room looked creepy now with all the people. Hung over and in the dark, they looked like zombies milling around. I was now glad I was on this side, who knows who would have eaten me alive over there? I chuckled to myself that the wall of cell bars separating us either kept me from that side or it was the other way around. For once, my side looked bright, vibrant, and safe.

There was one inmate close to me who kept watching me. His shoulder leaned on the cell bar wall and he intently studied me out through the bars. He wore a bright blue jacket, jeans and dirty, worn out sneakers. His hair was short, curly and fuzzy as if he had stayed up all night. I wouldn't blame him, the only guys sleeping on the floor were the ones already passed out.

I think it was the fact I was a Gringo in the jail that made me a matter of investigation. Yes, seeing a white guy in a Mexican prison would be weird, even for those Mexicans who had seen plenty of prisoners come and go. However, this guy didn't look drunk, nor did he look destitute. I smiled at him and said, *"Buenos Dias."* He smiled back and raised his eyebrows communicating "you're in trouble too?" I didn't know what he did to merit his being put behind bars, but there was regret and worry on his face. He was in trouble big time and he knew it.

By this time the two breakfast boxes were passed through the port hole. It seemed that Francis would count the number of inmates and pass just enough food for us. There was always plenty, but also just enough for us not to take it for granted. I looked back at my new acquaintance and waved a short goodbye. He nodded his head as I followed the box of food down the hallway.

Within a couple minutes, the cell was empty enough for me to take a turn at getting my breakfast. I still couldn't stomach the oatmeal, so I just took a banana and the bread and turned to go out of the cell. However, being the last again, and now that everyone was eating, I knew once again that no one would notice my cup going to someone else.

Putting the banana in my jacket pocket, and taking my bread in one hand, I grabbed my cup of warm oatmeal in the other and walked out of the cell and back to where the man in the blue jacket had been. He was still there, watching all of us come out of our cell rooms with handfuls of breakfast. I calmly went up to him and quickly slid the cup through the space between the cell bars into his waiting hands. In an instant he looked up at me with a quizzical look on his face.

He could feel the warmth immediately and wrapped both hands around the cup. In humble amazement he quietly said "gracias" as I quickly walked away. No sense staying around to draw attention or for others on his side to get jealous. It's not that I was embarrassed about it, I just didn't want to make a big deal out of passing food over to the other side. I was perfectly justified in giving my cup away, but I didn't do it for the recognition of the other inmates. If I could share something with others, then I felt good for at least doing what I could.

I sat down alone in the courtyard and thought while I ate. Eating provided such a good time to think. I watched the others, studied their habits, smelled the air and tasted more of my food. Sometimes we go through the motions of everyday life without knowing what we're doing. Today, I was fully aware that I had a banana and bread. That banana actually had a taste and the bread was sweet. Not that I was just high on life, but food tastes better when it's shared.

Christina

Eventually a call came from the main gate. "Roberto!" In fact this time quite a few voices from the hallway called my name, I guess all the guys in there really wanted me to come. I started toward the hallway when Ivan walked out into the courtyard. *"Roberto,"* he said excitedly *"there is a gringo woman here with your dad!"*

I smiled *"it's my novia!"* I replied. It looks like she had come and was starting to turn heads already. I thanked Ivan for keeping an eye out for me and gave him a piece of gum as I passed him and headed towards the main gate.

But, there she was. Christy was with my dad, talking to Francis the fat guard. He was jovial towards her. I don't expect that Mexican guards have many gringo visitors, nevertheless women gringo visitors at that. She looked as beautiful as ever.

Christina was a natural red head with a very light complexion. She had her hair pulled back and wore thin rimmed glasses. It was wonderful to see her for a brief moment without her knowing I was around. She was beautiful.

I finally approached the gate where Dad saw me first and came up to me. His spirits were definitely higher than I'd seen him in al of his visits. Christy looked through the gate and it took her a couple of seconds to recognize me in the darkness.

She came over as I put my fingers through the grate holes which she immediately squeezed them.

"Hi" I said. "Nice to see you!" My spirits lifted too. Even with only the touch of fingers through a metal gate, all worries melted away. She was here now and time stopped for a brief moment.

> Even with only the touch of fingers through a metal gate, all worries melted away.

She smiled, said hello and asked how I was doing. I

was still in a daze that she would come down and want to see me in such a state. "Are you Ok?" she asked again.

I smiled, "Of course I'm OK, never better," I declared. This made here giggle, but she had a questioning look in her eyes. I continued on, "I'm really ok, I've been treated well here and I could be a lot worse off." I was looking on the bright side, but honestly it didn't seem so bad now.

Dad finished talking with Francis and walked over to Christina to visit with us. She continued, "When your dad called on Tuesday, I got worried. You don't know how many phone calls I've made!"

She started to explain that she got into hysterics on Wednesday until dad called her late Wednesday night. "For two days, I just got sick. I told a colleague at work and cried on her shoulder for a while."

Christina continued, "My manager even told me to go home on Wednesday afternoon. I wasn't very productive, so I went home. I finally got a call from your dad on Wednesday night. I was really relieved that we found you, but knowing that you were here didn't help either."

I winced when I heard that Christina thought I was missing for two days. "I'm really sorry about this. I didn't mean to get you worried about me." I responded. She had been apprehensive about me going to Mexico on my own to see dad in the first place. She wasn't a big fan of the country and encouraged me to be careful while traveling. I guess I would have, if I had remembered to take the bullets out of my car! But no, here we were, separated by a set of metal bars so small that I could only get my fingers through.

At that moment, Christy's dad walked through into the guard room. What a surprise. I had not expected that he would come down too! He was a very tall man, properly built and had a slight country accent in his voice. An accountant by trade, he knew his business and held respect when he entered the room. As the boyfriend to his daughter, I had met him on other occasions but had some trepidation towards him because I was dating his daughter. Nevertheless he was a good man and a very honorable person.

He came up to my dad and Christina, and then called out. "Hello Robert, how are you holdin' up?" He asked.

"I'm not too bad today. Thank you for coming. It's really good to see you," I replied with great sincerity. "Of all the places to visit, I hadn't expected for you to see me like this." I told him. Part of me was glad to see him, but for the most part, I was just a little embarrassed.

"Well, you just hang tight, we'll get you out soon enough." He knew it was awkward for me to be seen like this, but he had a genuine smile and I appreciated his words of encouragement. I smiled at the irony that brought Christina and her dad here.

I was also happy for my dad that they came. For the first time in several days dad now had fellow American friends to help him on the other side. I was actually relieved to see her dad here to help mine.

After a few moments, the twin brother lawyers entered the room. "Hola, Mr. Sam!" they called out. Now the whole gang was here! The guards just kept out of everyone's way and didn't pay much attention to the number of people visiting the jail.

The lawyers could be heard throughout the jail, their voiced projecting at the right tone to ring through the guard room. Their smiles were contagious as Christina and her dad started to ease up from the situation too. The older brother came up to me, I still had a hard time telling the twin brothers apart, but by this time I could tell by which way they parted their hair.

"*Hola Roberto*" he touched my fingers in a sort of hand shake, "*how you doing?*" I nodded my head that I was OK. "*That's good, you stay happy OK?*" I nodded again. At least he was looking out for my welfare as much as my freedom. He then joined my dad who started a conversation with the other brother.

After a few moments of conversation, the brother lawyers waived goodbye. They had some things to do and both dad's were about to follow them away. Dad said he would be back later and I waved back to them. "We get you out Roberto!" was the words the lawyers left with.

Christina smiled as the men left the room. This left Christy by herself at the gate to visit with me. Francis and the other guard didn't seem to mind. "So, how's it going on the free side?" I asked her, I wanted to get a fresh opinion of what was before me.

Christina thought for a moment then looked over her shoulder to see if the Lawyers had really gone. "It seems the lawyers are really dragging their feet," she whispered. I already knew that, but it was interesting to hear this from someone else. She continued onward. "I don't know if they're friends with the Judge, or what, but they seem to be grandstanding a little bit."

"So, what can we do?" I was trying to think of alternative ways to improve the situation.

"Well, I think it was really good for my dad and me to come down. Now your dad is not alone and it seems like the lawyers are a bit uneasy to see us here advising and encouraging your dad."

I hadn't thought about it this way before. Not that dad was gullible, but it was a very difficult situation for dad to be alone, listening to foreign lawyers and not having any way to get much help.

We started talking about what life was like in the jail. I told her that I was well fed and that the guys were pretty nice to me. She wondered about being a gringo in an all Mexican prison.

"Oh, that," I thought back a three days ago to Wednesday when I first came here. "Well, one guy told me 'we are all friends here' and I seem to fit in." She was happy that I was taken care of, despite sleeping on a concrete floor.

I also mentioned that food came twice every day. She seemed relieved to think that I hadn't gone hungry either.

We were interrupted by her dad calling from the doorway. He informed us that it was time for Christina to leave. They would go back the hotel and rest. They had been on the road for about 6 hours and had not even unpacked yet.

She didn't want to leave me, but I assured her that I would be right here when she wanted to come back. I knew what she was thinking. It went through dad's mind when he first had to leave me too. How do you say goodbye to a man in jail when there is so much you want to do for him? How do you feel good about yourself by walking away from the situation when you know your loved one can't? By this time, dad was starting to feel more comfortable with walking away from me. Now it was Christina's turn.

I responded by letting her know that I was going to be alright and that there wasn't anything more she could do right here and now. I was OK, I was safe, and I was as comfortable as I could be. She might as well be productive in the other things she needed to do.

We said our goodbyes as her dad waved back at me too. I watched them as they left the guard room and was honored that her dad would love her enough to come with her. It was an uncomfortable situation for everyone, but he was making it easier for all of us.

Futbol Championship

As Christina left, I decided to get back to the others. I wondered what they were doing and walked through the hallway. What was a normal Saturday for a group of guys in jail anyway? Not too many were in the courtyard as they all seemed to congregate in the cell rooms. What's the deal? I immediately knew upon entering the cell room.

Throughout the week, I'd been hearing commercials of the National Futbol Championship for Mexico. Now the pre-game show was on and all the guys seemed to be interested in it.

Futbol, or soccer as we call it in the US, seemed to be a much different sport then I was familiar with. Many of the inmates lived and breathed this game. Amazingly, I never understood what the big deal was but everywhere outside of the US, soccer is the predominant sport. Citizens of the US could care less about the sport. I wondered which side needed to give in. However, for now I decided to join my fellow inmates and be a fan of futbol.

I leaned on the bunk bed, "Hey Ivan, what's going on?" I was curious about a Mexican's perspective on the game.

"It's the national championship," he answered and went on to inform me that it was the game of games, winner takes all the glory. And this was certain to be some game.

"So, who are you cheering for?" I asked. Rather than teams based on cities they're from like we have in the US for other sports, futbol was split up by teams based on the different states in Mexico. This championship was between a team from a Northern state and a team from the Southern part of Mexico. Most of the guys in the cell were from the local area and were rooting for the northern team. However, Ivan told me that he was originally from Southern Mexico.

"Really, you're from down South?" I didn't know that before, *"Where are you from?"*

"Puebla," was the reply. I knew Puebla Mexico was way down south, but how did Ivan get up here? That would be a story for another day. I guessed it would be similar to a New Yorker living in Los Angeles. Ivan shortly explained that he had come up to Northern Mexico for work, but he really didn't seem to want to talk, the game was on and all focus was on the players.

I watched the soccer game for a while as the players kicked the ball back and forth. Soccer is one of those low scoring games, most of the time you win because you maybe score three points on the other team's two goals. This seemed a little slow pace sport, and I kept hoping someone would score.

After a while one the Northern team finally scored. The cell block erupted with a cheer. So, at least someone had scored a point. I found the TV announcer the most humorous. Trying to say it as long as he could, he cried out "Goal!" This one word lasted for about 15 seconds. Everyone in the jail clapped and cheered, even our little section in the cell, except for Ivan. It was a disheartening blow for him. He just shook his head. Even in the first few minutes it seemed the game was over, maybe it was due to the fact that scoring was hard to begin with.

There is something about a soccer game that seems to mesmerize non-Americans. You watch a group of guys kick a ball back and forth hoping that it will get interesting by someone making a goal. I wondered what made soccer so exciting to so many people throughout the world. It seemed like it had a lot of activity but no one seemed to score. However, you watched so you don't miss any of the good action, hoping someone would score, but most of the time it was all rather bland.

I guess that's what Americans like so much about car racing. You just watch a bunch of adrenalin junkies drive in circles. It's pretty dull and I suspect most of us just pay attention as to not miss the crashes. And it's everybody's luck to look away right when a wreck happens. No one really wants to see the cars go round and round, they want to see when something goes wrong and the cars crash. So here I was, watching players I didn't know kick the ball, hoping someone would score a goal.

Corn on the Cob

While watching the soccer game for an hour or so, I got another call to go to the front. *"Roberto! Your novia!"* Ah, she had returned and still was catching the attention of the others. I smiled and went up to the front gate to see what was going on.

As I turned the corner, I saw Dad and Christina talking to each other while waiting. Christina was laughing from something that dad had said. Dad liked Christina, he thought I finally had some focus when I was around her. Christy had not yet met Mom because she was in England since the time that we had started dating. But dad had spoken well about Christina a number of times.

"Hi guys, what's up?" I was wondering what was so funny. Christina was holding a large corn on the cob on a stick. Even though she held it by the stick and had a napkin wrapped around her fingers, and you could tell it was loaded with butter.

"You're dad just told me about seeing you the first time on Tuesday. He didn't know if he should have left you there or helped you out." By now, I was used to jokes at my expense. This was a pretty humbling time and I figured I deserved some more jokes made about me. I guess I was a pretty pathetic sight that Tuesday when dad came and saw me for the first time.

In the couple of hours they had been together, Dad proceeded to tell Christina about the whole situation, from meeting me on Tuesday, to not getting out on Wednesday, to coming down to Rocky Point, to staying here a couple days. Christina also told dad what I missed at work and that my manager laughed when hearing about me being in jail and why. She was a welcoming sight for me as well as being an uplifting personality for Dad.

A cheer busted from the cell rooms and interrupted their little set of jokes. I looked back as Joker ran out of his cell room with his arms raised up, jumping up and down.

"What's going on?" dad asked. "It sounds like you're having a party in there."

"Well sort of", I replied. "The National Futbol Championship is playing today and most of the guys are watching."

Both dad and Christina looked surprised, Mexicans play football?

"Not American Football, Soccer." I explained. Oh now they got it. I explained that it was the final game and there was a lot of pride at stake on this game.

"Oh, we have something for you." Christina raised her corn on the cob.

"You've got corn on a cob on a stick for me?" This was a strange gift, but hey it was food. "Where did you get it?"

Christina started to explain that Dad had taken her to the outside market for a little shopping to relax from the trip. Dad was really good at being a tour guide. They got the corn on the cob from a vendor for me, and thought it would be fun to bring me a corn on the cob here in jail.

By this time, Francis the guard got up from his desk and came over with the set of keys. He opened up the small porthole door for Christina to pass my present through. I thankfully took it. Upon taking it, I knew it was going to be a chore. The butter had melted and was running down the stick and getting on my hand. The vendor had also sprinkled powered white cheese and salted it too.

The white cheese was like no other cheese I've had before, only in Mexico would you get this stuff. Mom and Dad raved about the powdered cheese, but I really didn't know why it was really special. It was a white, lumpy, powdery cheese that you sprinkle, similar to parmesan. Once on hot food it would generally get soft or melt in and add to the buttery flavor.

Handling my corn on a stick was fairly awkward. I felt like I was eating cotton candy at a punk rock concert. It just seemed out of the ordinary to be eating a corn on the cob on a stick that you get from a carnival market while in jail. Rather than complaining about it, I decided to take it and be grateful anyway.

"Thank you" I said as the port hole closed. I really felt that it was the thought that counted. Christy had taken extra effort to buy some corn so I could share in their adventures. I could stand a little butter dripping on my hand after I realized that it was a wonderful gesture of love.

Again, more noises came from the other rooms, this time it was the sounds of moaning. I guess most of them didn't like that last play. Christina looked past me as I started to take a bite. She knew I had been watching the game with them and didn't want to take much more time. I wanted to get back and watch, but I wanted to see Christina and Dad too. We visited for a couple of minutes more as I tried to make the best of what I could with eating the corn on a stick. But this time, it started dripping onto the floor and Christy pushed through her last paper napkin to me. It helped a little.

I finished about half of my corn before Christy said she would let me go. I was hoping that would happen. I didn't want to make her feel neglected by walking away, but I really needed to get some paper towels from the cell. It reminded me of a little kid who needs to go to the bathroom, but doesn't because he's having too much fun playing. Sooner or later something's got to give.

I said goodbye as my dad and girlfriend walked out of the guard room. I turned to head back to my cell while holding a corn baton in my hand and trying to hurry as best I could.

As I passed one of the cell rooms, Tito popped his head out. *"Hey Roberto, what do you have?"* He pointed to my corn. *"My novia gave it to me,"* I replied.

"Oh, that's good stuff man," He replied,

"You want some?" I asked. I guessed he liked the white cheese too. "Good stuff" is relative.

"Really?" Tito wasn't sure I was willing to share. I held the dripping, half eaten corn on the cob toward him. This was really awkward. Here I was, holding a corn on the cob with a stick ran through it with butter dripping on the concrete floor and offering a bite to him. He took the impaled corn out of my hands and took a couple of bites. He gave it back to me with a *"Gracias"* through a mouthful of food. He wiped his hands on his pants and went back inside.

I continued down the hallway and was then stopped by Pablo. He was watching the game in our cell with this others. *"Hey Roberto, Whassup?"* He was smiling as he saw me round the corner with my half eaten ear of corn. *"Oh man, where did you get that?"*

"My novia gave it to me. I'm full, you want it?"

Pablo's eyes lit up. *"Really?"* He asked, practically drooling. For the second time, someone wasn't sure why I would be giving up such a delicacy. Something so out of the ordinary, why would I part with it? It's not that I didn't like it, but I had about enough of all I could eat and didn't want it to go to waste.

"Sure, I can't eat any more," I replied as I gave him the rest of it. He took it graciously and started chomping to his heart's content. I left him to his pleasures as I tiptoed around those sitting on the floor of the cell to get a couple paper towels. I tried to hand Pablo one, but he had already found that his pants were a good substitute to a napkin.

I retraced my steps through the hallway and bent down to wipe up spots of melted butter and cheese from the concrete floor. I thought about what just happened. Christy felt so good about the effort she took to get me a corn on the cob. I really didn't want to take the corn from her, but it would have been worse had I rejected her offer. My choice was to surrender to how messy it was so that she would also be happy about what she had done for me.

Many times in our lives, we become martyrs to our causes by not allowing others to help us. I wondered how

> Many times in our lives, we become martyrs to our causes by not allowing others to help us.

many times in my life I had denied others the blessings of service when I denied them the opportunity to help me. Even at Christmas time we put so much energy on what to give others and still we say "Oh, you shouldn't have" when we receive anything. I realized that giving and receiving go hand in hand.

There was also a big difference between taking and receiving. Taking is when it's not offered to you. Receiving is the other end of giving. Like breathing, it's back and forth. If you gave more than you received, it would be like blowing out and forgetting to inhale.

This time, it was my turn to inhale. Tito and Pablo seemed as happy when I shared it with them too. For once I knew what was meant by win-win. Help everyone have a good experience. And it was all because I just learned that it's just as important to receive in order to have others receive their joys too.

Britney Spears

After cleaning up the butter spots, I walked back into the cell to see what the other guys were doing. I already knew the soccer game was still going on, and it seemed like about half the guys were watching the game now. The other half took a break and started walking around. Needless to say, the soccer game was still the most important activity in the jail.

The game paused for half time. It was a time for the guys in the cell to talk about the game, but their conversations were cut short because of what came next.

On the Mexican TV station, they announced the premier of Britney Spears' latest music video. As soon as we heard that her video was coming up, smiles were showing.

For me, it seemed like it was no big deal, other than I was getting a kick out of seeing the macho excitement about it. Well to be honest, I guess it was a big thing for me too. It had been a while since I had listened to any Non-Spanish music and even though I had heard Britney Spears' latest songs, I had not yet seen her newest video. So I admit I was looking forward to a Britney Spears music video too.

It finally came on the TV, and I soon discovered that this actually was one of the more conservative videos she had done. It was the one where she dances on a chair and spins it around. One of my first thoughts was: wow, I didn't know you could dance on a chair like that. That's pretty interesting. If I ever get bored, I can just pick up a folding chair, spin it on one leg and sit on it every which way. Not too bad!

For the next four minutes, not a word was spoken between the guys. All eyes were watching Britney's moves. I think we were all amazed at what she could do with a simple folding chair. I guessed that was the strategy of the video. Only Britney Spears could make a folding chair look sexy.

The music video ended and the Soccer game started up again. The guys started talking about Britney and the game. I walked away from the cell rooms towards the court-yard thinking that that it took me coming to jail for me to have the opportunity to see Britney Spears' latest video. I soon found myself drawn back to the cells by the sounds of cheers and groans. How could I miss the action?

To this day, I still can't remember which team won. I guessed the northern team won as most of the guys were jovial and Ivan was disappointed. I figured it was more important watching the different plays rather than remembering the stats of who won. I gave Ivan a piece of gum as he got off his bed and started for the courtyard. He smiled a thank you and silently left the cell. He later got over it, remembering that next year would be another season.

A Job Offer

That afternoon I found myself sitting on the floor of the cell along with three of The Kids. We got into a conversation of how we came to be in jail. Many of them had only been there a few days before I came and were waiting to be transferred to the State prison or to be released. They found my story to be really funny. They kept asking what I did with a gun in the United States, in which I replied the same way as my answers had been with any official. It was for pleasure, I go camping frequently and it's perfectly OK to own a gun in the U.S.

"But you got arrested just for the bullets," one said as they all started laughing. I did too, as it seemed ridiculously dreamlike once again. I enjoyed being their source of entertainment

I turned to Joey, "Can I ask what you are here for?"

The room quieted down. "Drugs", he said.

"What do you mean?" I was pretty curious about his situation.

He then started to explain that he had been hired to traffic Marijuana over the border and was caught before he crossed. He then started to explain how intricate the system was. He would get a shipment from Hermosio, Mexico or some other bigger Mexican city, then cross the border, where there would be another person waiting to take the goods into Phoenix or Tucson, Arizona.

The entire room was now intent on the conversation of how we all came to be there. The kid with the moustache started adding his comments. He too was a carrier for drugs and had been caught with Marijuana recently. Apparently both Joey and this Kid knew each other on the outside and had occasionally worked together, but were caught separately on different jobs.

I looked over to the other Kid. He had been quiet and contently listening to the other's telling their stories of how they would get drugs over the border. He started speaking quietly in Spanish.

I couldn't make it out and had to wait for Joey to translate. "He says he takes people across the border." This was a surprise to us all. With the help of Joey's translation, I became aware that this young man was a Coyote. Each Mexican wanting to get into the US without proper papers would pay him a fee of $1000 or so and the kid before us would supply a ride to across the border.

The reason behind it was that Mexicans could work in the United States, pay off the $1000 and even more to take care of their families who were still in Mexico. For the Mexicans who were transported, it was well worth the hassle and risks to get across. The service of going over the border was in such high demand that $1000 per head was an easy price tag for the Kid to receive.

This particular time, he had rented a U-haul type van and was carrying seven people. We really didn't fully understand how, but he was caught and ended up here in jail. It was still up in the air on how long he would have to stay incarcerated.

"Is it worth it?" I asked. Oh yes, with a thousand bucks a head, and costs of less than a few hundred with gas and preparation, he was making a good profit.

I turned to the other two, what about them, was transporting drug worth it for them? "*Yes, Roberto!*" was the reply. They started to smile, *"when the girls know you have money, they love you!"*

I started laughing with them. It was really interesting to see these guys and their attitude towards what they had done. It wasn't a matter of right and wrong. It was a matter of making money and lots of it, with no ethical or moral thought behind how it was accomplished. I first became aware that if you want to make money, you were either into drug trafficking, or some other illegal practice, or you were with the government.

After a few conversations to the others, Joey broke the silence again. "Hey Roberto, we've been talking, and we want to give you a job." I looked at him with a puzzled look.

"What are you talking about?" I asked. He started to tell me that they needed someone to meet them on the American side of the border. I would then take packages and drive them to Phoenix. I would have a phone number to call once I got there with a drop off point. "All you have to do" he said, "is to call and they will say, 'leave your car in some parking lot' and they will come for it. It is so easy, you can make lots of money!"

The other drug kid piped up too *"Mucho Dinero, Muchisimo Dinero!"* For a few seconds I thought they were kidding, but they kept on. Apparently they really needed someone on the American border to help transport drugs.

Ok I thought, how much is a lot of money to them? I asked, and was surprised with the answer. Five thousand a transfer, with thirty thousand average a month. That's why they only did it a couple of times. I really tried not to show amazement. That monthly amount was about my annual salary.

"Joey," I said, "The money may be really good, but what happens if you don't make it out of here?" He was at risk of going to the State prison for a long time. I then got a taste of how deep it went. He wasn't concerned. The money was well worth the risk. The higher ups within the drug organization had even paid Joey's lawyer's fees. And they were willing to do and pay more to get him out.

I learned a lesson that afternoon; crime unfortunately pays for many people. I thought it over for a few seconds and declined the offer. My reasoning to them was that if I couldn't get bullets across a border, how could I be any good with drug transportation? But deep down inside my reasons were different. I couldn't do it for any amount

> I learned a lesson that after-noon; crime unfortunately pays for many people.

of money. I felt a little sick inside that these guys couldn't find more moral opportunities for their income.

As we talked, Francis came in and locked up the courtyard. No one seemed to mind or notice him as we were still engulfed in our conversation and in the memory of the Futbol championship. Francis didn't say much this time as he passed the cells back to the main gate. I guessed he had rooted for the wrong team too and was bummed about the outcome.

Movies

Just then, Eddie walked in with some video cases in his hand. He had been visited by relatives this weekend and they passed through movies from a rental store. I knew from the families visiting that a lot of things were passed through to the inmates. However, this was the first time I ever thought of the idea of movies being passed though.

The TV in the cell had a VCR under it, but I thought it wasn't usable. Well not today, Eddie had videos and he announced the fact to the rest of us. The tall guy was still visiting his girl at the front gate, but many others congregated at hearing Eddie's announcement. The hermit with no teeth had not moved for the day. He was still in bed but his towel curtains were opened to watch the soccer game. They were quickly shut again after the game was over and I assumed he went back to sleep. But now, he was even awake and opened his curtains to see what all the excitement was about.

In a grand fashion, Eddie popped in a movie and sat on his bed. Several others filtered in the room. I guess this was a treat to watch something other than what came over the airwaves. And this time, Eddie picked out what was to be watched. I didn't mind, it seemed to be a diversion from the regular novellas on TV.

However, when the movie came on I knew that it would take some effort to keep my attention. Even though it was an American movie (they always are), the voices were dubbed over in Spanish. However, you don't need too many words when it comes to a military movie. I figured I would get a little creative by thinking up my own plot line as the movie went along. Besides, you don't need to be too imaginative to say "your terminated" when someone's shooting a gun. That phrase seems to go with just about any situation, even when Arnold Schwarzenegger is not in the movie.

Maybe it was the testosterone in the jail, or maybe it was just out of coincidence but Eddie said they all were shoot-em-up movies. I really don't think that a bunch of guys would be watching "Sleepless in Seattle" when you can get Rambo and Die Hard. I figured when there's a bunch of guys and so little opportunity to get movies, the fluffy ones wouldn't be the movie of choice.

I wondered about the family members that had to go to the rental store on Eddie's behalf. Eddie had a request to get some movies and gave them a couple of titles he was hoping to get, but I thought it would be a great joke for them to pass through a something totally different, like "Thelma and Louise." Chick flicks just didn't seem appropriate for a bunch of men in jail. Just imagine the late fees if Eddie didn't give them back at the conclusion of the weekend.

An hour through the movie, Francis came through the main gate again with his set of keys. He stood in the cell doorway for a moment watching what was showing on TV. I looked up from my spot. *"Hola Robert Deniro!"* I didn't know where this Robert Deniro thing came from, but most of the guys seemed to use it now.

I said "Hi" as I tried to focus on him, rather than going back to watching the movie. If Francis was talking to me, I wanted to pay attention to him. "You watching movies?" he asked. I nodded my head and said I was having a hard time understanding the words. "Well maybe you go home tomorrow and watch good movies, no?"

I looked at him. I was hoping to get out today, but once again it didn't seem to be the case. But tomorrow was Sunday and the probability of me getting out was slimmer than me getting out today. I thought for sure I was getting out today, especially now that Christina and her dad had come. "You think I'll get out tomorrow?"

Francis shrugged his shoulders, "Maybe tomorrow, but tonight, you watch Mexican movies," he replied as he slid the cell door shut. "Goodnight".

I waved him a goodbye as I turned back towards the TV. I could hear him sing some strange song with "Tomorrow" as the only word. He sure wasn't Annie, but I started thinking about 'tomorrow'. Once again, I was in here for the night, this time watching movies in Spanish and not wanting to be here. I knew I still needed to make the best of it, but my mind was racing with too many negative thoughts.

I felt resentment towards the lawyers, why were they dragging their feet about getting me out? It was Saturday and all odds had been that I would be getting out today. I guessed now that Christina and her dad were here, they had to start all over again. I was upset at the Secretary. He said he'd make his decisions today. I guess that by making no decision was still an action. I still was here for another night and now I wondered when I was ever getting out of here.

Dinner seemed a blur as we continued through the night. I don't even know who made the food. I just sat there, eating my food, it was the same two tacos I had eaten for the past three days. It didn't seem as tasty when I was in a sour mood. I know I should have been appreciative that I still had food, but I was in my resentment and I was upset at the fact that I was being controlled by being here for another night.

This was the one of the times I really felt down. I didn't want to be here, I felt sad, tired, and I missed Christina. She was trying to help by coming here but all I could think about was the distance between us, which was filled with concrete and iron bars.

I took a deep breath and said a silent prayer. I didn't want to get in the habit of being ungrateful. I knew that I deserved to be here, but wondered what more I needed to learn. I guessed because I was still here, there was more and I asked that I would be humble enough to continue onward with whatever I would have in store.

> I knew that I deserved to be here, but wondered what more I needed to learn.

I asked for increased strength to bear this burden of being here, when the ones I loved were in a hotel just a few miles away. I asked for patience to go through this and asked that I might be in the proper mind to help others too.

It was a heartfelt prayer, but I knew there was more for me. I was still here and would be for at least another night. There was not much else to do, other than be patient and join the others for the night.

The Tall Guy Leaves

My thoughts and prayers were interrupted by a voice calling from the main gate. Francis was yelling towards us and the tall guy from the top bunk answered back. The others didn't seem to mind this long distance communication and went back to the movie. Francis and the tall guy conversed like this for a few phrases and ended when a big smile came over the tall guy's face. He jumped down from his top bunk, grabbed his blanket, a bag of personal items and slipped his shoes on. Within a minute, Francis was at the cell door again, fiddling with the lock.

I didn't really understand what was going on, but after a few moments I realized the tall guy was leaving. Was he finally getting out? He sure smiled like a free man! Well good for him. I was really happy that at least someone was leaving. This was the first person who had gained his freedom since I came on Wednesday. I wondered how long he had been here, but no matter how long, it was now his time for him to go and his face beamed.

The others waved goodbye as Francis let him through the cell door and through the hallway. The cell door was locked behind them and soon the sounds of the main gate rang through the jail. This left us alone again to watch the movie. However, Joey started talking to the kids. They shrugged back at him. In one smooth move, Joey grabbed his blanket, and jumped up to the bunk bed where the tall guy used to be. Eddie and Ivan didn't seem to mind being below him now. They had their own beds and now Joey was privileged to have a bed. I thought it was fair. Joey had been here longer than me, and had been helpful during the past few days. It seemed appropriate for him to have the next vacant bed.

The movie ended and Eddie got up and changed it out for a new one. While up, he unscrewed the light bulb, leaving all of us in the glow from the TV. My mind was still thinking about who gets out, who stays here and who gets a bed. I wondered what factors there are that determine seniority. Was it just someone who is here the longest? Or does seniority depend on your level of involvement in the group?

I thought back to work, school and other group settings and realized that seniority and rank advancement comes from those that step up to the requirements. Some people call it playing full out, and I became aware of those times I held back and those times I really participated in what life gave me. I soon fell asleep with the resolve to once again live life to my fullest capacity.

CHAPTER 7

SUNDAY

Spending Time with the Gang

The Tall Guy Again

I woke up Sunday morning to the song of a bird nearby. It was actually a peaceful sound as the bird tried to compete with the sounds of cars in the vicinity. It must have been near the courtyard as its singing didn't sound too far away. As quickly as it started, the bird stopped singing and must have flown off. I was left to hear the snoring of those inside, combined with the sound of distant cars.

Today was Sunday. Normally I would go to church today. Even if I was unable to attend church, Sunday was still special. Believing came from the heart, not from the day of the week.

I laid in my sleeping bag, thinking until the others started stirring. Today, Eddie wasn't the first one up. He had stayed up late last night watching movies. Ivan did also, as well as Joey who had inherited the top bunk from the Tall guy. It was the kids on the floor that got up first. We didn't want to get stepped on, nor could we go back to sleep once we were awake.

The snores from the sleeping guy still came from above Rocco. The sleeping guy was the one man I had seen the least. He kept to himself, except when to eat, watch Britney Spears videos and take care of personal things like go to the bathroom. It was funny to watch when this hermit came out of his cave. Like the Groundhog in February, it didn't last long. He came out, did his business and went back into his hole.

After we folded up our blankets, we huddled inside our jackets. There was little room to move around in. You usually had to say "excuse me" while making your way from one side of the cell to the other. I needed to go to the bathroom, so I meandered around the others and slid the curtain behind me. My hands were cold, making the whole process difficult.

Francis seemed to be taking his time opening the cell today. He should have let us out by now. I wondered if there were any guards for us today, being that it was Sunday. Maybe on Sundays they didn't let us out. Who knew? It seemed like the right time of day, given the amount of light that filtered through hallway, but I couldn't tell one half hour from the next. Maybe we woke up earlier than usual, but that didn't seem right, given the fact that we had watched more TV than normal last night. Or did we? Usually, we went to bed after the last novella ended. But last night, who knew how long a couple movies were anyway?

This whole lack of knowledge about time really threw me off. I had been so adjusted to the fact that I could manage my time, but now in jail, it was a different story. Time really didn't matter much anyway, other than the fact that we were anxious to have the cell door open. I felt like a racehorse squeezed into its metal box ready for the race to start. I was chomping at the bit and had to tell myself to calm down. "Easy boy".

Finally, after a while, the sounds from the front gate told us that it was opening. Soon, Francis came to let us out. Oh, what a relief. I was comforted to know that I would be allowed the small freedom of stretching my legs. With good mornings and "Hello's", Francis the fat guard was jovial as ever. He must have had a good night's rest considering yesterdays Futbol disappointment.

As we soon filed out of the cell, others trickled out from the other cell and we all stretched near the wall of sunlight in the courtyard. It seemed like a slow morning, but it gave me time to think. Thinking was all I could do. While walking the circle, I continued to think of all the things I wondered about last night. I was glad that Dad finally got some companionship with Christina and her dad coming down.

Breakfast was called and we went back inside the cell rooms. Today, breakfast was different. Rather than bread and oatmeal, we had something wrapped in tin foil and our regular bananas.

Each of us took a tinfoil wrap and a banana and headed out again to the courtyard. Eating in the sunlight always seems better than eating in a darkened cell room. With the banana in one hand and my foil package on my lap, I unfolded the edges to reveal a breakfast burrito of scrambled eggs wrapped in a tortilla. Not bad, I thought. It had been a while since I had one of these, and it looked inviting.

I took a couple of bites and was content without the oatmeal being served today. Breakfast was really good today. It's amazing how something different, even like a breakfast burrito could feel like it was gourmet food. It was something new for breakfast and variety was welcomed today.

I was interrupted by some cheers from inside, and got up to investigate. My name wasn't called yet, but Christina and dad might have come already. Once entering the hallway, I could see no one special in the guard room. Christina wasn't there, but there still seemed to be a lot of conversation coming from the cell. Joey was finally off his bed and standing in the doorway. To my surprise, the tall guy was back in the cell. But didn't he just get out yesterday?

The Tall Guy was talking to Eddie who was still in his bed. The tall guy had his shirt off with a towel hung over his shoulders, combing his wet hair. The guy also seemed happy as a lark. He was all smiles as he passed the comb back to Eddie and started whistling as he approached the community food box to get his breakfast.

I didn't get it, I thought he was just released yesterday. Did he get in trouble again? If that's the case, he must be a really lousy criminal to be caught so soon. But why was he so happy? I decided I was more curious about it than to just let it go. I had a half eaten burrito that didn't seem as interesting anymore.

I didn't think anymore about eating. I quickly walked over to the wall of iron bars and looked into the drunk tank. The guy with the blue jacket wasn't there anymore, but right in front of me was a man who was watching us. I quickly folded the tin foil around what was left of breakfast and passed it through to him. He quickly took it with a set of the dirtiest hands I had ever seen. They were encased with black soot and grime. I was glad that he could eat the burrito out of the tin foil without touching it. It was a little shocking to see how dirty hands could get. However, I left him with breakfast in his hands and turned my attention back to the cell.

I nudged Joey. "Hey, didn't he just leave yesterday? Why is he back?"

Joey smiled and shook his head. "He just went to the married room last night."

"Married room?" This was an unfamiliar phrase.

"Yes, it's a room you can go to be with your woman for the night. Last night he was there with the lady that came yesterday. It's his wife." Joey said matter-of-factly as he explained that the jail had a small cell that you could get locked up with your wife. She would stay with you for the night, and in the morning, you are back here and she goes home.

Well, no wonder this guy was so happy. He just spent the night with his wife. A flood of images went through my mind that I wish hadn't. But still I got the idea that if you wanted to, you could be alone with your wife in the "Married room." It didn't seem too romantic, but maybe some women liked the wild criminal type. Besides, I always imagined that in US prisons you had to go abstinent until you got out.

I really couldn't tell if this married room was a good thing or not. Obviously to the Tall Guy it was great, he'd be smiling for the next couple days. But in the prison system, did this allow a privilege to a prisoner that shouldn't have it? That was a pretty special privilege. Or did it keep prisoners just sane enough so they wouldn't turn abusive, crazy, and homosexual? Who knew? Now the tall guy was back here and had bragging rights that he had been in the Marriage room. Within a couple of minutes, the cell was empty again. It seemed like a normal thing to the others for the Tall Guy or anybody else for that matter to go to the married room for the night.

Reading Luke II

It still didn't seem like Sunday. I usually go to church, but this particular day, there really wasn't anywhere I could go. Many ask why they have to go to church to worship God. This is basically an excuse so they don't have to go to church. Now that I was prevented from going to church, I really wanted to.

I found a Santa Biblia near the TV in the cell. I picked it up and headed to the courtyard. I sat down on the step and started to read from the Good Book. However I didn't read Spanish well, especially religious words.

I thought of what I should read. It was now Christmas time and because of it, I decided to read something about the Nativity. I turned the pages and found Luke Chapter II.

For a moment the world stopped around me and I felt the still calmness that comes from reading scriptures. My problems seemed to dissipate and I felt as if I was OK for the brief moment. Even in Spanish, I could make out that angels appeared as shepherds were abiding in the field. The message of a Savior wrapped in swaddling clothes was the same in Spanish as it was in English.

Many people throughout my life always had different ideas about Christmas. Sometimes it was just the end of the year, sometimes it was about presents, sometimes it was getting to see family. I wondered throughout the years, how many Christmases I had focused on one thing or another. What was it really all about? And what should be the focus?

I looked down at the Bible again. The words in Spanish *"good tidings of great joy"* held my attention. What tidings did they bring, what joy was theirs to tell. Was the birth of Jesus important enough for angels to declare to even the lowliest of shepherds? The answer came back, yes. He was the Messiah who had come and it was time for the entire world to know. Even two thousand years later, the message was still important.

I thought about my friends in church back home. I really wanted to be with them rather than in Jail on a Sunday. I learned much later that the church congregation had a Christmas party the night before and I missed it. I even was scheduled to sing in a men's quartet. I guess it became a trio.

The Bishop of the Singles Ward told the group that night that I would not be with them as I was 'detained in Mexico'. My name was mentioned in the opening prayer. I also heard later that a couple girls cried for me during the party. For some reason, the thought of girls crying over me stile makes me smile to this day.

I wondered what the Ward was doing today. It was a couple Sunday's before Christmas, and most of the hymns sung in December were appropriate Christmas hymns. There was vibrancy in going. So many times we ask ourselves, what benefit will it help me? Why should I go to church when it's the same old things announced and discussed over and over? Like fuel to a flame, it keeps the fire burning. You can only last so long as a burning ember by yourself. But with others, you're collectively better off.

Jose

Just then, a man came up to me as I was reading the Santa Biblia. He smiled and said, "H*ola*". I recognized him as the guy I gave food to on Saturday morning. He was in the temporary room on Saturday and I now discovered that he moved over to our side this morning. He was still wearing a blue jacket and had hands in his pocket. He really hadn't talked to anyone since he came in. I knew how he felt. It was strange being in jail and not knowing anyone. I motioned for him to join and sit with me.

We started with the simple greetings. His name was Jose and he didn't speak much English. He thanked me for the food I passed to him on Saturday.

"*Do you have family?*" I asked.

"*Si, I have a wife and two children,*" he replied. He lived in a nearby town with his wife, children, his wife's mother and a couple other people that I couldn't understand who they were. Usually when I couldn't understand I would mumble an "*Oh, OK*".

He then went solemn. "*It is hard to have my family see me like this.*"

"*Is this your first time here?*" I asked. He nodded his head yes and then explained that he was planning on going to the store to get food, but he didn't have gas for his car. So he

203

went to his neighbor and stole gas from his neighbor's car. He got caught and was taken to jail.

"It is very hard," he kept saying as tears filled his eyes. This was an emotional situation or me too, I just finished reading about the Nativity and this guy had no tidings of great joy to tell.

"We must have faith and hope," I tried to encourage him. He looked at me and then to the Santa Biblia in my hands.

He nodded and replied *"When I leave, I will change".* I truly hoped he would be better from this experience. I knew that he was a different type of person than the rest of the guys I met in jail. When you take responsibility and move on, you can improve rather than being victim to your situations. Rather than finding excuses for himself, Jose admitted that he had done something wrong. He was remorseful and wanted to do something about it.

> Sure we all deserved coming here. But the real question is what are we going to do about it after we leave?

Jose taught me a valuable lesson right then. Sure we all deserved coming here. But the real question is what are we going to do about it after we leave? Do I become a better person when I leave than when I came in, or do I go home callused, hardened and justified?

"I know you can change," I said reaching into my pocket. I pulled out a stick of gum and handed it to him. He took it and thanked me as he got up and walked away. Throughout the rest of the day I saw him smiling and chewing on his gum.

Grace vs. Works

Later that morning I started to read the little book I had stuffed away between the folds of my blanket. The "Mere Christianity" book asked the main question: what's the benefit of believing in God? Did I believe? Yes, but now that I believed what was I going to do about it? There is a big difference between believing and doing.

Maybe this is where a lot of people get confused with Grace versus Works. Throughout the religious community, this has always brought a much heated debate. Did Salvation come through grace or could you actually work your way to heaven? Was there one without the other, could you separate them? What was Grace and how does Works fit with it? All these questions ran through my mind.

I tried to apply what I was learning to my situation of being here in Jail. Those in authority said I had broken the law. I was at the mercy of a Secretary who made the decisions on how much time and penalties I would incur. To this extent, there was nothing I really could do about it until the Secretary made the decision.

I was locked up, feeling my own guilt and remorse, but that still wouldn't get me out of jail. However, while here I found satisfaction by helping others. I gave gum and food away when I could, smiled at others, and honestly tried to get to know those around me. Did it make any difference to the Secretary that I was being proactive here? Not really. Did I do these things so I could get recognition and a reduced sentence from the secretary? No, he didn't even know about these things.

But by so doing these small and simple gestures, it made the process a bit easier. Even though I was at the mercy of the Secretary, sooner or later I could come free. However, waiting around for someone else's ability to set me free didn't stop me from trying to do my best while I am here. And if I was to be let go today, it wouldn't stop me from being friendly to those around me in the future.

Of course I knew I would still make mistakes when I got home. I think I would always do something wrong now and then, but that wouldn't give me allowance to give up. Also, even when I would get set free from jail, that wouldn't give me a blank check to wreak havoc as I left the country. Being pardoned of my crime meant I had to do and act according to the law, which meant doing good things, even when I was forgiven by the kindness of a Mexican Secretary. I realized that for me, Grace and Works go hand in hand. We are forgiven by the Grace of God, but that does not eliminate our responsibility to be kind to others, help others, keep the commandments and be obedient, all these actions define the works we do. I knew that many times I would fall short of any eternal destiny if I was on my own. It's by the grace of Him that I could be freed of any spiritual prison I was put in.

However, after I'm allowed out, I still have a responsibility of helping others along the way. This also meant staying the course and calling for help when I stray. Many call it 'enduring to the end'.

I sat in the courtyard for a while thinking about what I had just discovered. It shook me to the core. The lessons being in prison were far more than just physical.

I was called away by voices from the hallway. Pablo peeked his head out and called for me *"Hola Roberto! Is that your novia?"* I looked up and nodded my head. I figured Christina came to see me again.

"Man, she is beautiful" Pablo called as he whistled in amazement. I thanked him for getting me as I started towards the door. It was nice to hear a compliment about my girl, I was sure to tell her too. I pulled out some gum from my pocket and pulled out a stick. His eyes lit up as I handed him his piece. He smiled but didn't have to say anything else. His countenance said it all, we give, we receive and both are edified.

Staying with Christina

Christina, as well as both dads were waiting for me at the front. Dad had a troubled look on his face, Christina was all smiles, and Christina's dad never showed much emotion anyway. "Hi guys, how's it going?" I asked.

Dad came up and started small talking. The three of them were having as good a time as they could. "Well, the lawyers say they can get you out tomorrow," Dad said with some confidence, but I could tell there was something else.

I asked again, "What's going on dad?" He seemed to be a little closed down today and I knew sooner or later it would come out.

"Robert, I don't want to leave you, but there are some things I HAVE to do today and tomorrow. I still don't know yet if I'm going to London on Tuesday, but there's no way I can possibly go unless I go home and get some things straightened out anyway." Dad was between a rock and a hard place. He was leaving on Tuesday for England, and I was to get out of jail on Monday. However, if dad waited around until I got out tomorrow, he would have no time for packing, paying bills and getting everything set up to lock his house down for his stay with mom through Christmas. On the other hand, it was hard to acknowledge you have to leave your son in jail in Mexico while you travel as a free man back to the United States.

Dad continued, "Christina's dad will take me back to Arizona today and Christina will stay here until you get out. I've left the car with Christina so she has transportation, as well as paid for her hotel room for the next couple of nights." It seemed they had this all well planned out. These were bold moves, knowing that Dad didn't want to go home without me, and Christina's dad didn't want to leave without her. But still both men were brave enough to let go of their kids for the time being.

I nodded my head. I stuck my other set of fingers through the gate for dad to hold onto. This was a bonding moment, but was ever so brief. "I understand Dad, it's OK for you to go to England. I'll be alright. You can't make the decision to go or not to go without getting your own house in order first." I knew he had to go to England to be with mom for Christmas and I tried the best way I could to explain that he was OK by leaving me behind as he went back.

Dad nodded his head. "I'll talk to you tomorrow after you get out, then we'll decide."

I interrupted him. "Dad, even if I'm still in process, you need to go. It would break Mom's heart for you not to spend Christmas with her. I'll be OK, if Christina's here. Besides, you need to be with Mom." I kept encouraging him to make his flight on Tuesday.

> Deep down inside, I hated the idea that I could be the cause of a drastically changed itinerary.

And if I was still here, I knew it seemed strange to leave for England while your son's in Jail, but he would be missing a paid flight, hotel bookings in London with Mom, as well as a missed opportunity to go to Europe, all because of me. Deep down inside, I hated the idea that I could be the cause of a drastically changed itinerary.

"Well, we'll see" Dad said as he said his last goodbye.

By this time Christina's dad had come closer to me also. Out of earshot from dad, I looked at Christina's dad and pleaded with him, "Please encourage him to go. He really needs to go. It would be worse if he didn't go, please talk to him on your way back home." Her dad understood my plea and nodded in agreement.

"You take care, Robert. Your dad will be alright with me," He said as he turned to Christina, "You going to be OK?" He was a little unsure about this whole situation, but Christina remained strong and replied back a yes.

Christina seemed especially happy to stay with me. She was comfortable to be the one left behind, and quite frankly I was happy to see her too. We said goodbye to our dads as they left us still clasping fingers through the front gate.

Francis watched us talking for a moment and knew that Christina would be here for a good while. As a service gesture, he took the chair from the security desk and moved it right next to her. She thanked him as she sat down, and we began to visit, as privately as possible with the guards and cell mates watching.

Visiting

For the rest of the day, Christina stayed with me at the gate. One of the kids found the white five gallon bucket and slid it over for me to sit on. I turned it upside down and with both of us sitting, we tuned out everything else and just talked. The others went about their business as if we weren't even there. I could hear the basket ball bouncing on the concrete courtyard and by this time, the TV's in each cell were turned on to their various programs. It seemed like the others had plenty to do, and all I wanted to do was focus my attention on Christina and spent the day with her.

"How's your mom?" I began.

Christina got animated. "Oh Robert, you wouldn't believe what she has gone through too."

"What do you mean?" I asked. Her mom was a sweet lady and I felt her mom liked me. She had a good sense of humor and seemed to be a happy person. But I worried that if she found out that I was here, she would be upset about all the commotion I brought to myself.

"Once I heard you were missing on Tuesday, she got scared too. She made a lot of calls on your behalf." Christina then explained that her mom was worried that something wrong had happened. Well obviously it did, but she was thinking that I might have been the victim to Drug Wars or the Federales or mugged or even killed. They finally found relief when they called the US consulate in Nogales late Wednesday.

Oh yeah, I had forgot about those guys. I didn't blame them now and was grateful that they had at least called me at the Sonoyta Jail despite me being resentful that they couldn't help me more at the time.

"But they wouldn't give any information!" Christy was upset about this as she went through the whole dialog her mom had with the Consulate. It seemed that when her Mom called the Consulate, they told her that they were aware of my being in Mexico.

"Well is he alive?" her mom had asked.

"*Si.*"

"Can you tell me where he is?"

"No."

"So, what can you tell me about his situation?"

"Not much, unless you are his mother."

"No, I'm not his mother, she's in England but I'm the next best thing."

"Unfortunately I can't help you with this information" the Consulate answered.

Christina continued with the story. By this time, Christina's mom was getting worried and frustrated. "Please help me as a mother then" she pleaded. "If I was his mother, should I be worried about his health or worried that he has gotten into trouble?"

There must have been something in her voice, because the Consulate answered that if Christina's mom *would have been* my mom, then the worry would have been that I had gotten into trouble. Satisfied with the answer, they waited to know how much trouble I was in. This was verified when Christina got the call from Dad late Wednesday night.

I wanted to crawl in a shell and hide. "I'm sorry, I was the one who ordered the Consulate not to say anything."

Christina blew up! "Why did you do that? We were worried sick not knowing!"

"Well, I really didn't know you would be trying to find me." I tried to explain. I didn't know that I would be here this long. It was hard to explain that I thought I would get out on Thursday at the latest, so I thought it best if no one knew. I should have been out before Christina discovered I was missing. I didn't think that Christina's family would actually call the US/Mexican Consulate and ask about me.

Christina seemed to be satisfied with my answers. She actually began to find it funny after all. Trying to find out information on me was harder than they thought, and to know that I was the one who had prevented it. "You're going to have to explain this to mom yourself!" she laughed.

Christina also explained what she had done for the past couple days. She had taken sick days on Wednesday, Thursday and Friday. While doing so, she contacted my manager at work, and my church leaders. All were very grieved that I was in trouble and offered to write letters. She picked up the ones written in Phoenix and had received a fax from Dad's hometown. Christina let me know that all of them asked how I was doing and wished me the best.

When Christina came down yesterday, she presented the letters to the lawyers who said they would in turn pass them over to the Secretary. She was a wonderful girl and I was so grateful for her help.

After a while, Christina looked at her watch and exclaimed, "Oh, I need to get ready!"

"For what?" I asked.

She then explained that she had been invited to dinner with the Lawyers. I found this odd that they were trying to pick up on her, but was soon corrected when she told me that the Secretary was going to be there too. A little socializing while here didn't hurt. I wished Christina good luck and encouraged her to have a good time.

She left me pondering on the fact that the Secretary and the lawyers had planned this dinner for a couple of days. But I thought they were working for me to get out yesterday? I guessed not. It seemed that the lawyers and the secretary were working out the best way to make it the beneficial for all of them. I wasn't surprised or upset about this, I knew I was a prize fish in the small pond and the right price had to do with it just as much as anything else.

Asking Joey a Question

Within time, we were interrupted by Francis coming through the main gate, this meant that it was time to close up the courtyard. However, it caught Eddie off guard, as he finished smoking a marijuana joint just minutes before Francis came in to lock up. Joker and a couple others took drags as they joined Eddie for a smoke. The scent was still in the air, but it was quickly mixed with the open air of the courtyard, the open sewers and the others smoking regular cigarettes. Francis never caught wind of Eddie's marijuana, but it gave Eddie something to brag about later that he finished in the nick of time.

Once again we were confined to the hallway and the cell block for a few more hours before we were to be locked in the cells. I paced the floor walking back and forth. Jose was walking too, thinking about his situation. His hands were still stuffed in his pocket as he passed me a few times with a "Hola" and a nod of the head. He didn't say much to anybody else. This was his first day and he seemed a bit shell shocked about being here.

The Kids got out a deck of cards and played War in the hallway. I think games could have pacified them for hours, at least it was something entertaining for them to do. Joey was seated nearby on the floor watching the card game.

I squatted down to watch the kids play cards. "Hey Joey, can I ask a question?"

His eyes still fixed on the card game replied a quick "sure".

I spoke softly, "how do the guys get drugs passed through?" I couldn't understand that if we had limited freedom, how can something like that come in and where was the source in which most of the guys get weed? It seemed that by this time, most everyone had taken a drag here and there, now and then!

Joey looked around as the kids looked up from their game too. No one else heard, but considering our conversation yesterday with the drug job offer, I thought Joey would know.

"When families come, they bring food and stuff, right?" Joey asked back.

I nodded my head. I saw quite a few family members visit the Tall Man, Rocco, one of the kids, even Eddie had a motherly like visitor on Friday afternoon. Come to think about it, most of the time, someone was at the gate talking to visitors.

Joey continued with his explanation, "It gets passed through with the other things given to us. If food gets passed in, it's in the food, usually in a small plastic bag or something. When clothes get passed in, they put it in the pocket and fold the clothes around it. There's lots of ways, but it gets passed in by those that visit us."

I looked at the kids, with a discrete nod of their heads, they agreed with Joey's account. It made sense. Obviously, there had to be others on the free side that would have to get it for them. Francis and the others didn't look through my things very closely either. Not that the guards were not doing their job, I was more focused on the inmates and their demand that created the supply.

I wondered who would pass in drugs to their very own family member? All of it was weed rather than harder drugs, but it still seemed rather odd for those on the free side to support a negative habit of a loved one in prison. I wondered what message that sent us, knowing that if someone really wanted it, they could get it. Forget right and wrong, it was about who could get what. Even when in trouble, others support us in those things that created the problem in the first place. It was about secretly maintaining the trouble rather than helping to change it.

I thanked Joey for the information and watched the others play cards. I really didn't feel like participating, just watching this time. It seemed like many of the guys had inherent personalities. I wondered how much toughening up each would do here. I think most of us became who we are long before we came to jail. There are many times in our lives when we've already made a choice far before the opportunity arises. For me, I decided that I wouldn't play victim to my circumstances.

> There are many times in our lives when we've already made a choice far before the opportunity arises.

I sat there, on the concrete floor of the hallway, watching the kids play cards. A flood of noises came to my ears as I tried to absorb the sounds filling the air. The cards shuffled on the floor, the TVs turned on, someone coughing in the bathroom, Joker laughing. For a brief moment I tried to look at the big picture. I was just one prisoner in this jail, insignificant to most of the world, but I still knew who I was and was aware of my personal choices and the many blessings I had.

Lockdown

After a few hours, Francis once again entered the hallway and shooed us into the cells for the evening. Once again, I wasn't getting out tonight. I had spent my Sunday with the guys in the Rocky Point Jail. It also meant tomorrow was Monday, I wouldn't be going to work and I wondered if tomorrow would be any different. My heart sank as the sliding door shut behind me, locking us in the small cell for the night. I took a deep breath and told myself, "I can do this."

"Goodnight Robert Deniro!" Francis was still jolly. "Maybe you go home tomorrow". Well, sooner or later Francis would be right. However, he wasn't yesterday, who knew about tomorrow? I nodded my head anyway as he said goodnight

The others pulled out their folded blankets and sat on their temporary cushions. I followed and slowly sat on my bedding while two of the kids were preparing the dinner. I was feeling really disheartened tonight. It had been spiritually draining day. I had learned a lot about myself and the world around me, now it was time to absorb it in and take personal inventory.

I was still here, seven days in jail, tomorrow would be number eight. The lawyers were partying with the Secretary and my dad was gone. I missed church today and honestly didn't know when specifically I would get out. I really felt low.

I asked myself what was going well for me and tried to think about the good things in life. Christina had spent most of her day with me. We held fingers and I loved what touch I had from her. I had a sleeping bag and was in more comfortable clothes. Dinner was cooking and I would soon have something to eat again. I had met a friend named Jose and had a thought provoking conversation with him. I had a toothbrush and a razor the lawyers had passed through, and I still had my can of Coke.

I smiled at the thought of my can of Coke. I forgot it for a while as it remained concealed in my sock in the clothes bag. Looking forward to the victory drink gave me renewed hope again. I wished to get out of jail, just so I could have my Coke. Very rarely did I drink much soda with caffeine, so every now and then when I did it was special.

Life didn't seem so bad after I listed some of what I thought were blessings. I was deeply blessed just to have a girl who cared enough to stay alone in a foreign country to be nearby. All these things combined into a great desire to continue onward. Tomorrow would be another day in jail, but tomorrow would at least be a new day. I felt really cheesy thinking about it, but I could understand that if you have hopes, the current situation is brought into positive perspective.

One of the kids handed me a paper towel with some meat stacked in a bread roll. Like my bread for breakfast, the bread made a good sandwich. The meat was good and they had used quite a few limes as seasoning.

Just then Eddie yelled out to Francis who was in the guardroom. They exchanged a few loud words which were followed by the front gate opening. Within seconds Francis stuck his head around the cell doorway looking through the bars.

Eddie didn't have to yell so loud now and handed Francis a couple of dollars. I couldn't imagine what in the world was going on, my worst fears were that Francis was in on the drug smuggling too and Eddie needed a quick fix! Giving them the benefit of the doubt, I just watched what was going on. Francis thought for a moment and said OK and left with Eddie's money. As quick as the whole thing started, the transaction ended in a whirl. I was left to my own devices to guess what was going on, the others didn't seem to mind as they knew what Eddie had asked of Francis.

Watching the Volcano

Tonight wasn't the usual news on TV. Instead, there was a special live presentation about a volcano in Southern Mexico that had erupted earlier this morning. I remembered seeing the news yesterday and at that time, the volcano had smoke coming out. I guess tonight it opened up enough to start spitting lava.

Being filmed at night, the volcano was actually spectacular to watch. We were mesmerized by the sight of lava spewing out of a mountain in Southern Mexico. The TV program mentioned that this one wasn't too serious. But I wondered how bad it had to get for it to be considered serious. The officials had already evacuated the back half of the mountainside which consisted mostly of impoverished farmers. The report stated that when the volcano stopped erupting, the residence could go back to their homes. This wasn't anything new to them as the volcano spitted like this before.

But this time it was a little more significant, the news said, because there was a lot more lava flow. As I sat there, pondering the turn of events, I wondered how long a volcano usually lasts. There were interviews from seismologists and the local residents, but once again all in Spanish. My mind went wandering.

Here I was, in a Mexican jail seeing volcanoes erupt in the country I was actually in. Needless to say, it was erupting a good thousand miles away, but it still

> Any way I evaluated my situation, I figured I was going to make it just fine, even if this was going to be "The End".

worried me because I was in jail. What if this was "it", The Big One, the end of the world. I figured I had a couple options. Any of which I would come out on top.

First, there would be mass chaos from the volcano not stopping and then from more eruptions. The Mexican government would be over thrown by the people and all the government workers including the secretary would quit and the Jail guards would abandon their posts. But they would let us out first of course. Then we would be free to go home.

Or better yet, I thought of some epidemic like Toxic Volcano Ash Rash for all the people of the Western Hemisphere, but the few of us in jail would survive because were indoors, out of the courtyard. Any way I evaluated my situation, I figured I was going to make it just fine, even if this was going to be "The End". I found myself grinning slyly, all because I was watching a volcano erupt on TV while sitting in a Mexican Jail.

Francis Returns

About 10 minutes later, the front gate opened again. Francis came back and was now at our cell door. With keys in hand, he fumbled with the cell lock and seemed out of breath, but that was to be expected as he was a rather heavy man. Wherever he went a few minutes ago, he did it in a hurry. I didn't think anybody was going to the married room, so why was he opening the door? After it slid open a crack, Francis held out a bottle of soda. It was the generic orange soda found in convenience stores.

Eddie took the soda with a *"Gracias"* and held it up like a trophy. All the other guys watched with smiles. Looks like Francis made a grocery run for Eddie while the other guard watched the main gate. Eddie brought his new possession over to the community food and started pouring soda into several community cups. The gate slid shut, and Francis said goodnight again as he locked up.

Once each of us had a cup, we raised our glasses to Eddie's health and Francis' good nature. We thanked Eddie as we sipped a cup full of orange soda. This also meant taking turns going to the bathroom once dinner finished.

With a full belly and a sweet taste in my mouth, I unrolled my sleeping bag and got in. I said a silent prayer, thankful for the blessings of the day, and even for Eddie and his good fortune in getting soda for us. I finished up and tried watching the novellas for the night, but didn't pay much attention. I soon found myself asleep before the TV was turned off.

CHAPTER 8

MONDAY

Making the Best of the Day

More Oatmeal

I woke on Monday stiff and tired. I slept long through the night, but the concrete floor was getting to me. I always thought that you adjusted to it as you slept on a flat surface. But sleeping on a rock hard floor is still sleeping on a rock hard floor. It didn't get any better for me and by this time I even felt my body was out of whack.

I didn't want to get up today. I just laid there, not wanting to move. Eddie got up and walked over me to get to the bathroom. I didn't mind, everyone walked over the legs and bodies of those sleeping on the floor. The only rule was to not move or else the others might misjudge their step and land on you.

Even though I really didn't want to get up, sooner or later I would have to. I slowly got dressed in my sleeping bag and finally crawled out. By this time the others were stirring too, except the hermit with no teeth. As usual he spent the morning with his towel curtains drawn. By now, I didn't expect anything different from him. It was nice to know he was true to his character.

Soon the front gate rattled open and footsteps could be heard through the hallway. Francis unlocked the court-yard gate and then came to our cell door with his usual

"Buenas Dias". We all grunted back a hello, still sleepy and not ready for conversation. The door was opened and most of us shuffled out of the room.

I was still groggy as I wandered out to the courtyard. Without thinking I started walking the circle. Within minutes, after going round and round, the blood started flowing, and my limbs found circulation. I stretched as I walked, it was now nice to be in the air getting my faculties fully restored.

I didn't walk long when the call came for breakfast. This morning, it was back to the banana, bread and oatmeal. I decided to take all three with me today. With the cup in my hands, and food in my pockets, I proceeded out the door and sat with Jose on a wall.

"Buenos Dias, Jose" I smiled, *"How did you sleep?"* I was glad to see Jose eating a good meal.

"Hola" he replied. His hair was messed up from the sleep but probably wasn't any worse than the day before. It was apparent he was doing better now that he was on this side. I couldn't imagine another body in our cell, so I guessed Jose found a spot somewhere else to sleep. He nodded his head that he was doing well and was focused on his breakfast.

I sat and ate in silence with Jose. These few moments were precious to us. Time seemed to stop when you eat breakfast in jail with a friend. It's your moment when you still feel like you are king of the castle.

After finishing my banana, I turned to Jose. I knew he had been talking to the guards yesterday. "Any luck on getting out?" I asked. I was wondering what his next steps were.

He couldn't understand my English and looked at me with a questioning look.

"When are you leaving?" I asked again, this time in Spanish.

Jose shook his head, *"I don't know, maybe in a couple days"* then his countenance brightened. *"But my family is coming today!"*

"That's great!" I knew it meant something for him to able to see his family. He was certainly excited about it, and I would be too. I knew how much it meant to have family and friends come to visit. *"Tell me when they come?"* I gave him a piece of gum as he walked to throw his banana peal away.

I thought that I could try my oatmeal, but it just wasn't appealing anymore. I quickly walked inside and looked at those in the other room.

By this time, most of the guys from Friday and Saturday nights had been let go. Now that it was Monday, the drunk tank was back to holding only a few men. As always, they looked longingly over to our side of the jail. Quietly I passed through my cup to one of the men who was leaning on the wall. I was accustomed to this now and it didn't matter much now if others watched. I was comfortable in giving to others as I passed my oatmeal through the bars. The man took the Styrofoam cup with a *"gracias"* and quickly consumed the warm contents.

Today was different. Within a few moments as I started back to the courtyard, I noticed Jose coming out of the other cell room. He too had an oatmeal cup and passed it through the iron bars to another man in the drunk tank. With gratitude, the man took it and walked to the other side of the room, to consume his meager meal undisturbed.

I don't think Jose was aware that I was watching him from a distance as he made the food transfer. I could tell there was a deep satisfaction for Jose as he served someone else like he once had been served. He walked towards the courtyard with his head held high and a smile of confidence.

Joker and the Bunny

After breakfast, I decided to walk around the court yard again. It was still early and Christina had not come to the jail yet. The others were there and I started walking with Rocco and some others. As many times as everyone had gone around the courtyard, we were surprised that there wasn't a worn pathway. However, it probably would take a long time for a group with regular shoes on to make any impressions in concrete.

Eddie was also in the courtyard sitting with some others and started to light up their morning Marijuana. By now I was familiar with the aroma and it now seemed as normal as breakfast itself. Two of the kids got out the white domino set. Seeing those two with dominoes seemed traditional as well.

While walking the circle, I continued to think. It was Monday, and I expected to get out today. After all, it was the beginning of the week and Christy had mentioned that she would see what she could do while she was partying with the lawyers and the Secretary. That still seemed a bit weird. What a vacation, I thought to myself. No one at home is going to believe this. I had to keep pinching myself to believe it too.

Loud laughter coming from the hallway distracted me from my thoughts. I couldn't make out what was going on, but it seemed that everyone inside had all burst into laughter at the same time. Those of us walking the circle looked around, wondering what was going on in there? At that moment, the Joker jumped out from the hallway door with a "tah-dah!!!" I definitely thought I was dreaming because Joker was wearing a bright pink Bunny Suit!

Standing before us, Joker was wearing a bunny-rabbit costume. It was a full sized, pink, fuzzy jumpsuit with pajama style feet and a large white cotton ball tail. His hands were gloved in fuzzy pink mittens and he had a headpiece covering his head with fuzzy pink floppy ears. His dark Mexican face with mustache and missing tooth grin was the only part of him to be seen.

We all stopped and dropped our jaws. Our disbelief quickly turned into laughter which made the Joker grin even more. He started cavorting and dancing in the middle of the courtyard while shaking his "tail". Some of the guys whistled cat calls and tried to pinch his cotton tail. It was such a ridiculous sight to see a Mexican prisoner dancing in a pink bunny costume!

The entertainment finally died down and Joker took a seat near Eddie. He pulled out a cigarette and lit up. He too was worn out from the animation and took a break. Rocco called out, *"you have to have some big cajones to be in that,"* another added *"or you are crazy!"*

I thought it was a lot bit of both! He seemed like the guy who would do something like that, but my other question was where in the world did he get a bunny costume? He must have had someone pass it through the bars, but what an unusually strange item to pass through the bars! My other guess was that the costume might have been someone else's left behind from another time, but Joker was the only one gutsy enough to put it on and dance around in it!

Voices called my name from the hallway *"Robert Deniro!"* What a welcome bit of news to hear that my girl-friend had arrived. I left the circus in the courtyard and walked through the hallway.

I stuck my fingers through the gate and said "Good morning!"

Christina took my fingers in hers and replied back. It was nice to see her.

"How did you sleep?" I asked, knowing that she had stayed at the hotel because dad had arranged for her to stay at the hotel as long as she needed to. Maybe she would check out today, maybe not.

"The hotel room is really nice." She was grateful to Dad for allowing her to stay in the hotel as it was more of a resort than just a hotel. But I was glad she had gotten a good nights rest. "Oh yes," she added "I also had a run on the beach this morning".

Christina was an avid runner in high school and continued as she got older. She could out run me, but that wasn't saying much as I can't run to save my life. She always said her dream was to run on the beach. I guess today she fulfilled that dream. She was excited about the fact that she had a run in the morning. Coming from Arizona, running on the beach was a rare experience, well so was waiting on your boyfriend to get out of a Mexican Jail.

After a couple of minutes in the courtyard, Joker came back inside. Christina caught a glimpse of the costume and her eyes widened at the sight of a Mexican man walking in Jail with a bunny costume.

"What in the world...?" she asked. I explained that he just came out of the cell like that. I guessed that the costume might have been here for a long time and then every few months it gets pulled out again. With a new crowd coming in so often, the bunny suit would get laughs every time it was worn. Hopefully it didn't happen too often! Joker saw Christina and came up to us at the gate. "Hello pretty girl, how are you?" the Joker asked in a hard Mexican accent. He was playing again and found her as a new audience. "You like my new look?" He asked.

By this time Christy was giggling. This added fuel to the fire and Joker turned around to show off his tail.

"Oh that's a good look for you!" She managed to say through her laughter.

"You think so?" Joker turned around again and started to evaluate himself. "Does it make me look fat?"

Christina couldn't breath, she was laughing too hard, so she just nodded.

"Maybe you're right, thanks pretty lady!" As quickly as Joker came, he darted back into the dark cell to change back to normal clothes. However, I didn't think that Joker could ever be normal!

What if...

Christina tried to gain her composure but she was still thinking about Joker and kept snickering. I watched for a couple moments until she caught her breath. It was just as funny watching her reaction as it was seeing Joker running around.

Finally she calmed down, "I'm sorry," she said, "but that was just too funny." Changing the subject, she continued on, "Oh, I almost forgot, I wanted to tell you about last night."

"What happened, how did it go?" I asked. I was curious about her dinner date with the lawyers and the secretary.

"It was nice" she replied. "You would have been proud of me!" She explained that she went to an outdoor barbeque with the three men and some women she didn't know. Christy didn't know if the women were girlfriends, or just one time dates, either way, they weren't good for much accept hang on the arms of the men. Most of the conversation was about how much beer they could drink, and what they were doing for Christmas.

She continued on, "The secretary asked how long I was planning on staying here, I responded that I was staying as long as you were in jail." She was all smiles, and feeling confident. "Then I asked him, can't you just let him go? It's been several days, and it's about time to let him go."

I smiled as this was a side I knew Christina had mastered. Last night, she was on top of her game. She continued, "He seemed to think about it and just shrugged his shoulders saying 'maybe', I really tried, and I think sooner or later you'll get out.

"But after dinner, the lawyers and the secretary wanted to go to a discotheque, but I went back to the hotel, leaving them drunk and on their way to go dancing."

I could imagine the lawyers and the secretary dancing in some smoky filled dance club with their dates with them. Even at that, the image of these three men dancing around with beers in their hands was a little disconcerting. They were supposed to be professional, and yesterday they let their hair down.

I really wasn't upset that the lawyers were having a good time, but deep down inside, I couldn't tell what the lawyers' motivations were. Was it really the fact that they wanted me out, or was it that they were determining a way for all of them to benefit from a gringo being in jail? I guessed only time would tell.

My questions were soon to be answered as the lawyers walked in the guard room. Surprisingly, the secretary came with them too. Well speak of the devil, this was the time I was sure to get out! They had come to give me the good news! Within a few minutes, I would get my things and get out!

"Hola Roberto," the older brother called out as the other brother smiled at Christy. The secretary had a couple of words with Francis and stayed back by the door to the outside.

"Hi guys, how's it going?" My heart was pounding and I was getting ready for them to say the words, 'you're free'.

The lawyer nodded his head. *"Good, gracias,"* from his blood shot eyes, I could tell he had a wild night and was paying for it now. "Eh, Roberto, we need to take the Secretary up to Sonoyta, to the border again." The lawyer said somberly, it was a combination of a hangover and bad news.

"What?" I asked, "Why do you need to go away?"

"He wants to talk to the border guard and see the car." So the secretary had more questions. I could tell this was more a matter of dragging his feet and not wanting to let a trophy fish get away.

My heart sank. This meant more time here, but how much? What did the

> I could tell this was more a matter of not wanting to let a trophy fish get away.

secretary need to do, and what were the lawyers waiting for? Questions ran through my mind. I looked sternly at the lawyer, what more surprises did he have?

"OK," I said. "So will I be able to leave today?"

The lawyer sank back and with a sly voice explained, *"I don't know."* He was between a rock and a hard place as I was a bit heated and knew I needed to cool down. On the other hand, he couldn't make any promises he knew the Secretary wouldn't keep.

I looked back at the secretary, who was watching us from a distance. It seemed that there was something else that he was trying to hide. I guess he just didn't want me out yet. Without even acknowledging being there, he soon left the guard room, followed by good-byes from the lawyers.

As the lawyers left with the secretary, Christina and I were left to pick up the pieces of what just happened.

"What was that all about?" I asked. I didn't think that Christina knew, but I needed to vent a little.

"I don't know, but last night the secretary asked a couple of questions about the car. I couldn't understand them, it was all in Spanish," she replied.

Whatever was going on, they wouldn't let us know yet. For the next couple minutes, Christina and I discussed my situation and how we didn't know which way was up. I assumed that I would leave today, but now it seemed unrealistic. It would take the men an hour to get to the border town, and then who knows how long it would take for them to stay and talk to the border patrol and inspect my car.

Afterwards they had an hour drive back down, which would result in me staying here a while.

I also knew that the trip would stop any more progression today. The secretary would be too tired from the trip and not make any decision today. I became frustrated as the hurry up and wait mentality kicked in once again. I probably wasn't going anywhere and I could almost bet on staying here another night.

Christina saw that my mind had negatively wandered and offered some encouragement. "Listen, it's going to be OK," she said.

"I will miss more work" I replied. The idea had first crossed my mind this morning when I remembered that it was Monday.

"You'll be fine, your manager said take your time." She was trying to comfort me, but it sounded funny. We both smiled. Oh, take as long as you want in jail, come back when you're ready.

My mind started to wander, what happens in the worst case scenario if I was never to be let out? What would happen if I was sent to Caborca, Mexico and serve time there, just because I crossed the border with bullets? Would I ever get out, would I ever return to the United States, did I have a job when I returned?

"Christina, what happens if they keep me here?" I didn't want to alarm her, but this was weighing on my mind. There was a chance that I would still be here as not much has progressed since I'd arrived here. "I know it's a little far fetched, but what if...?"

Christy squeezed my fingers. "Robert, don't..." She replied. Christina was getting serious. I knew this was not the time to panic, and she wanted to make it clear that I needed to stay positive. "You're going home soon and don't get down on this."

I nodded my head and knew she was right. Besides, all the lawyers and the Secretary were doing was taking a trip back to Sonoyta, it didn't mean that I was going to Caborca. Even though I knew it meant another day here, I could go on. Each day I told myself, "I'm getting out tomorrow", and even Francis said that each night. Sooner or later I would, it just was a matter of when.

Jose's Visitors

At that moment, another family came into the guard room and was greeted by Francis and the other guard. The family consisted of a woman with a baby in her arms, and an older woman holding the hand of a little girl that looked to be three years old. Francis and the women exchanged words and Francis called out "Jose!"

"Hey Christina," I spoke, trying to overcome the commotion of the guardroom. "Give me a second to go and get the guy for this family?"

Christina nodded and I raced through the hallway to the courtyard. Others were starting to call Jose's name from the hallway as I came through the courtyard and found him leaning against the far wall.

"Hey Jose," I called out. By this time, he was looking around, but couldn't tell if it was really his name or not. *"You're family is here!"*

Jose's eyes lit up and dashed across the courtyard and joined me at the door. Looking down the hall, he squinted his eyes and cried out *"Yes, it's my family! Gracias!"* We both hastened back to the gate and I watched as Jose saw his family that he'd not seen in a couple days.

To Jose, seeing his family was a wonderful sight. It seemed like he hadn't seen them for weeks. I knew his feeling, it was of joy, overcoming any temporary guilty feelings for being behind bars. The family seemed relieved to see him too, the woman with the baby was his wife and the other must have been a mother in law. I wondered what she

231

thought of all of this. The petite little girl was darling. She held on tight to her Grandma's hand and still didn't understand why her daddy was not with them. Still, she stayed quiet in her new surroundings.

After a few words, Jose turned to me and proudly pronounced *"Roberto, this is my family!"*

I nodded to them and smiled *"Nice to meet you."* All feelings of awkwardness went away as they smiled back at me.

"Jose, this is my girlfriend." I pointed to Christina as she greeted them too. Christina then said hello to the women on her side and we all went back to talking to our individual loved ones.

However, the eyes of Jose's little girl were glued to my girlfriend. After a few moments Christy became uneasy. She didn't know what to do about the little girl staring at her.

"It's your hair," I commented. Christina didn't understand, so I had to explain. "She's rarely seen red hair before." The little girl was accustomed to most Mexicans with dark hair and this was probably the first time she had seen a girl with naturally different hair color.

"Go ahead, let her touch it" I challenged Christina. Christina thought a moment and then bent down. Her wavy red hair was pulled back in a pony tail, so she grabbed the end and motioned towards the little girl.

Slowly, the little girl reached her hand up and touched it, just to see if it was real. After doing so, she quickly drew back her tiny hand and buried her face in the legs of her grandmother. Both Christina and I smiled.

I remember the first time I came down to Mexico. I was about 9 years old and had a great time. However, I too have red hair and got looks from many of the youngsters. I once caught a kid trying to touch my hair from behind. He touched the back of my head and quickly moved away before I could turn around. The kid was with a group of friends who dared him to go ahead and touch the redhead before them. I knew that it would be a long lasting memory for the little girl to touch the red hair of a woman.

The Nuts

Christina interrupted my train of thought. "Oh, I brought something down from Mom."

"What?" I asked.

"Well," she announced, "Mom and I didn't know what kind of food you had here, and so dad and I brought some things down with us just in case. Mom especially thought these would be nice." She pulled out from her bag a large bag of pistachio nuts.

This bag wasn't just large, it was huge. The bag had to be holding at least a gallon of nuts. I don't know if a bag of nuts is measured by weight, or volume, but this one was the biggest bag I had ever seen.

I called out to Francis to open the small door. He looked at Christina and the bag. "Whoa" he said under his breath as he reached for his keys and moved towards us. Within a minute, the door was open and the bag was passed through. I took the pistachio nuts and thanked Francis for opening the door and for Christina and her mom for thinking of me.

I quickly made a hole in the bag and knew it was more than I could eat alone. Besides, who eats a gallon of nuts by himself? I looked at Jose who had been watching me receive a year's supply of nuts. "Hey Jose, have some nuts!" He cupped his hands and I poured him a handful.

Joey and a couple of the others walked out of a cell and saw my treasure. "Hey, come have some," I called out. I poured each a handful as I went from person to person. I walked away from Christina as she patiently watched me share my good fortune. "Christy, I'll be back," I called out as she waived goodbye.

The word spread through the jail that *"Roberto has food!"* I went to the courtyard and was the focus of attention as the others received their share of the pistachio nuts. Everyone cheered as the contents of the bag were passed out.

Eddie waited at the edge of the courtyard, I soon made my way around him as he looked up from his cigarette. "Eddie, have some," I motioned the bag to him and he thought for a moment. He guessed because I was giving some to everyone that he wouldn't be in debt to me for taking some. He cupped out his hand and I poured a larger handful. He nodded a *'gracias'* and I moved on to the next person.

> The word spread through the jail that "Roberto has food!"

I completed the courtyard and walked into my cell. Ivan and a Kid were watching TV. The kid was excited as he held out his hand. I poured some for him and moved to Ivan. He looked up from his TV and focused on the bag. Without expression, he tapped his finger on the corner of his bed. I poured some on the bed as he took one and unshelled it. He nodded his head in thanks as I gave him an extra portion too.

By this time, Joey had finished his first course and held his hand out for more. I knew there was plenty to go around again, so I gave him more. He smiled with a gracias and turned to out to the courtyard. I guess I made his day too.

The guy with no teeth parted his curtains to see what the ruckus was all about. In front of him, the gringo had a bag of pistachio nuts and was sharing with the others. I looked at him with a hello and a smile. He looked at me, then to my bag then back to me. He still didn't know what was going on, so I moved closer, offering him some nuts. He finally got the idea and put out his hand for me to fill up. He said a quick 'gracias' and went back to his world behind his veil. I was glad that I could do at least something for him. He didn't have his front teeth, but I didn't think that it would be too difficult to unshell and eat a nut. I left that challenge up to him.

As I started walking down the hallway, I passed near Pablo who was standing in the doorway and filled his hands.

"Gracias Roberto!" He was amazed that pistachio nuts were flowing to everyone.

"Don't thank me, thank my novia," I said as I pointed towards the front gate.

Pablo took a couple steps closer, *"Gracias, novia!"* as he unshelled a nut with his teeth. Christina giggled.

By this time, those in the drunk tank room wondered what all the amusement was about over on our side. Some of them had come over and leaned on the metal bars, watching us. I couldn't leave them out, so I came over gladly poured nuts into their hands too.

I finally returned to Christina, who was all smiles. She knew that it was a big bag and was happy that I could share them. She was a good sport and got a kick out of watching me empty most of the bag into the hands of others. I still had a quarter of the bag left and finally took one for myself.

"Thanks Christina, I really appreciate it. Would you thank your mom for me?" I really wanted her to know how much that bag of nuts meant to me.

"You're welcome, but thank my mom yourself," she said. She pointed to the rest of the bag. "I think that will keep you for a while. I need to go. I have to call dad to tell him how we're doing."

Telling her dad that I would be here for another day would be somewhat of a shock to him. He expected me out today too, so it was time for Christina to let him know before it got too late. I put my fingers through the gate again, she squeezed them one more time as she said goodbye.

I walked away from the gate, leaving Jose to visit with his loved ones.

Basketball

I finally found my way to the courtyard as Ivan came up, dribbling a basketball. I had seen the basketball a couple days before, but was surprised that one would be in this small jail.

On one wall of the courtyard about 10 feet up was a large circle drawn with a black magic marker. This circle represented a makeshift basketball hoop for the guys to play. It seemed kind of weird, but with a little imagination, you could visualize a horizontal place to shoot a ball through rather than a circle on a vertical wall.

"*Hey Roberto,*" he said, "*let's play one on one?*" Ivan asked.

"I'm no good," was my reply. However, he kept insisting and I finally agreed. .

Making baskets was a little harder than I thought. The rule was you couldn't just throw it up there to hit the circle. I tried a couple times and was told, "That's not how you make a basket!" You had to arch your shot so that the ball hit the circle on the way down. It was a little easier said than done.

Ivan didn't turn out to be much of a basketball player either. He was not very tall, and he was husky. As we started to play, I noticed he had a couple of other handicaps which I wasn't first aware of. When he first came into the jail, the guards didn't give back some of his personal things. So he improvised by using white plastic grocery bags and making shoelaces and a belt. It was amusing to see laced pieces of the plastic bag laced through every other shoe hole.

His makeshift belt worked too but you could tell that his pants were still too loose. He was always pulling them up with one hand.

Despite the crude articles of clothing, it really didn't stop Ivan from playing basketball. I think it made him feel right at home with a circle on the wall for an improvised hoop and it probably improved his game. When I had the ball, he would back me into a corner, steal the ball, and make a shot. Soon the score was six to nothing before I realized that I was really glad that I didn't have to create my reputation and respect based on a basketball game. Others came into the courtyard and watched.

Another basket for him, then another one. No matter what I did, I couldn't make a basket. Many times I would have the ball, but I just couldn't get the idea of making a basket in a circle on a vertical wall. I was getting a little flustered as all of the guys watching were starting to notice how really bad I was.

After a while, Ivan again had the ball and I was between him and the basket. He had his back to me, dribbling and thinking of how to get around me. I came up with a brilliant plan. I reached forward, grabbed his pants at the waist and pulled down. It caught him off guard as he grabbed for his pants. He wore boxers and a very long shirt, so I knew I could get away with a bit of nonsense. It surprised him long enough for me to run around, steal the ball, run to the basket and make my only point in the game.

All the others started laughing when they saw what I had done. I was complimented for such a smart strategy. We played for a bit longer until I got tired and finally conceded him to be the winner. We shook hands with a *good game.*

I sat on the sidelines watching the others play as I grabbed a handful of nuts. Despite the unfortunate events of the lawyers needing to take the secretary to take my car, it had been a relatively good day, especially with the bag of pistachio nuts from Christina. I was amazed how easy the emotions of worry and distress could be replaced with feelings of good spirits and jubilation right after a game of basketball.

Sweeping

Francis came through the front gate to close up the courtyard for the day. As always, he was smiling as he ordered us back into the hallway. It was time to lock up and as I passed him, he saw my bag of macadamia nuts. *"Hey, Robert Deniro! How's it going?"*

"Hi Francis, you want some?" I asked the obvious question as I offered him a handful of nuts which he graciously cupped his bulky hands. I wondered how he would carry his new snack and manage to lock up the courtyard. I figured it would be fun to watch as I gave him a good portion.

Francis watched as the rest of us filtered in from the courtyard and left him to lock up. He dropped a few nuts along the way as he fumbled for his keys. Finally after a bit of effort, he used one hand and his belly to hold the nuts and managed to grab his set of keys from his hip with the other hand. After some struggle, he closed the gate behind him and worked the lock. A couple of us chuckled under our breaths as we saw the comedy before us. He soon walked back down the hallway and through the main gate.

Happy that I had been of service to others in the cell, I turned to place my bag on the community food table for the others. Eddie met me in the cell. "It's your shells, you clean up," he said as he handed me a broom.

I left the bag of nuts with the community food and went to work sweeping. Once I began, I noticed there had been a lot of nut shells dropped on the concrete floor. Everyone had just let them drop, but I guess Eddie determined it was my responsibility to clean up. I didn't mind, I figured it was about time to sweep for the day anyway.

Most everyday, before lockdown, someone would grab a broom and sweep the cell rooms and the hallway. I guessed this time, it was my turn.

I started at the front gate and worked my way back. I did a sweep of each cell and continued onward. When I got to the courtyard gate I had a nice pile of dust and shells. Ivan saw me cleaning up and he came out of the cell room with a dust pan. He helped me with the last bit of shells and dust and then dumped the dirt in a small trash can.

I thanked Ivan for helping me out and gave him a stick of gum as we put the broom and the dustpan back in its place. The excitement of the day had died down and most of the guys were watching TV or playing games on the hallway floor. I decided to walk the hallway, since I had spent most of the day sitting with Christina at the front gate and had not gotten much exercise.

I pulled a few pistachio nuts from my jacket pocket as I paced up and down the hallway. I put the shells back in a pocket to dump in the trash can later. I didn't want to get any more shells on the floor now that they were swept. My lesson learned was that we you have something to give, you might as well go all the way and make sure you finish what you've started. I guess for me, sweeping was the final step and it was part of what I could do. Rather than just giving out nuts and letting the trash go to the wind, it was best that the shells were swept up too. I guessed even Eddie gave me opportunities to find the lesson in the moment.

> You might as well go all the way and make sure you finish what you've started.

Joey Goes Away

After a while, I knew it was getting time for the Francis to come around and lock us in the cells. I tried to get as much walking in as I could. Christy said that she was going to be back before we were locked in for the night. I guess she got tied up with some of her errands that she said she had to do. I wondered if she would be back before I would have to go into the cells.

Francis stepped up to the gate, however this time he had another guard with him I had not seen before. This guard was actually in uniform and stood properly. He looked hurried as he waited for Francis to get a move on. Francis called out Joey's name.

Joey came out from one of the cells where he was talking to some of the other guys. He came over to the gate where Francis gave him some instructions. Joey turned back and started towards the cell again. "I'm going," he said to all of us. We knew Joey's time was up. He told us he was now to be transported to the State Prison located several hours south in Caborca, Mexico

I remember the comments of this State Prison made by the Joker. It was not too bad of a place, for a prison. However, there are a lot more prisoners. The Rocky Point jail was a temporary jail and most of us stay here until the locals can find out what to do with us. However, Eddie, Ivan, Rocco and some others had been here longer than just a week.

Joey's destiny was to go to the State Prison. We guessed that the locals couldn't resolve his crimes of drug trafficking, so he was being shipped elsewhere.

I watched him get his stuff and grab his blanket. By this time, all of the others knew he was going and started coming by to wish him well. He said thanks and seemed actually happy to be going. I guess it would be a change of scenery. He also enjoyed being such a center of attention, even if it was for a brief moment. It seemed strange for one of us to actually be going. We were all becoming like family and now it had to change.

I finally got out of feeling the nostalgia and back into reality. This was a temporary situation, hopefully. How easy it is to get into a mindset that we should all stay here forever. Still there was a risk of me following Joey to the State Prison if these lawyers couldn't get me out. I was still praying for my issues to be resolved here.

Joey took his stuff to the main gate as Francis opened the gate and let him though. The other guard handcuffed him, and took him and his stuff away.

By this time, Christy came to the front room and saw them leaving. She came up to the gate where we met for a few minutes. I told her that the Joey left for the state prison and I was now getting worried that I would join him. She smiled, but said that there is no way she would let them! That gave me a bit of confidence, knowing that I had a great girlfriend nearby.

We were soon interrupted by Francis as he started jiggling his keys. He really liked seeing Christina here. She was the only gringo visiting and Francis was now on a first name basis with her. But, he was always nice to everyone.

"Hello Roberto! Hello Christina! Sorry but it's time to lock up!" He called out. Christina and I smiled. He was trying to make light out of a sad moment.

"I tell you what, I will open the small door for you!" he said, trying to be nice. With that he took the key to the small 2 x 2 foot small porthole part of the gate. This door could be opened so families can pass food through and would also allow the main large gate to stay shut for security purposes.

He opened the small door and smiled at Christy. "Hurry, Kiss him! I no look!" He smiled and put his hands over his eyes playfully. Christina and I looked at each other with puzzled looks. Oh, the guard was giving us time to say goodbye!

I stuck my head out the small opening and Christina got the message. She leaned over and we kissed. It had been over a week since I had kissed her goodbye in the United States and we both had not thought of kissing while she had been here in Mexico.

As we kissed, I knew it was a small, appropriate kiss. But for me, it was a much needed kiss goodnight.

We finished when Francis took his hands off his eyes. "You guys done? OK. Say goodbye, Christina!" By this time the night guard came as Francis closed the small gate door. The night guard opened the lock to the main gate while Christina left the guardroom.

The gate was closed behind Francis and we were led back into our cell rooms for the night. "Good night Roberto, maybe you get out tomorrow," he called to me as the twelve of us were locked into our cell.

I sat on my bed roll near Eddie's bed while the others were getting situated. With Joey gone, there would be one less in the room. I started to count, 10- 11- 12? There was one extra person here. I looked around and found him. Another young Mexican was sitting on the floor with us. Ivan, Eddie and the rest had already moved to their beds for dinner and the newcomer made six of us sitting on the floor.

This new guy was a young man the about the age of the other "kids". I knew he had been here today, but couldn't remember when he came into the jail. He might have come yesterday, but spent last night in the other cell. I guess he didn't want to spend the night in the other cell. I couldn't blame him.

I asked him if he had a blanket. He shook his head, "no". I reached under Eddie's bed and pulled out my extra blue blanket and tossed it over to him. He didn't have any belongings with him, so he assumed he would sleep in his clothes on the concrete floor, without any blanket. I knew how bad that could be and just couldn't see him doing that. He folded his new blanket and sat on it for the night.

Eddie called my name and announced that dinner was up to me tonight! I looked at him a bit puzzled. He was serious and he expected me to make dinner for the group.

I said Ok, I really didn't want to fight him about it. I got up and moved around toward community table and the cooking supplies with the food that was brought in earlier this evening.

As soon as I started getting the food ready, I got overwhelmed. This seemed like such a big chore. I was up for the challenge, but it wasn't as fun, now that Eddie dictated that I was in charge of dinner. Still, I determined to make the best out of everything and that meant cooking dinner for the night too.

As soon as my attitude changed, I noticed that my new friend I gave the blanket to got up and offered to help. I thanked him and welcomed whatever he could do. Together we started heating up the meat and stuffed them into the corn tortillas provided. Other than Eddie not wanting anything to eat, dinner seemed to go as smooth as it could.

My new friend took the broom out and finished by sweeping up. I was glad that he helped out. After clean up, we sat back down to watch the rest of the novellas for the night.

Rocco's Bed

It was Monday night. A week ago, I crossed the border with bullets in my car. A flood of memories raced back, the border patrol guards, the gang member police that put me in jail the first night, the clean white toilet in the first jail cell. It had been a full week and I felt that little had progressed. I wondered what the secretary wanted with my car, then it dawned on me, maybe he wants the car!

My thoughts quickly changed to the fact that I got a kiss from Christina tonight. Let them take my car, I thought with a smile. I don't mind whatever happens now because I got a kiss tonight! What a strange trade off, but I thought there was no cement ceiling strong enough that could keep my spirits from flying high tonight. My liberty was taken from me, my car possibly too, but tonight I considered myself fortunate from a single kiss.

Some noises of the chinking metal gate being opened interrupted my thoughts and Rocco's name was called. All of us looked at Rocco. He sat up in his bunk-bed and looked around. A few moments later Francis peeked his face through our cell bars.

What was going on, I thought to myself. Was Rocco being transported like Joey? The guard and Rocco exchanged words and Rocco's face was all smiles. He called to the rest of us and grabbed only his pillow and blanket and put on his slippers. I finally figured out that his wife was waiting for him in the "married room". Not bad, I thought.

From a bunch of guys stuffed in a cell, Rocco was given "manly" encouragement with grunts and whistles. Seems like this was common practice for an inmate to get a break every once in a while. Especially if this was just a temporary jail before you go somewhere bigger (or worse), I could understand that this jail could afford to give its prisoners some more liberties now and then. Besides, it also gave you bragging rights when you came back.

Rocco said his "See ya later's" and followed the Francis through the now opened cell door. The door closed again and the two of them went out of sight and down the hallway.

Soon, the smiles went away and my focus was brought back into the cell. The other guys on the floor were looking at each other rather curiously. It didn't take long for me to figure out what they were thinking. With Rocco gone, this meant his bed was up for grabs tonight. This also meant we had to determine who would get to take Rocco's bed. I started wondering who would take the opportunity to get off the floor.

Just then, one of the Kids cleared his throat and said *"Roberto, you take the bed."*

I looked at him. At first I thought he was kidding around, as anyone could hop in there faster than I could even think. He wasn't joking, he was being serious. His face was solemn as he knew what he was giving up. Anyone on the floor would have given tomorrow's banana to get the bed for the night. The room fell silent. The others on the floor looked at me too with an affirmative vote.

> Anyone on the floor would have given tomorrow's banana to get the bed for the night.

"You sure?" I asked them. The Kid with the mustache nodded and the new guy that helped me cook dinner was smiling about it too.

"Gracias," I said as I got up. I didn't know what else to say. This seemed like an early Christmas present they were giving me. I could tell that they seemed fulfilled as they offered this gesture of kindness.

I took my sleeping bag with me I hopped over to Rocco's bed. However, I really didn't feel the need for my extra blanket, so I tossed it to my friend who helped with dinner. Now he had two blankets. What a deal. He thought he was in heaven too.

As I laid out the sleeping bag and started to lie down, Eddie piped up "OK, Robert. You get to sleep there tonight only, and don't touch anything."

"Ok, thanks Eddie," I said trying to keep the sarcasm out of my voice. Deflecting his controlling personality was actually becoming fun. Eddie was trying to push my buttons and I still didn't let it get to me. The thought crossed my mind "A soft answer turns away wrath". I used this approach with him and it seemed to work. It wasn't that I was being a pansy about it, I just wouldn't let his digs get to me. Besides, if I was Rocco's friend, I didn't need Eddie to tell me not to touch Rocco's stuff.

I've seen movies where the main character spends years in prison on a hard floor, then gets released only to find that he can't sleep in a soft bed. Whoever wrote that stuff was way wrong. Anything is better than a hard floor I soon discovered as I laid down for the rest of the night. Even if the mattress was a folded blanket against the metal mesh grid frame, it seemed like I fell into a pile of hay. Well, not exactly, but I was feeling pretty comfortable about being off the floor.

I started to sink in to my new contentment when a flood of gratitude filled my heart. It was the first time in seven nights that I had a chance to sleep on a bed instead of a hard floor. I glanced down at the guys below me. I wondered how long they had been there and how long we all would have to sleep on concrete. I had been given the opportunity tonight to relax. The feeling came that I would be just fine tonight and I should cherish what the others had given up.

I turned over, my face towards the wall. My eyes got teary as I said my prayers for the night. I was grateful to see Joker in a Bunny suit. I was grateful that I got a kiss tonight, I was grateful that I had help with dinner, and I was grateful for my friends who gave up the chance to sleep on a bed so I could. Most importantly, I was grateful to still be loved from above. And even though I was in a predicament, I still felt a love that let me know that I could make it, even for just one more night.

I fell asleep while counting my blessings.

CHAPTER 9

TUESDAY

Finally Saying Goodbye

Off the Floor

I was really warm that night. Rocco's bed was a foot off the concrete floor and with my sleeping bag around me I felt pretty cozy. I finally woke up to Eddie's coughing in the bathroom.

I really didn't want to get up today. I was warm, I was off the floor, and I was comfortable in Rocco's bed. At least being off the floor allowed me the ability not to have to get up first. So this time, I waited a while for the others to start moving around.

Those on the floor finally got up. Now I was in a dilemma. I wanted to stay in bed, but I knew I couldn't forever. Besides, Eddie would probably say something and Rocco would be back later this morning. So how long could I stay here? It was like eating a great dessert, you savor every bite, but get disappointed the closer you are to finishing.

Soon Francis came with his keys jingling. As he opened the gate to the courtyard, I began getting up. I finally got my clothes on and sat up in bed. I didn't have much clearance between the bed and the bottom of the bunk above me which belonged to the hermit with no teeth.

The kids soon trickled out of the cell door and I put my feet on the ground cold ground. It was probably not much different from the other mornings, but today I wasn't used to the cold concrete. I slipped my sneakers on, proceeded to roll up my sleeping bag and left Rocco's bed as if it was never touched. Silently I thanked Rocco for the use of his bed last night. I figured he was also in a much happier place last night anyway.

Walking in the courtyard wasn't half bad this morning. My body had a great night's rest and I found myself a little more awake than the previous mornings. Today was Tuesday, another morning in jail, another series of hopes and anticipations. Would I get out today? Every evening I thought that tomorrow I was getting out, every morning I wondered if that day had come. Not that I didn't like it here, but it felt like my life was on hold until I could be free again.

I didn't want to think about this much longer and I knew if I did, I'd get myself frustrated. My attention refocused on positive things when breakfast was called. I went back into the cell after the others and took my banana and bread. By this time, Rocco had come back to the jail and looked refreshed and ready for the morning. It was amazing what a married room would do for an inmate.

I walked out to the courtyard and sat with Ivan as he ate breakfast. A couple of minutes later, Jose joined us as we ate in silence. Breakfast tasted extra good for some reason, maybe it was because I had a good nights sleep. I kept thinking about last night. I was grateful to the others for letting me sleep on Rocco's bed and was glad that Rocco had left for the night.

After eating my banana, I sat for a while letting my food digest. After a few days of bananas and bread in the morning and small tacos in the evening, your eating habits get pretty ordinary. I watched as Eddie sat in the corner and lit up another joint. Joker and Pablo joined him in his daily ritual. I watched in amusement as each would take a drag and pass it to the other one as they tried to hold their breath for a while. However, as soon as they started to cough, they would let their breath out and start coughing until fresh air got back in their lungs.

Many people in the world say that marijuana should be allowed for medicinal purposes, but what kind of smoke is good for you at all? Maybe it was the effects afterwards. Eddie just stayed seated quietly for several minutes after the joint was finished, all relaxed and calm. I didn't mind the calm relaxed Eddie, he was much better than the controlling offensive Eddie. But I was sorry that he paid such a high price to get tolerable.

I left the courtyard and my breakfast companions and went back to the cell to pick up my cup of oatmeal. By now, I had no desire to consume the stuff. I was now in the habit of giving it away and just didn't have an appetite for it anymore. Not that giving oatmeal away was bad, I was just thinking that any way I looked at it, I just didn't want it.

As I walked out of the cell room into the hallway, I saw Jose giving his cup of oatmeal to someone on the other side in the drunk tank. The wall of iron bars separating the drunk tank room from our side didn't seem so cold now. There were now very few men in the other room as most of them from the weekend had been released. I quickly found a man leaning on the wall, hands clasping the iron bars. I held out my cup and the man took it with a quick *"gracias."*

> The wall of iron bars separating the drunk tank room from our side didn't seem so cold now.

I looked up to find that Jose watching me. He raised his eyebrows in a silent hello and walked into the cell closest to the front gate. I guess what goes around, comes around.

The Old Man

I finished breakfast and started walking circles in the courtyard. After turning the corners a couple of times, I looked into the hallway while passing the entrance between the courtyard and the hallway. At the other end of the hallway, I could see that there was some commotion at the front gate. I expected that it was family visiting at the gate because some of the inmates had gone to the front gate to greet them. I would find out what was the excitement soon enough.

One of the 'kids' came out of the hallway and waited for me to come around the circle to where he was standing. *"Roberto!"* He called to me and said there was another gringo coming into the jail.

"To visit me?" I asked. I was the only gringo that these guys had seen here and all the other gringos who had come this week came to see me.

"No, to come into the jail!" He answered in excitement. This was the most stirred up the group had been in a while.

I was confused. *"What, a gringo is coming inside, here?"*

"Si!" was the reply as he motioned for me to come see for myself. I followed him into the hallway.

Sure enough, there was a gringo on the inside. Not every day did a new person come into jail, let alone a gringo. He hadn't even made it five feet from the front gate and a crowd of other inmates had already gathered around.

This man was old, but he probably appeared older than his actual years. His uncombed hair was grayed out and white whiskers revealed that he hadn't shaved in several days. He finally saw me and looked at me with as much as wonderment on his face as I had about him. The other prisoners around saw me coming up and called out my name, "Roberto!"

For a moment, time stood still as I saw the expression on his face, his demeanor, his appearance. I knew he felt like me almost a week ago. It was the scared deer in the headlights look. I could tell what he was asking himself "what am I doing here?" I knew it would take a while for him to find his answer. Nevertheless, I made my way up to him.

I got near him and said, "Hello."

He replied with a "Hello." He was glad to hear something in English. His hands were trembling. I asked him his name, and he replied "George." It was nice to meet him.

"Welcome to the Rocky Point Jail" I exclaimed as I tried to create a different mood. He smiled sheepishly, not knowing how to respond.

At this time, the main gate was opened and a backpack and a blanket came through. The old man looked at me with a puzzled look as to ask "what do I do?" Although it now seemed so long ago, I remember I had the same feelings. I offered to help out and took the bag from him. He seemed a bit apprehensive about what I was going to do.

I started walking to the cell closest to the main gate. I turned to him and spoke, trying to calm his nerves "You see, everyone here are friends. You should be fine here. They are all friendly and we're fed well." I smiled as I remembered someone mentioning that to me when I first came. The lesson I learned was that you live, you learn and pass it on.

I took George into the cell where a couple others were watching TV. Jose was sitting on the bed. I looked at him and held up the bag. He motioned me over and we found a place under the bed and stashed his bag. George handed me the blanket and I placed it along side the bag. It was out of sight and most importantly out of the way in such a crowded cell. I instructed George that his things could stay there out of the way until tonight. If he needed anything, go ahead and get it, but usually it would stay out of the way under the bed.

I wondered why I put George's things in the fist cell rather than mine? It seemed like there was more room in that cell as we had twelve in our cell. I couldn't keep count of the inmates in George's, but it seemed appropriate since he had originally stopped so short after the gate.

Afterwards, George followed me out of the cell, through the hallway towards the courtyard. By this time, the others had dispersed as the other inmates started finding other things to do. We talked for a bit. He said he was originally from Wisconsin but had been living here in Mexico with "family" for a few years. Seemed pretty normal to me.

I showed the old man around, informing him that, "This is another cell were the other 12 of us stay and this is the courtyard were we walk in circles for exercise and play basketball when we can." That was pretty much it. Nevertheless, he was appreciative that I was being friendly to him.

I was dieing to ask him and finally I couldn't keep my questions in. "George", I began, "you're really a strange sight to see here, what happened?"

"It's a blur to me." He said as he started with his story. He was driving from Rocky Point to the border town, Sonoyta. He was feeling charitable, so he picked up two Mexican hitch-hikers. He thought everything was going fine, until a police car pulled him over. As soon as he stopped, the two Mexican hitch-hikers jumped out of his car and ran away. The police tried to go after the runaways, but got George instead who was still sitting in the driver's seat and oblivious of what was going on. The two hitch-hikers had left their bags in the car, only to be discovered by the police. The bags contained about five or six kilos of Marijuana. Not being able to explain the bags, George was arrested for possession of drugs.

I sympathized with him and wished him the best of luck. He asked me what I did to get put here. I smiled and told him that I transported bullets on accident into the country and was caught by the border patrol. I'd made the mistake by not checking my car after target shooting with friends in the US before I crossed. But hopefully, I should be out soon. I told him that I was in Sonoyta for a couple days last week and had been here since last Wednesday.

He nodded his head and exclaimed, "I spent two days in Sonoyta jail too!"

I smiled and wondered if he had seen the message I left in the cell. "I guess those guys up there just pass the buck and send all of us down here." How weird, two gringos in the same set of jails within a week of each other. I wonder how much gringo criminal traffic comes through here anyway.

By this time a man came to the guard room and approached the front gate. George recognized him and headed towards him. "There's my brother," he stated.

"That's your brother?" I questioned in disbelief. The man at the gate waiting for George was oriental and looked like he was just out of college.

"Yeah, my adopted brother," he answered. "We live in a commune and we consider all of us as family."

Now that explained things. I had heard of these groups before, but never really got the chance to see it first hand. There are some Americans who just get tired of the rat race in the US and move to Mexico to live in group communes. I really hadn't witnessed this "adopted family" life style before, but it made sense. At least the old man had some support on the other side of the jail.

I let George go talk to his "brother" and got distracted as Christina walked into view. I caught a couple of words spoken between these two men. It wasn't good news. The young guy on the outside was frustrated. "There's not much I can do" he would say and "I don't know what else to do". I felt sad for George, they were in a predicament and didn't know how to resolve it.

The Gift

I turned my attention to Christy who seemed rather serious. Once again I put my fingers through the front gate and she squeezed them a hello. "Get your bags packed," she said. She had an anxious look on her face.

"You're joking right?" I asked. I knew she wasn't, but I wanted to get her reaction. You could tell she was a bit frazzled, but I wanted to see the 'How dare you think I'm joking' look!

Just then one of the lawyers came into the outer room and came up to us. *"Hola, Roberto, we get you out soon."* He sounded excited too.

"Today?" I asked. I knew each day I was getting more and more difficult to work with, but it was a half serious and half heckling question.

"Well, we are working on it," the lawyer explained.

Christina interrupted, "They want to give your car away," you could tell she was now in a sour mood.

"Is that true?" I asked as I looked at the lawyer. This was getting interesting, the lawyer before me was in the hot seat and now he had to explain this one.

He shrugged his shoulders, "Well, the secretary may need to keep the car here still." Yeah right, justify the car staying here as evidence. However, as soon as I leave, it becomes the property of the Secretary as "a gift."

"OK," I said to the lawyers, I was a little frustrated with this, but didn't want to make a big deal of if it right now. I was aware of stories told of small "bribes" or "gifts" as they would officially be called. Depending on the severity of the circumstance, "gifts" were many times the way things got done.

The lawyer seemed relieved with my answer and quickly walked away. That left me alone with Christina who had gotten heated by now. "What's going on?" I asked.

As most redheads are, Christina was very outgoing and passionate. However, I knew she also had a temper and I usually tried not to get her mad. Nevertheless, she was now upset. "They are playing poker with your life" she replied.

She then explained that she talked with the lawyers last night before she had left. They proposed to give the car to the secretary as a 'gift'. This would speed up the process and maybe push the secretary over into letting me go. Christina got upset about it because she thought now that the lawyers were looking out for the secretary too. I was beginning to agree with her. She called her dad last night and cried to him about the car and the situation that I was still here for Tuesday. So her dad offered to come back down.

"Your dad's here?" I asked.

"Yes, he's talking with the other brother and trying to figure how he could help speed this up." Christina's voice quivered. Her frustration last night, turned to anger today and was now turning into holding back tears.

We were interrupted by George, "Hey, is that your lawyer?" He had watched us as we discussed the car issue.

I nodded my head, "Yeah," I replied, "one of them found me in Sonoyta and have been with us for several days."

George got a bright idea, "Hey, do you think they can help me out?" There was desperation in his voice.

I shrugged my shoulders, "Probably," I replied. "But you have to hire them."

This was a different concept for George. He had been living where everything was shared, away from the buy and sell world that he once knew. He thought for a minute, "Well, I don't have much money."

I didn't know what to do for him, "Well, the next time they come back, go ahead and talk with them, I don't know what they would negotiate for, but give it a chance."

George nodded his head and went to check on his stuff in the cell as his visitor on the other side took a cigarette break. Christina watched as the old man talked about his situation. She felt bad for the guy but was still concerned about our circumstance.

Just then, Christina's dad walked into the guard room. He greeted the guards as they said hello. I was really happy that the guards had a 'come and go as you please' policy with visitors.

He put a hand on Christina's shoulder, "Hi Robert, how're you doing?" His voice was concerned, but his face was expressionless.

"Hi, I'm still hanging in there. How was your trip down?" I knew he had to have left early this morning to be here by now. I didn't really know what mood he was in and was trying to test the waters.

"Uneventful, thank goodness." He continued "Robert, the lawyers say they want to keep the car, I think they want to give it to the secretary as part of the payment. Are you going to be alright with that?" I guess he didn't know that Christina and I had already talked about it, or he wanted to make sure about it.

A hundred thoughts a second filled my head as I thought over my situation. The car had been my first car. I had most of it paid off with about a thousand dollars to go on the payments. The financial value really didn't faze me, it was the whole thought of how much I had done in that car. The dates, the road trips, and the stories I could tell about that car all came back to me. I had to deal with a sentimental value that was far greater.

I looked at her dad and replied "I'm OK with it." Sure the possessions we have may be valuable, but that's not all there is to life.

I continued, "If giving up my car means I can be released sooner, then I think that's a good trade off." Christina's dad nodded his head understandingly.

There was more I had to say, "Listen, I think you are in a better situation to make these decisions. If you think this is right, then please go ahead." I tried to make it so that her dad would feel comfortable taking control of the situation. He came here to help out and I wanted to give him my full vote of confidence. He understood what was going on far better than I did.

"OK thanks," he replied, "Come on Christina, there's a couple of other things we need to talk to the lawyers about."

She really didn't want to go, but I figured that she could do more with her dad than just by staying with me. We said our goodbyes and Christina left with her dad.

Joker's Final Joke

As I focused my attention back to the jail, Joker came up. He was followed by one of the Kids.

"Hey Roberto, you going home today?" Joker was trying to hide a smile but the kid was chuckling softly.

"Yes, what's going on?" I wanted to know what was so funny.

"Well you know there's a rule here. When you go, you get water poured on you!"

I put my hand on Joker's shoulder, "Sorry buddy, but I'm not going yet!" I thought there would be some initiation rite to getting out, but Joey didn't get any yesterday. Was that the deal today? I think Joker was trying to pull a fast one on me, so I didn't want to spoil it for him and just played along. I left Joker and the kid snickering to themselves in the hallway. I would deal with the water issue later, but for now I needed to make sure that I had all my things in order.

As I walked into the cell room, I realized that I had only two bags full of things. It wasn't like I had to pack a lot of things, I originally was only going to be staying a few days. Now that couple of days turned into more than a week. I sat on the floor and pulled out the bags holding my possessions from under Eddie's bed.

My book, "Mere Christianity" was among my possessions too. I had finished the book on Sunday and was quite pleased that I had filled the time with reading. It made the days go by faster and the time here more tolerable.

An idea came to me and I quickly took off my sneakers and put on my black shoes. I felt like wearing those when I got out and decided to wrap my sneakers in a plastic bag I found under the bed.

The other bag contained my clothing. The black pants I wore last Monday still had a button missing, and my blue button up shirt was folded up. It had been a couple days that I wore my T-shirt so it was time to come off too. I changed back into my button up shirt and put my T-shirt in a bag.

As I put the t-shirt in the bag, my hand hit something hard. Oh yes, the sock containing my smuggled can of coke! I had put it in the back of my mind the past few days and now remembered that there was a sock containing my soda. I smiled at the accomplishment of keeping it for so long.

A thought crossed my mind: "What if Eddie's right?" I hadn't seen others drinking out of cans and wondered if there was truth to his no can rule. What if the guards checked my stuff and found the can? My worst fears were that I would get thrown back in and start my jail time all over again. But what was I going to do? How could I get a soda can out of jail? It seemed hard enough to keep it, now I had to get it out too!

> A thought crossed my mind: "What if Eddie's right?"

My eyes turned to my sleeping bag. It was rolled up and in its own bag, still under the bed. Quickly I took the sleeping bag out of its place. I took my sock with the can and stuffed it in the center of the sleeping bag. I felt around the outside of the bag, and sure enough, no hard spots. I could only feel the padding of the rolled up sleeping bag in its stuff bag.

I kept wondering why I would go to such lengths to protect a can of soda? To somebody else it was just another soda can, but to me there was a value far beyond its content. It reminded me of my past experiences, the afflictions, my ability to feel comfortable here and the victory of overcoming any challenge I had. My time here would soon end, and I knew drinking it would be sweet in many ways.

With the Coke can safely stowed away, I checked my clothes and set all my things in one corner. My sleeping bag was on top of the grocery bags containing the clothes, ready in a minute's notice. I was ready to go, the problem was that I didn't think that the others were ready to let me go yet.

I went out to the courtyard and paced around. I was getting anxious and needed to calm down. But I couldn't, I just kept thinking over and over that I would get out today! My heart beat harder and harder as it kept time with the seconds passing.

A Captive Audience

Ok, when was I going to get out? I really didn't know, but I knew it was coming soon. I started watching the front gate. Something strange was going on and I decided to take a closer look at what was happening. As I approached I saw two other guys in the front room, I didn't recognize them, but they seemed to be friendly with the guards. By this time they started bringing in some electronic equipment.

This caught the attention of some of the other inmates, while many others didn't seem to take any notice. I watched for a few moments and soon realized that they were setting up a small sound system consisting of two guitars and two microphones hooked up to an amplified speaker. The speaker was positioned flush to the front of the gate and definitely pointed down the hallway towards us. I guessed they were going to put on some entertainment. Ok this should be fun for a while, I thought to myself.

One of the entertainers strapped on a guitar and strummed a chord, and his first word was "Hallelujah!"

Oh, I thought to myself, these guys are preaching ministers. Well, I guess it's appropriate to preach to prisoners. Talk about speaking to a captive audience!

The two preachers had set the speaker right next to the gate and cranked the volume up. The two of them went right into a song, of course in Spanish. I could recognize some of the words "Jesus, faith, holy spirit." Even though I couldn't understand the whole song, I got the message.

These guys were not bad, they had good voices and they seemed to be in tune. I got amused as they were pretty animated with the whole experience. Their body language and the amount of energy they displayed were pretty high. However, their vigor seemed to drown out the message for me. I was more focused on what they were doing, rather than what they were saying.

The song was over and the leader went right into his message. I didn't seem to mind until I realized that his "sermon" would delay my departure! My heart panicked temporarily. These guys were keeping me from going free and as long as they were right in front of the gate preaching to us, there would be no way the guards would let anyone in or out. How could they do this? Don't they know I was going to get out today?

Just then the other guy said another "hallelujah!" in support of whatever the other one said. Oh, that just set me off. This was the last straw, I was getting out today and now I had to wait for these guys to finish preaching!

I decided to change my situation by going into the cell rather than stay in the hallway. I walked past Rocco who had taken a seat on the floor and was listening intently to the message. The guy with a buzzed haircut was sitting on the other side of the hall with a content smile on his face too. Amazingly the hermit with no teeth had come out from behind his towel curtains and was sitting on the floor of the hallway!

In the cell were Pablo, Tito and Eddie. The sound reverberated not only the hallway but the cell too. Pablo had a disgruntled look on his face while smoking cigarettes. But my stomach turned over when I looked at Eddie, his look was more of hatred than anything else. My attitude shifted. I now could choose to keep company in the hallway with those that wanted to listen to the spoken word, or join the group in the cell who would rather welcome the devil himself.

At that moment, I got humble really quickly. What was I thinking? This wasn't so bad. I started rethinking my priorities.

These were just activities I was not used to. Many times, I've heard others bad mouth "holy rollers." I really don't think negatively on such liveliness, I guess I just worshiped in a different, quieter way. Rather than showing my emotions through randomly shouting "Praise the Lord" and waving my arms in the air, mine was more of a reverence and inner peace.

I remembered as a young man reading in the Old Testament where Elijah went to the mountain. There was wind, and earthquake and fire, but the Lord came afterwards in a still small voice. The lesson was that the Lord comes by subtle means, rather than large outrageous ways. I liked the preachers before me, but their performance reminded me more of the wind and earthquake more than the still small voice.

> I figured if there was earth, fire and wind right now, I might as well enjoy that too.

I figured if there was earth, fire and wind right now, I might as well enjoy that too. I couldn't go anywhere and I didn't want to disrupt the others either. I walked back into the hallway and sat down near the door to the courtyard. If I was a captive to the message, I might as well make the best of it too.

Soon, the two preachers ended their presentation and packed up to leave. They shook hands with the guards and left. The sermon had finished for the prisoners. After it was all said and done, I admired the two gentlemen for taking their time to come visit us and doing what they felt was the right thing to do.

The 9 of Spades

My mind slowly turned back to the situation at hand. Any minute now the lawyers would come down the hall and I would get released. Oh, the wait was agonizing! The brief moments when I finally knew I would get out seemed longer that those moments when I didn't know. What was taking them so long? Wait a minute? I had been here for a long time, what were a couple more hours? I determined to not be so impatient and just wait, however long the wait

I went back inside the cell to see what was going on. All of the others had left the cell and were now in the court-yard except for Ivan. He was on his bed watching TV. He watched me as I entered. I nodded my head and he replied back with a silent nod.

I sat down on the ground and started watching TV with him. However, my mind was on other things than what I was watching on Mexican TV.

It was now Tuesday. Probably afternoon by now, but I couldn't tell. Counting the first night last Monday, it had been a total of nine days that I had been "in jail". Whoa, nine days! Being in the jail at the border town for the first three didn't make the time seem so long. But still, I was about to go home. What was my manager at work going to say? Would I even have a job? The thought of being fired really wasn't in my mind. Christina had said my manager was cool about the situation. He had even written a letter, so I knew that my job would be ok, but talk about stories around the water cooler!

Nearby was a small trash can. I glance over and saw a handful of playing cards had been discarded in the trash. I remembered that two of the kids had played with them. However, some of the cards were missing and now the rest were in the trash. I rummaged through the cards and a few cards deep, I found the Nine of Spades.

I pulled the card out and studied it for a while. Nine black spades on a playing card, Nine days in jail. I decided to keep this one as my souvenir to remind me of my experience in Mexico and put it in my shirt pocket. I got up and pushed the waste basket back in its place and went back to my seat on the floor.

I became restless again and left the cell room with my shoe bag, I caught a glimpse of the secretary in the guard room. Without thinking about the rest of my stuff, I walked quickly to the main gate. As I approached, Christina, as well as the lawyers and the Secretary, came through the doorway.

"*Roberto!*" the lawyers called out. They were all smiles again, even Christina seemed a bit more cheerful.

"Hi guys, how's it going?"

"We get you out now!"

Oh what a relief, I was beginning to wonder if it was going to be today or not. I looked at the secretary. Ok guys, open the door, I thought to myself.

The door didn't open. Francis and the other guard just stood there. What was going on? When the lawyers said "we get you out now!" does that mean right away now or sometime later now? The secretary and the lawyer came closer to the gate. I leaned in, puzzled by what was going on.

The Secretary said something and the lawyer had to interpret. However, the English vocabulary of the lawyer was worse than my Spanish.

"Eh, He says, you go out today, but you pay, how you say, a fin to get out."

I looked at the lawyer, "a fin?"

Christina caught on to what they meant and interrupted, "I fine."

Oh, a fine, I was wondering how much a fin cost and hoped it wouldn't cost as much as an arm and a leg!

The secretary spoke again and the lawyer continued with his translation "Eh, he says your fine is $1000 dollars to get out." Well, that was the first tangible piece of progress that I've heard so far. At least we were getting somewhere.

"OK," I said, looking at Christina.

"I'm working with dad on that." Christina answered. "Your dad left a check and so that's all set." Christina seemed like she was on top of things as she knew what was going on far before they came to the front gate.

The lawyer continued, "OK, so you wait a minute, we pay fine and get you out." That statement told me that I wasn't getting out just now. I guess they wanted to tell me what they were going to do, but by this time I really didn't care. Dad and I had discussed that there would be a fine in addition to lawyer's fees and I was grateful that he had prepared for this. Right now, I was unable to organize all of this and was deeply grateful for everyone else who coordinated getting me out.

But there was one more thing, I looked at the secretary and with the most confident voice I could muster, and asked: *"And the car?"*

The secretary looked at me, then at the lawyer and then back at me. I could tell the lawyer was cringing at this. With certainty in his voice the Secretary replied *"the car remains here."* I could understand at least that much Spanish. With that, the secretary ended the conversation by walking away. He was playing hard ball and everyone knew it. I guess he had me over a barrel, but it could have been worse.

So with a thousand dollar fine in addition to giving up my car, I was to be released soon. The lawyers left with a "We be right back" and followed the Secretary out the door. Christina left with them and I was now left alone again, still waiting to leave. At least I had some sort of resolution on this. Within due time, I would be released.

Giving Things Away

While waiting, I decided to go back into the cell and grab the bag that held my sneakers. With the bag in my arms I went into the courtyard to look for Jose. He wasn't there and I then went to the other cell to look for him. I hadn't seen him since breakfast and was wondering if he was OK. I soon found him in the other cell. The TV was on and several of the inmates were sitting on the beds watching, Jose was sitting on another bunk and watching from a distance.

"Hey Jose," I whispered as I interrupted what he was watching. Jose looked up and smiled. I didn't want to create a scene but wanted to talk to him privately.

"Hola Roberto!" He said softly. His spirits had been lifted from the visits with his family yesterday. It was good to see them and you could tell Jose had been encouraged by them.

"This is for you," I whispered as I passed the bag of shoes to him and placed them on the bed at his side. He opened the bag, trying not to make noise with the rustling plastic. His eyes grew wider as he looked at the clean pair of shoes.

Jose's shoes had certainly seen better days. They were low tennis shoes and were stained, filthy and caked with old dirt. Sooner or latter they would fall off his feet so I thought he would like to have mine. It was a small gesture to give him my shoes. They weren't too old and seemed to be his size. He looked up at me and remained silent for a moment. To him, it seemed like I had given him the deed to a house.

I continued, *"I want you to have them, you remember our conversations. When you get out of here, remember to do good things."* My Spanish was terrible and I knew I barely had the proper vocabulary to get my point across. It seemed like I was talking like a four year old, but I still wanted to give him one last piece of encouragement.

Without much hesitation, I left him with his gift. I didn't want him to be a martyr and refuse, and I didn't want to cause commotion with the others that I was giving things away. I felt lighter as I left the cell room. A burden was lifted from me, just by the simple gift of giving.

Quietly, I walked into the cell and found Ivan lying on his bed watching TV. There was no one else in the room, and I made sure Eddie was in the courtyard.

"Hey Ivan," I quietly called out. He rolled from his stomach onto his side and gave a nod of his head.

"Hola Roberto, You leaving today?"

"Yes, I should leave in a couple of minutes." I replied as he nodded his head. *"Listen, I want to thank you for helping me. You are a good friend."*

Ivan didn't change expression, he just watched as I spoke. I pulled the rest of the gum I had from my pocket. I pulled back a fold of Ivan's blanket and deposited the two packs, out of sight for him. As I folded his bedding back in place, signifying that the rest of the gum was now Ivan's. I didn't think I needed it anymore and thought it best to give it away.

Ivan watched me as I made his bed right again. I think one thing I liked about him was that he was constant. He was a good man, not wavering. I still don't know why

Ivan was here or what he did to get here, but he seemed like a man of honor. I knew he would have my back if anything went bad. There was not much he ever said, but he didn't need to. I said goodbye to Ivan and walked out

> For some reason, giving away my car just didn't feel so difficult anymore.

of the cell. Now that I had given away my gum and my shoes away, for some reason, giving away my car just didn't feel so difficult anymore.

With the sleeping bag in one hand and two blankets under my arms and two bags in the other hand, I made my way to the front gate. I might as well wait there for the others to return. I also thought if they saw me with my things, it would give them some sense on urgency. Who knows, maybe some complications would come up and I'd have to put the stuff back inside a cell for the night again. By now, I had given my favorite pair of shoes and gum away, so who knows how long the lawyers would take on this.

I stood by the gate and waited. One of the kids came up and shook my hand goodbye. Pablo came up and thanked me for his gum throughout the week. Tito came up, the back of his hair still had his hometown carved in and by this time most of the others knew I was leaving today too. I was glad for the farewells, but I was trying to keep calm and not get restless.

Soon, Eddie made his way up. He heard that I was leaving and finally investigated the truth of it. Sure enough, I was at the front gate with my things ready to go anytime now.

Eddie motioned a nod of his head, "Hey you leaving?" He asked. I really wanted to say something sarcastic just for the fun of it, but instead just nodded my head yes.

"Well, are you going to leave your sleeping bag here?" He pointed down at my feet.

I looked down at my rolled up sleeping bag and knew what he wanted. "No," I replied, "I'm taking it with me."

"Well you know," he continued. "If you leave it, it will keep us warm after you go away. All of us stay here in the cold at night." He was painting sad story playing on my sympathy. The real truth of it was that he would get first dibs if I left it.

"I know, but I'm taking it with me, I'm not giving it up, so it's not staying here." My voice was calm and clear. There was no reason for me to give him the sleeping bag. Come to think of it, the blue blanket I gave to the new guy last night was still under the bed. It was his now and I think that was enough bedding to leave behind. I made sure the new guy was taken care of and I really didn't think Eddie went cold in the night either as he had a good set of blankets and a good bed.

There was no further discussion about giving up my sleeping bag, I saw right through his private agenda. After a few moments of stare down, Eddie walked away. If he only knew the contents of the bag, I thought to myself and silently smiled as he disappeared into a cell room. This was my last interaction with him.

I didn't hate Eddie, it was just that he was used to a different lifestyle than I chose to follow. Eddie looked out for himself. He was programmed to do it that way, but I decided early that he wasn't going to control my situation. If he had a different look on life, that was fine, but for me, I chose another.

Soon after, Christina came for me. She was alone but seemed content.

"How's it going out there?" I asked. I was hoping for some good news.

"Well other than the secretary settling payment with Dad, things are almost complete." She said, a little exasperated but seemed to be handling it in an honorable manner. "It seems like the Secretary was really dragging his feet..."

Then she smiled, "Until we told him that dad was really thinking about calling the TV crews in Phoenix to come down here and do a story about this. As soon as the Secretary heard that the tourist season might be at risk, something clicked! "

So that was the trump card. Sooner or later something had to give, looks like the Secretary had a vice after all. Unfortunately, most Mexican authorities have conflicting commitments. They are not put in position until they know someone higher that gives them the job. After thinking about it, a negative TV story about an Arizonan who came down to Mexico for vacation and got in trouble didn't seem like the publicity that the local Authorities would want. Rocky Point was driven by the dollar of the American tourist. If word got out that I was still here after all this time, this would be a really bad fly in the soup.

I grinned with Christina's train of thought as she mentioned that the lawyers were on their way back to us. Just then, Christina looked behind me in the hallway as her eyes got bigger.

"Look out! " she cried, but it was too late.

Joker had come up from behind, a white bucket raised above his head. There was no where for me to run as I was in a corner by the front gate and couldn't move anywhere to get out of his way. Time seemed to slow way down as I saw the grin on his face as well as others behind him, laughing at his attack.

It was time for me to get wet, looks like Joker was right after all. The size of the bucket and the effort it took to carry it said it all. I would come out soaking wet and stay that way for the drive home. Before I could duck and with a fluid motion, Joker dumped the bucket over me.

However, rather than gallons of water pouring out, the bucket had about four tablespoons. In a light trickle, the water flew out of the bucket and hit me in the chest.

Everyone started laughing, I don't know if it was because Joker got me wet with a little bit of water or from the shocked expression I had, thinking that I was going to get the full load. Either way, everyone who watched exploded with delight! After collecting myself together again, I watched Joker as he raised his arms in victory, appealing to the others. He had done it again, the clown of the Jail had pulled one over on me. He turned back to me and shook my hand. I gladly took it, hoping that would be the last from him.

By this time, the lawyers had come back and saw the tail end of the fun. However, they seemed more focused on the guards than what was going on behind bars. With a paper in hand, the lawyer requested Francis to open the gate.

Francis looked at the paper, found everything in order and grabbed his keys. I guessed tomorrow had come, it was time for me to leave. He looked at me as he placed the key in the hole, "Robert Deniro! Looks like you get out!" The door swung open.

I grabbed my sleeping bag, my blankets and my other bags and walked across the threshold. Could I finally leave? A cheer from the other inmates sounded behind me as they wished me goodbye. I was so caught up in the excitement that the only thing I could think of was to grab Christina and pull her tight. Right in front of Francis, the lawyers and the prisoners now on the other side of the bars, I kissed her. That brought a bigger clamor from those around. The lawyers smiled and the prisoners clapped while Joker whistled.

We ended the kiss and looked around, Christina was caught off guard from the whole thing and blushed. I waved to my friends in the jail as Francis closed the gate.

The lawyer brothers informed me that we had to go back to the secretary's office to sign some paperwork. They took us out of the jail where we met her dad on the sidewalk. I had forgotten about him when I had kissed Christina. It was nice to see him now, knowing that he wasn't aware that I planted one on her in front of everyone. He smiled as we proceeded across the street towards the municipal building and the Secretary's office.

The Phone Call

Walking down the sidewalk reminded me of last Thursday. I retraced my steps from the jail over to the office building. However, this time I wasn't handcuffed and I knew I wouldn't return back to the jail. Walking hand in hand with Christina, we crossed the street and headed towards the other building. Our smiles were interrupted when the cell phone of one of the brothers rang.

The lawyer stopped and answered, "Oh Mr. Sam, good to hear from you!" He listened for a moment, and then continued, "Yes, he's right here!"

> I thought dad was on a plane crossing the ocean, how could he possibly be calling me?

He passed the phone to me as I looked at Christy in amazement and wonder. I thought dad was on a plane crossing the ocean, how could he possibly be calling me? Had he canceled the flight? Christina didn't have any answers either.

I put the cell phone to my ear, "Hi dad! Where are you?"

The familiar voice on the phone replied "I'm in New Jersey. The more important question is where are you?"

"I just got out of jail just five minutes ago!" I replied. "We are on our way to sign my release form and will drive home later." I continued on, "I'm out and I'm OK!"

I could hear a large sigh from dad on the other end of the phone. This was really good news to him. I didn't know how good it was until he explained his situation.

"I had a layover here in New Jersey and I made a pledge to myself that I would call before the flight to London." He said. "If you weren't out by this time, I would cancel the rest of the flight and turn back. I'm glad you're out, I have to board my international flight in twenty minutes! " Dad had a hard time leaving me while I was still in jail. Christina's dad had talked him into going on the flight from Phoenix, but his conscience got the best of him. So he decided to change plans during his layover in New Jersey. If I was still in jail, he would have hopped on a flight back to Phoenix and cancel the London plans altogether.

Within an amazing window of twenty minutes, I had gotten out just in time for dad to make his flight. Now it was my turn to sigh. I was really glad dad would make his next flight. I had a brief conversation with him about the next steps. He would get on the flight and be with Mom for Christmas. I would sign the release forms and drive back to Arizona.

I was humbled by dad's call and gave the phone back to the Lawyer. I explained the conversation to Christina and her dad as we followed the two lawyer brothers to the other building.

Looking around, I could tell the sun was low in the sky and soon it would get dark. It had taken all day to get me out. Christina came in the morning and spent most of the day with her dad, negotiating with the lawyers to help motivate the Secretary to get me out today. In a short while, we would be on the road back to Arizona driving in the dark.

We entered the door of the municipal building and down the corridor to the Secretary's office. Unfortunately the lady at the front desk, who had flirted with one of the lawyers the other day, had already left. The thought crossed my mind that maybe she was one of the women partying with them on Sunday night, why not? The five of us walked into the Secretary's office where he was waiting at the desk.

A few words were spoken between the lawyers and the Secretary. The older brother spoke up. "OK Roberto, you need to sign and then you are free to go." I looked at the secretary, as he looked quite satisfied with what was going on. With pen in hand, I signed and dated the line. It was official, I was now released and that was it. There were several other spaces on the form and the lawyers instructed that if I ever came back to Rocky Point, I would have to sign in with the secretary. However, after talking with Christina and her dad, I thought it best that I wouldn't come back. Who knows what trouble they would conjure for me, just to get me back in jail to pay another fine and loose another car?

So, with my named signed I said 'gracias' to the Secretary and then walked out of the building. I kept thinking of that first Monday, where the border patrol guard asked me to sing in front of the whole group. What a big difference there was between singing and signing.

One of the brothers turned to Christina's dad, "Ok, you meet us later, Roberto you have a good trip home." I thanked them for all they did and the two brothers walked across a street and out of sight, leaving me with Christina and her dad.

"What was that all about, they want to still see you?" I asked her dad.

"Yes," he replied "they paid the $1000 fine and now they want reimbursement. I promised them I would meet them up north at the border town to settle up." He answered.

I thanked him for all his hard work. I think this was not how he expected to spend a random Tuesday, but I was glad he helped out.

Nearby was the dad's van. He left it for Christina to use when he went away on Sunday with Christina's dad. Next to the van was another car which was the one her dad came down in this morning.

"Listen," he said, "why don't you take Christina in your car and just cross the border? I need to finish up with these guys and I will meet you at the gas station on the other side." I nodded my head, sounded like a good plan to me. The sooner I could cross back the better. I remembered the gas station on the US side. It was the one I should have stopped at to clean out my car. I guessed I would have to stop now!

We got into the van and left Christina's dad. As we sat in the front seats, my mind swelled with all of the thoughts of the past day. It seemed like an eternity since this morning when I had a slight hope of going home.

"Robert" Christina interrupted my thinking. "Are we going?"

I nodded my head, said a quick prayer and turned the key. Was it really time to leave? I guessed so, because Christy wanted me to hurry up.

We drove away from the Rocky Point Jail and I couldn't help but look back, it seemed so surreal. The jail floated out of sight in the rear view mirror as I turned my attention to where I was driving. It would take a good hour to reach the border town where we would wait for her dad. We then had several hours driving from the border to Phoenix where I could finally be home. It was now dark and the remains of the sunset lingered in the Western sky. I left Rocky Point, Mexico disappointed that I had not seen the ocean on this trip. I soon dismissed the let down, considering all the other things I had seen. I guessed the ocean will have to wait for another time.

Crossing the Border

Before long, we came to the border town of Sonoyta, Mexico. Just for fun, I wanted to drive by the first jail to show Christina where I had spent the first few nights. But come to think of it, I didn't even know where the jail was. My sense of direction was really messed up and I couldn't tell one building from another. Rather than look around or ask for directions, I decided to just cross back into the United States.

My heart raced as we approached the border. We had to go through the Mexican patrol station as well as the US. I knew that I wouldn't have any problem with the US, but what happens on the Mexican side? Would they stop me again? Obviously, I didn't have any more bullets, but I didn't want to go through the searching all over again.

I slowed down following a car in front of me. A Mexican guard stopped the first car and leaned on the driver's door. You could tell they spoke a couple of words and the border guard motioned the car to proceed through. Now it was our turn. My heart pounded, my hands sweat as I gripped the steering wheel. There was nothing for me to be scared of, but I couldn't get the recent experience out of my mind.

I rolled down my window and waited for the Mexican border guard to say something. However, he just looked at the two Americans in the car and flagged us onward. The tires of the van didn't even completely stop as we proceeded onward. Oh what a relief, I looked at Christina and the color was coming back to her face too.

> There was nothing for me to be scared of, but I couldn't get the recent experience out of my mind.

We then proceeded on to the US border station. It was a little more lighted and a man in uniform stopped us. Most of the US border patrol guards were bilingual and Hispanic looking. However, this man had fair skin and light colored hair.

"Hi guys," he said as he stepped up to my window. I was so relieved that he spoke English. It was the first official American I had seen in a while. "Where are you coming from?" He asked.

'From jail' didn't seem like the most appropriate answer, so my mind wondered how much I would tell the US border guard. There was no reason for me to be worried, I was now on US soil and Christina and I were both citizens.

But, did I need to explain that I was a former prisoner in the Rocky Point County Jail and that I was now returning after nine days?

I decided to keep it simple and replied "We're coming from Rocky Point." Considering this was the road to Rocky Point, the guard knew that it was the truth.

"OK," he replied, "Do you have anything to declare, any Drugs? Any Mexican Stowaways?" You could tell he was being witty but official in his questions, and still polite about it.

I shook my head and said, "No, we're just going back to Phoenix." He shined a flashlight behind me into the empty seats of the van. Sure enough, I was good to go. He wished us a good night and stepped aside. He was really nice and I was relieved to have someone in uniform that friendly. Maybe I was just worked up, either way, it was nice to be on the US side again.

About fifty yards away on the US side is a gas station with a convenience store. I pulled the van into a parking spot and turned off the engine. The silence was eerie. As I looked at Christina, she leaned over and gave me a big hug. We had made it! I was elated to finally be back in the US. What a liberating feeling to be back on your own soil. I'm as patriotic as the rest, but this time I was especially grateful I was a US citizen and finally home again.

We ended the embrace and I found Christina was crying. I didn't know if she was sad, happy or hurt, so I held her hand and gave her a tissue from the glove box. For a few moments we sat in silence as she sobbed.

"What's going on?" I asked.

With a gasp for breath, she whispered "I don't know". I left it at that, thinking that the stress and emotions of an intensely serious day had finally caught up to her. My heart went out to her as she opened up and let her emotions go. Within a couple of minutes, she calmed down and sat with me, watching the traffic on the road cross over the border.

Just then I had an idea! What if I could get my car back from the Mexican Border patrol? Could it be that easy to go over and get it? It was worth a try, so I got out of the van.

Christina questioned my actions and pleaded with me to stay with her. However I needed to find out. Besides, I was no longer a criminal.

I walked toward the US border station. It was on the northbound side of the road and looked clean compared to the Mexican side across the way. A Hispanic gentleman in uniform was on a cigarette break at the side of the road.

"Excuse me," I called out. He looked up from his thoughts and looked surprised that a random American was calling for him. "Do you have a minute?" I asked. He nodded and I began explaining my situation.

"A week ago, I crossed the border and got in trouble with the Mexican border patrol. I've been in jail at Rocky Point and now I'm finally out. I was wondering if you know how I can quickly get my car back tonight if it's on the other side?"

He looked at me and thought for a moment, "What did you do to get in trouble?"

I decided to give him the information. "I accidentally had bullets in my car and crossed the border."

The US guard smiled, "No gun?"

"No, just bullets, it's stupid I know, but now everything's been cleared up with the Mexican Authorities in Rocky Point.

He thought again for a moment, still smiling, "Well, I know that just on the other side of the fence they keep cars that are confiscated. If you let the Mexican Border patrol know you are set free, you might be able to see if you can get the car."

The US guard was nice, but he knew that my car was on the other side of his jurisdiction. With that, he pointed just left of the fence, giving directions where on the other side most of the cars were parked.

"Thanks!" I said as I walked away. Christina watched me from near the van. She got out when I left and stretched her legs. I could see her wince as she watched me walk across the border again to the Mexican side.

Standing near the little office where I was originally held for several hours last Monday night were several guards, their hands in their pockets to keep warm. A couple of them I recognized from a week ago. I waved hello as they watched me walk across the border towards them. They had no problem with me approaching as we were in the open and they had watched me walk from the US border station.

"Hi guys, remember me, I came here last week?" I called out to him.

The guard peered at me for a moment and then smiled as he said "Oh yes, you had bullets." Another guard I recognized from last week meandered over.

I smiled, "Yes, everything is OK now" I said as I pointed to Christina who was across the way at the gas station. The others looked and nodded their heads in agreement.

"I was wondering if I could get my car?"

The border guard had a puzzled look on his face as I realized that he didn't know much English.

I tried it again in Spanish. *"My car, can I get it?"* I pointed a cross the street where there were several cars parked just a stones throw away.

The Mexican border guard spoke a few words to the other and then back to me. *"I'm sorry, but no."* He shook his head, *"Because it has been parked here, we need to know it's Ok from Rocky Point to let it go."* That's not what I wanted to hear. If I had to get permission from Rocky Point, then there was no point as the secretary wouldn't release it.

I weighed my options. I wished I had gone straight to the car in the first place and just opening the door with a spare key I had in my wallet. Now that the border guards knew that I wanted the car back, it would be difficult to drive it away.

While thinking about what to do, I saw Christina's dad drive up across the street. He was being inspected by the Mexican guard before he could cross into the US. I knew that I had to get back. He probably saw me and would meet Christina at the gas station after crossing the border.

I thanked the guards and turned away. They were nice to me tonight and didn't seem to mind talking with me. Come to think of it, they were just as nice when I crossed the first time and wouldn't have made a big deal about me crossing had I been clean in the first place.

I got back to Christina just as her dad parked his car next to ours. He got out and Christina gave him a big hug. He looked at me with a questioning expression.

"I tried to see if my car was over on the other side and if I could get it back," I responded. I didn't need to explain, but felt I needed to break the silence.

"I had thought about that too, but no luck?" He asked.

I shook my head no and we both realized that it was no use tonight.

"What took you so long?" Christina asked. It had been a while since we crossed before her dad finally came.

"The lawyers wanted more money," he replied, he was in good spirits but you could tell he was winding down. "They said they needed to be paid, so I gave them the extra $1000 check from your dad and I gave them my palm pilot." It seemed to satisfy them. I really didn't know how valuable his palm pilot was, or how important it was to him, but I had an increased sense of gratitude towards him for all of his help today.

"Thanks," I said as Christina still had her arms around her dad.

"Well, we're glad you're safe now," he said in a fatherly deep voice.

We made a plan to leave the border now and drive back to Phoenix. It was getting late and we didn't want to delay our trip any longer. All of us were in agreement that Christina would ride with me and we would head home.

We climbed in our cars and headed deeper into Arizona. I said a silent goodbye to the prison life I had taken on for the past week. It wasn't a good fit for me anyway. I decided that I was far better off as a normal citizen, rather than an inmate. A smile of relief crossed my face as we continued onward.

I then realized that I had something hidden away. With one hand on the steering wheel and another hand reaching to the back seat, I caught hold of the sleeping bag and pulled out the Coke can. My victory drink, the one I had saved all this time!

Christina looked at me, not realizing what this was all about. "Where did that come from?" She asked.

"I've saved it since last Tuesday!"

She looked in amazement as I held the can of Coke in my hand. Finally, I could enjoy it.

I popped the tab and took a sip. It was the best beverage I have ever had!

Epilogue

A few days after my return to the United States, I went down again to the Mexican Border with several hundred dollars. I thought I could buy the car back from the Border Patrol. This time, I parked on the US side and walked over. The Border Patrol looked at the paperwork and said it was not possible, as the car was still tied up in the legal process.

I asked to clean the car and take my belongings that I had left behind. As a border guard watched, I cleaned under the seats, in the trunk and glove box. While the guard turned his head away, I found one spare bullet in my glove box that had been overlooked. I quietly slipped it into my pocket and finished up. I walked back over to the United States and headed back for Phoenix. I still chuckle at the fact that I took a bullet from Mexico and crossed back into the United States. To this day, I still have the Nine of Spades and one un-seized bullet as tokens of my experience.

It's been a few years since my encounter with the Mexican Jail System. Since then many events have happened. US relationships with Mexico have changed for the better and sometimes for the worst. September 11th happened in New York City, forever changing how countries interact with each other. Borders have become stricter in their policies, including the requirement of passports to travel almost anywhere. Even though situations and physical circumstances change, the lessons learned only grow.

The value of my experience in Mexico will remain with me for a very long time. Sometimes I honestly realize that my nine days in jail were probably one of the best experiences that have ever happened to me. Understanding that I can continue to make great experiences out of negative situations will be used in many different ways in the future.

Many people have asked why I chose to write a book and share this story when it was so embarrassing at the time. I guess this is a way to embrace and learn from my past rather than to run from it. Each day, I continue to realize I'm still not perfect. I guess if I was, I would at least have had the knowledge of taking bullets out of my car. I guess that's why personal growth is a journey. Even after writing this book, I still have my everyday challenges.

Christina and I have since separated paths, she is a wonderful woman and I will always continue to think of her as the noblest of ladies. She taught me that even when relationships come and go, you can still be of service in every moment. Her dedication and compassion for me in my situation was truly inspirational.

Dad continues to be the greatest of dads. Now that I have a family of my own, I realize how smart dads really are and I give him more credit the more I grow up. And at the same time, I'm also aware that no one has a "how to" book on parenting. I don't think the book would be useful anyway, because love comes from the heart.

Recently I crossed back into Mexico with a group doing a humanitarian project by building houses for the less fortunate. It's seemed the Border Patrol was unconcerned with the group, including me as they were very gracious as we crossed. I knew it wouldn't be an issue, as it was more an internal struggle from my own fears rather than anything else.

For the humanitarian project, we raised over one-hundred-thousand dollars including building materials and supplies. With our own manpower, we helped several families in the community and our impact on them will hopefully give them a better future. We also realize it's a drop in the bucket compared to the need that is truly out there to help the less fortunate in the world. However, at least it was a small contribution.

Everyone asks why bad things happen to good, unsuspecting people. My answer is that sooner or later something unfortunate will happen to everyone. This is to test us, to try our faith and most importantly to make us stronger. My question now is not why these things happen, but what we will do with them when they come?

ABOUT THE AUTHOR

Robert Messick grew up in Northern Arizona. He received his Bachelor's degree in Finance and received an MBA in Global Management. After verbally sharing his story about Mexico, several friends and family members said, "You've got to write this down and get it into a book!" So, Robert took the next little while writing and finally getting the story published.

Robert is married, has a family and currently lives in Northern California.

Robert is available for speaking engagements. You can contact him at Robert@BulletsAtTheBorder.com. Additional copies of *Bullets at the Border* are available online at www.BulletsAtTheBorder.com.